McGraw-Hill Ryerson

PRISM
MATH

CANADIAN EDITION

purple

McGraw-Hill
Ryerson

Toronto Montréal Boston Burr Ridge, IL Dubuque, IA Madison, WI New York San Francisco
St. Louis Bangkok Bogotá Caracas Kuala Lumpur Lisbon London Madrid
Mexico City Milan New Delhi Santiago Seoul Singapore Sydney Taipei

McGraw-Hill

*A Division of The **McGraw·Hill** Companies*

Prism Math – Purple

Copyright © 2005, McGraw-Hill Ryerson Limited, a Subsidiary of The McGraw-Hill Companies. All rights reserved. No part of this publication may be reproduced or transmitted in any form or by any means, or stored in a data base or retrieval system, without the prior written permission of McGraw-Hill Ryerson Limited, or, in the case of photocopying or other reprographic copying, a licence from The Canadian Copyright Licensing Agency (Access Copyright). For an Access Copyright licence, visit www.accesscopyright.ca or call toll free to 1-800-893-5777.

ISBN 13: 978-0-07-096047-3
ISBN 10: 0-07-096047-X

http://www.mcgrawhill.ca

3 4 5 6 7 8 9   MP   1 9 8 7 6 5 4 3 2

Printed and bound in Canada

Care has been taken to trace ownership of copyright material contained in this text. The publishers will gladly accept any information that will enable them to rectify any reference or credit in subsequent printings.

Library and Archives Canada Cataloguing in Publication

Prism Math – Purple.

One of a series of non-grade specific workbooks for use in grades 1–12. The level of difficulty increases throughout the series in the following order: gold, brown, red, orange, yellow, green, blue and purple.
ISBN: 0-07-096047-X

1. Mathematics–Problems, exercises, etc. 2. Mathematics–Study and teaching (Elementary) 3. Mathematics–Study and teaching (Secondary)

QA36.5.P758 2005   510'.76   C2005-900445-2

PUBLISHER: Diane Wyman
MANAGER, EDITORIAL SERVICES: Linda Allison
SUPERVISING EDITOR: Kristi Moreau
COPY EDITORS: Julia Cochrane; Write On!
EDITORIAL ASSISTANT: Erin Hartley
PRODUCTION SUPERVISOR: Yolanda Pigden
PRODUCTION COORDINATOR: Janie Deneau
COVER DESIGN: Dianna Little
ELECTRONIC PAGE MAKE-UP: SR Nova Pvt. Ltd., Bangalore, India

COPIES OF THIS BOOK MAY BE OBTAINED BY CONTACTING:

McGraw-Hill Ryerson Ltd.

WEB SITE:
http://www.mcgrawhill.ca

E-MAIL:
orders@mcgrawhill.ca

TOLL-FREE FAX:
1-800-463-5885

TOLL-FREE CALL:
1-800-565-5758

OR BY MAILING YOUR ORDER TO:
McGraw-Hill Ryerson
Order Department
300 Water Street
Whitby, ON L1N 9B6

Please quote the ISBN and title when placing your order.

Student text ISBN:
0-07-096047-X

Contents

PURPLE BOOK PRETESTS
Readiness Check

NAME _____

Complete.

	a	b	c	d	e
1.	$\begin{array}{r} 25\ 647 \\ 8\ 016 \\ +95\ 648 \end{array}$	$\begin{array}{r} 65\ 137 \\ -9\ 849 \end{array}$	$\begin{array}{r} 65\ 000 \\ -13\ 296 \end{array}$	$\begin{array}{r} 847 \\ \times 60 \end{array}$	$\begin{array}{r} 9365 \\ \times 478 \end{array}$
2.	$8\overline{)2736}$	$63\overline{)5295}$	$\begin{array}{r} \$16.85 \\ 2.16 \\ +4.78 \end{array}$	$\begin{array}{r} 0.3694 \\ +0.87 \end{array}$	$\begin{array}{r} \$14.03 \\ -7.57 \end{array}$
3.	$\begin{array}{r} 0.9 \\ -0.375 \end{array}$	$\begin{array}{r} 0.456 \\ \times 1.7 \end{array}$	$\begin{array}{r} 25.37 \\ \times 6.02 \end{array}$	$6\overline{)1.572}$	$0.05\overline{)16.5}$
4.	$0.45\overline{)3.474}$	$\dfrac{4}{7} \times \dfrac{7}{10}$	$1\dfrac{2}{3} \times 2\dfrac{1}{2}$	$\dfrac{5}{6} \div \dfrac{5}{9}$	$5\dfrac{3}{5} \div 4\dfrac{1}{5}$
5.	$\begin{array}{r} \frac{7}{12} \\ +\frac{2}{3} \end{array}$	$\begin{array}{r} 3\frac{4}{5} \\ +2\frac{2}{3} \end{array}$	$\begin{array}{r} \frac{7}{12} \\ -\frac{1}{3} \end{array}$	$\begin{array}{r} 5 \\ -1\frac{5}{6} \end{array}$	$\begin{array}{r} 2\frac{5}{18} \\ -1\frac{5}{6} \end{array}$

Solve each of the following.

	a	b	c	d
6.	$\dfrac{n}{4} = \dfrac{6}{8}$	$\dfrac{5}{n} = \dfrac{15}{21}$	$\dfrac{3}{7} = \dfrac{27}{n}$	$\dfrac{9}{27} = \dfrac{n}{81}$
7.	$\dfrac{12}{17} = \dfrac{120}{n}$	$\dfrac{7}{10} = \dfrac{n}{100}$	$\dfrac{9}{n} = \dfrac{75}{100}$	$\dfrac{n}{25} = \dfrac{64}{100}$

Complete. Write each fraction in simplest terms.

	a			b		
	percent	fraction	decimal	percent	fraction	decimal
8.	16%			8%		
9.		$\frac{3}{4}$			$\frac{1}{20}$	
10.			0.09			2.2

Complete the following.

          a   b   c

11. _____ is 25% of 84.   7 is _____% of 140.   8.5 is 17% of _____.

12. 64.2 is _____% of 150.   3.2 is 8% of _____.   _____ is 90% of 160.

	principal	interest rate	time	interest	total amount
13.	$800	7%	1 year		
14.	$1000	$9\frac{1}{2}$%	2 years		

Complete each of the following. Use 3.14 for π.

          a   b   c

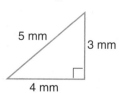 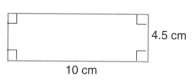

	Perimeter/ Circumference	mm	m	cm
15.		mm	m	cm
16.	Area	mm^2	m^2	cm^2

Find the volume of each.

          a   b   c

17.

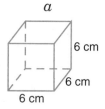 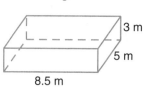 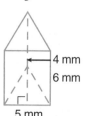

_____ cm^3 _____ m^3 _____ mm^3

PURPLE BOOK PRETESTS
Mixed Facts Pretest

NAME _____

Add, subtract, multiply, or divide. Watch the signs.

	a	*b*	*c*	*d*
1.	$\begin{array}{r} 58 \\ +76 \\ \hline \end{array}$	$\begin{array}{r} 83 \\ -27 \\ \hline \end{array}$	$\begin{array}{r} 68 \\ \times 9 \\ \hline \end{array}$	$8\overline{)3696}$
2.	$\begin{array}{r} 503 \\ -86 \\ \hline \end{array}$	$7\overline{)9457}$	$\begin{array}{r} 857 \\ +98 \\ \hline \end{array}$	$\begin{array}{r} 80 \\ \times 97 \\ \hline \end{array}$
3.	$40\overline{)8974}$	$\begin{array}{r} 678 \\ +954 \\ \hline \end{array}$	$\begin{array}{r} 608 \\ \times 79 \\ \hline \end{array}$	$\begin{array}{r} 520 \\ -298 \\ \hline \end{array}$
4.	$\begin{array}{r} 698 \\ \times 605 \\ \hline \end{array}$	$\begin{array}{r} 5948 \\ +673 \\ \hline \end{array}$	$\begin{array}{r} 4012 \\ -689 \\ \hline \end{array}$	$70\overline{)4760}$
5.	$\begin{array}{r} 865 \\ \times 79 \\ \hline \end{array}$	$39\overline{)940}$	$\begin{array}{r} 875 \\ 903 \\ +678 \\ \hline \end{array}$	$\begin{array}{r} 8001 \\ -4237 \\ \hline \end{array}$
6.	$\begin{array}{r} 35\ 174 \\ -6\ 498 \\ \hline \end{array}$	$\begin{array}{r} 9617 \\ +5289 \\ \hline \end{array}$	$\begin{array}{r} 3078 \\ \times 95 \\ \hline \end{array}$	$91\overline{)6643}$

	a	b	c	d
7.	1793 8065 +7689	48 205 −13 978	973 ×100	21)275
8.	598 ×507	23 986 6 070 +34 689	76 000 −19 356	82)2 550
9.	91)6 643	679 ×896	63 742 86 009 +73 658	826 300 −97 513
10.	7095 ×846	27)97 362	842 000 −267 194	706 052 +39 868
11.	986 745 +776 988	531 006 −89 438	43)86 840	4706 ×800

PROBLEM-SOLVING STRATEGIES
Multi-Step

Sometimes it takes **multiple steps** to solve problems.

A wooden fence is to be built around a 30-m by 50-m garden. If the wood for the fence costs $36.95 per metre, how much will the wood for the entire fence cost?

The total distance around the garden is ___160___ m.

It will cost ___$5912___ to fence the garden.

Find the total number of metres of fencing needed.

$30 + 30 + 50 + 50 = 160$

Next, find the total cost of fencing that distance.

$160 \times \$36.95 = \$5912$

Solve each problem.

```
SHOW YOUR WORK
```

1. On her first five science tests, Maria scored the following: 92, 86, 78, 94, and 95. What must she score on the sixth test so that her average for all six marks is 1 point higher than her average is right now?

   Maria has a total of _____ points on her first five tests.

   One point higher than her average on the first five tests is _____.

   Maria needs a total of _____ points on all six tests.

   Maria must score a(n) _____ on her sixth test.

2. A carpet cleaning company has eight homeowners that want their carpets cleaned. It takes one worker 12 h per home to clean a house full of carpet. If a team of three workers is assigned to each house, how many hours will it take to clean all eight homes?

   Three workers can clean one house in _____ h.

   The carpet cleaning company can have the carpet in all eight homes cleaned in _____ h.

PROBLEM-SOLVING STRATEGIES
Draw a Picture

Sometimes you can **draw a picture** to solve problems.

A rectangular piece of cardboard is 8 cm wide and 16 cm long. Squares measuring 2 cm on each side are cut from each corner of the cardboard. Then, the sides of the cardboard are folded to make a box. What is the volume of the box?

After cutting a 2-cm square from each corner and folding the cardboard into a box, the new width is ___4___ cm, and the new length is ___12___ cm.
The height of the box is ___2___ cm.
The volume of the box is ___96___ cm^3.

Draw a picture of the rectangular cardboard with squares cut from the corners.

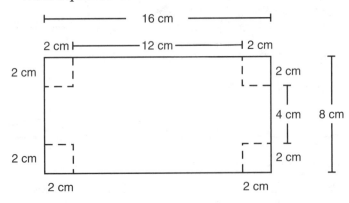

Then find the volume.

V = length × width × height

$V = 12 \times 4 \times 2$

$ = 96$

Draw a picture to solve each problem.

SHOW YOUR WORK

1. A baseball diamond can be described as a square that measures about 27 m on each side. What is the perimeter of a square whose sides are drawn inside the baseball diamond at a distance of 1 m from the baselines?

   Each side of the inner square is _____ m long.

   The perimeter of the inner square is _____ m.

2. Mr. Story designed a flag that is 250 cm by 375 cm. After the flag was completed, he decided to attach 15-cm-long fringe around the edges of the flag. What are the dimensions of the flag including the fringe?

   With the fringe attached, the flag has a width of _____ cm and a length of _____ cm.

PROBLEM-SOLVING STRATEGIES

Look for a Pattern

Sometimes you must **look for a pattern** to solve problems.

Jordan designed the following pattern.

Fig. 1   Fig. 2   Fig. 3

What will the next figure in his pattern look like?

The number of triangles on the bottom of each figure increases by ____1____.

The number of triangles on the top of each figure increases by ____1____.

The number of squares in each figure increases by ____2____.

The next figure in Jordan's pattern will look like this:

Look for a pattern.

Number of triangles on bottom:

1   2   3   4
 _/ _/ _/
 +1   +1   +1

Number of triangles on top:

1   2   3   4
 _/ _/ _/
 +1   +1   +1

Number of squares:

1   3   5   7
 _/ _/ _/
 +2   +2   +2

Solve each problem.

| SHOW YOUR WORK |

1. Brianne designs jewellery. Below are three of the five steps she followed in making a silver barrette from links.

    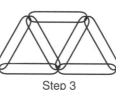

Step 1   Step 2   Step 3

How many links did Brianne use to make the barrette?

Step 1 uses _____ silver links.

Step 2 uses _____ silver links.

Step 3 uses _____ silver links.

After finishing step 5, Brianne used _____ silver links.

PROBLEM-SOLVING STRATEGIES

Guess and Check

Sometimes you must **guess and check** to solve problems.

Roberto used an equal number of quarters, dimes, and nickels to buy a $2.00 greeting card. How many of each coin did he use?

Guess possible numbers of each coin.

Check to see if the value of the number of coins is $2.00.

Roberto used __five__ quarters, __five__ dimes, and __five__ nickels to buy a $2.00 greeting card.

Guess: 4 quarters, 4 dimes, and 4 nickels
Value: $0.25 × 4 = $1.00
$0.10 × 4 = $0.40
$0.05 × 4 = $0.20

Total Value:
$1.00 + 0.40 + 0.20 = $1.60
Incorrect guess.

Guess: 5 quarters, 5 dimes, and 5 nickels
Value: 5 × $0.25 = $1.25
5 × $0.10 = $0.50
5 × $0.05 = $0.25

Total Value:

$1.25 + 0.50 + 0.25 = $2.00
Correct guess.

Guess and check to solve each problem.

1. The volume of a rectangular box is 693 cm³. The length of the box is 2 cm more than the width, and the width is 2 cm more than the height. What are the dimensions of the box?

   The dimensions of the box are _____ cm, _____ cm, and _____ cm.

2. Leanne drew an isosceles triangle with one angle twice the size of the sum of the other two angles. What is the size of the largest angle in Leanne's triangle? Hint: The sum of the angles in a triangle is 180°.

   An isosceles triangle has _____ equal angles.

   The largest angle measures _____ degrees.

PROBLEM-SOLVING STRATEGIES
Identify Missing Information

Sometimes there is **not enough information** to solve the problem.

On a map, Shelly used a ruler to determine the distance from her town to her grandmother's town. She measured the distance as 5 cm. How many metres is Shelly's town from her grandmother's town?

<u>   Not enough information   </u>

Missing information: <u>how many kilometres 1 cm represents on the map</u>

Use a proportion to determine the number of actual kilometres equivalent to 5 cm on the map.

$$\frac{1\,cm}{?\,km} = \frac{5\,cm}{?\,km}$$

Information on how many kilometres on the map each centimetre represents is missing.

Identify the missing information in each problem.

1. Last softball season, the Jets won nine of the games they played. What percent of games played did they win?

   _____

   Missing information: _____

   _____

┌─────────────────┐
│ SHOW YOUR WORK │
└─────────────────┘

2. Carl leaves home at 7:30 A.M. to travel to the lake where he has a summer job. If he drives at an average rate of 70 km/h, when will he arrive at the lake?

   _____

   Missing information: _____

   _____

PROBLEM-SOLVING STRATEGIES
Make a Table

Sometimes you can **make a table** to solve problems.

Archie mows Mr. Chun's lawn every third day. Every Monday and Thursday he has trumpet lessons. Every fourth day Archie helps his grandfather repair clocks. If he does all three activities on Monday, June 1, when is the next date that he will do all three activities?

Archie does all three activities again on June ___25___.

Make a table to determine what date Archie does all three activities.

Mon	Tues	Wed	Thurs	Fri	Sat	Sun
1	2	3	4	5	6	7
8	9	10	11	12	13	14
15	16	17	18	19	20	21
22	23	24	25	26	27	28
29	30		O = mow		/ = repair clocks	
			\ = trumpet lessons			

Make a table to solve each problem.

SHOW YOUR WORK

1. Marshal puts $2 into his savings account every 3 days. Karen puts $3 into her savings account every 4 days. They both began their savings account on Monday, September 1. At the end of 30 days, how much money will they each have in savings?

   After 30 days, Marshal will have _____ in his savings account.

   After 30 days, Karen will have _____ in her savings account.

---

2. At a store's grand opening, every third person entering the store wins a $5 gift certificate. Every fifth person wins a free ice-cream cone. Out of 30 people, how many people will get both a $5 gift certificate and an ice-cream cone?

   Out of 30 people, _____ people will get both a $5 gift certificate and an ice-cream cone.

PROBLEM-SOLVING STRATEGIES
Make a List

Sometimes you can **make a list** to solve problems.

There is a certain town called Quatreville where every family has exactly four children. In how many different orders of birth can boys and girls be born into the families in Quatreville?

There are ___16___ possible orders of birth in Quatreville.

Make a list of all possible combinations. Let B stand for boy and G stand for girl. Start by listing the oldest child first.

4 boys	3 boys	2 boys	1 boy	0 boys
BBBB	BBBG	BBGG	BGGG	GGGG
	BBGB	BGBG	GBGG	
	BGBB	BGGB	GGBG	
	GBBB	GBGB	GGGB	
		GBBG		
		GGBB		

Count the combinations in each column.

| 1 | 4 | 6 | 4 | 1 |

Make a list to solve each problem.

1. A vending machine at Riley's school sells yogourt cups that cost $0.55. The machine accepts only loonies or correct change. It only gives nickels, dimes, and quarters for change. How many different combinations of nickels, dimes, and quarters could it give?

   The machine must give _____ in change when a loonie is used.

   There are _____ different combinations that the machine can give change in quarters, dimes, and nickels.

---

2. Two number cubes, one numbered 1 to 6, one numbered 7 to 12, are tossed. How many different ways are there to get a sum of 14?

   There are _____ different ways to make a sum of 14 when rolling the two number cubes.

Solve a Simpler Problem

Sometimes you can **solve a simpler problem** to solve problems.

Motega is helping the scouts with a project. He needs to cut a 200-cm length of wire into 1-cm pieces. How many cuts will he have to make?

Motega would need to make ____1____ cut in a 2-cm length of wire.

Motega would need to make ____5____ cuts in a 6-cm length of wire.

Motega would need to make ____9____ cuts in a 10-cm length of wire.

Motega would need to make ____199____ cuts in a 200-cm length of wire.

Solve a simpler problem. Determine how many cuts Motega will need to cut in a smaller length of wire.

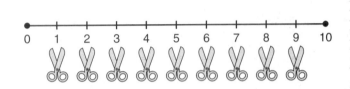

Solve a simpler problem to solve each problem.

1. For its fundraiser, the soccer team sold raffle tickets. The tickets were numbered in order. The first ticket Jorge sold was numbered 299 and the last ticket he sold was numbered 355. How many tickets did Jorge sell?

Jorge sold _____ tickets.

SHOW YOUR WORK

2. Alma and her family are going to plant 28 fir trees around a square lot. They want to plant one tree at each corner and then space the remaining trees 3 m apart around the perimeter of the lot. What is the area of the lot?

If 4 trees are planted, the lot has _____ × _____ = _____ m^2.

If 8 trees are planted, the lot has _____ × _____ = _____ m^2.

If 12 trees are planted, the lot has _____ × _____ = _____ m^2.

If 28 trees are planted, the lot has _____ × _____ = _____ m^2.

PROBLEM-SOLVING STRATEGIES

Work Backward

Sometimes you can **work backward** to solve problems.

A company that made a very good profit this year gave half to a local charity. They gave an overseas charity half of the remaining money and kept $3.4 billion. How much profit did the company have this year?

The company had a profit of $\underline{\$13.6 \text{ billion}}$ this year.

Work backward.

Before they gave half to an overseas charity:
$3.4 billion + $3.4 billion
= $6.8 billion

Before they gave half to a local charity:
$6.8 billion + $6.8 billion
= $13.6 billion

Work backward to solve each problem.

SHOW YOUR WORK

1. Michael cashed his paycheque. He spent half his pay on new clothes. He spent a third of what he had left on a gift for his mother. He put the remaining $25 in his savings account. How much was Michael's paycheque worth?

    Michael's paycheque was worth $_____.

2. After deductions, LaToya's paycheque for 40 h of work was worth $372. She paid $68 in provincial taxes, $18 in federal taxes, and $42 in city taxes. How much does LaToya get paid per hour?

    LaToya earned $_____ before deductions.

    LaToya is paid $_____ per hour.

3. Building A is 3.5 m taller than Building B. Building B is 2.5 m taller than Building D. Building D is 15 m taller than Building C. Building C is 37 m tall. How tall is Building A?

    Building A is _____ m tall.

PROBLEM-SOLVING STRATEGIES

Use Estimation

Sometimes you can **use estimation** to solve problems.

When Tamoko visited Mexico, $1 in Canadian money could be exchanged for 6.875 pesos. If Tamoko exchanged $95 in Canadian money, about how many pesos should she receive?

Tamoko should receive about ____700____ pesos.

Estimate. Round 6.875 pesos to 7 and 95 to 100, then multiply.

$7 \times 100 = 700$ pesos

Use estimation to solve each problem.

1. A 400-g box of Corn Frosties costs $3.79. Another brand, Sugared Corn Flakes, costs $4.99 for a 600-g box. Which cereal costs less per gram? About how much less per gram does it cost?

_____ costs less per gram.

It costs about _____ less per gram.

2. When Leona went to Japan, $1 in Canadian money could be exchanged for 91.845 yen. If Leona exchanged $45 in Canadian money, about how many yen should she have received?

Leona should have received about _____ yen.

3. A 675-g jar of Best spaghetti sauce costs $3.59. Another brand, Better spaghetti sauce, costs $4.89 for a 950-g jar. Which brand of spaghetti sauce costs less per gram? About how much less per gram does it cost?

_____ spaghetti sauce costs less per gram.

It costs about _____ less per gram.

> SHOW YOUR WORK

PROBLEM-SOLVING STRATEGIES
Use a Formula

You can **use a formula** to help solve problems.

A formula for the number of apples in a box is $N = S^3$, where S is the number of apples along each side of the box. Find N when there are 11 apples along one side of the box.

There are ___1331___ apples in this box.

Use the formula given to find the number of apples in the box.

$N = S^3$ or $S \times S \times S$

$N = 11 \times 11 \times 11$
$\quad = 1331$

Use a formula to solve each problem.

SHOW YOUR WORK

1. Kyle uses the formula $C = 15x + 25y$ to find the cost C, in cents, of x oranges and y apples. How much would Kyle pay for 9 oranges and 7 apples?

   Kyle would pay _____ for 9 oranges and 7 apples.

2. A box has a volume of 240 cm^3. The height of the box is 3 cm and the width of the box is 5 cm. What is the length of the box?

   The formula for the volume of a box is

   _____.

   The length of the box is _____ cm.

3. Using $\pi \doteq 3.14$, find the volume of a cylindrical tank having a diameter of 14 m and a height of 10 m.

   The cylindrical tank has a volume of about _____ m^3.

PROBLEM-SOLVING

PROBLEM-SOLVING STRATEGIES
Use Logical Reasoning

You can **use logical reasoning** to help solve problems.

Ann, Seung, Yolanda, and Denny each have a pet. They each have a different pet: a beagle, a cat, an angelfish, and a gerbil. Yolanda lives next door to the person with the gerbil. Denny and Seung have pets that live in small habitats. Ann cannot have a dog because of allergies. Seung is afraid of animals that bite. Which animal does each person own?

Use a table to keep track of the facts. Then, indicate your conclusions.

	Beagle	Cat	Angel-fish	Gerbil
Ann	no	yes	no	no
Seung	no	no	yes	no
Yolanda	yes	no	no	no
Denny	no	no	no	yes

Ann has a(n) ___cat___.

Seung has a(n) _angelfish_.

Yolanda has a(n) _beagle_.

Denny has a(n) ___gerbil___.

Use logical reasoning to help solve each problem.

SHOW YOUR WORK

1. Jarod, Scott, and Rick each ate either a hamburger, cheeseburger, or a cheese pizza for lunch. Rick did not have any meat for lunch. Jarod does not like cheese. What did each person eat for lunch?

   Jarod ate the _____.

   Scott ate the _____.

   Rick ate the _____.

2. Four letters, A, B, C, and D, are each written with a number, 1, 3, 5, or 8, though not necessarily in that order. The letter A is written with a prime number. The letter B is written with a number less than 5. Neither A nor D is written with a number that is an odd factor of 40. What numbers are the letters B and D written with?

   Letter B is written with the number _____.

   Letter D is written with the number _____.

CHAPTER 1 PRETEST
Whole Numbers/Decimals

Add or subtract.

	a	b	c	d	e
1.	4815 +7263	15.8 +23.9	165 975 45 336 +64 821	48.62 3.94 +5.75	64.559 61.947 +83.827
2.	1286 +576	45.88 +8.90	126 783 +267 854	14.892 −7.698	1000 −256
3.	4296 −853	8.3 −2.7	526 794 −64 288	15.21 −5.76	561.341 −279.648

Multiply or divide.

	a	b	c	d
4.	264 ×13	957 ×816	16.23 ×4.8	1.867 ×23.1
5.	1658 ×623	21.79 ×25.4	49)15 729	35)481
6.	113)2488	2.5)412.5	0.088)53.68	3.81)9.3726

CHAPTER 1 PRETEST Problem Solving

Solve each problem.

Park Ticket Prices
$1.50 per ride
$13.00 day pass

1. There were 4129 ride tickets sold today at the park. How much money was collected for the ride tickets?

   $_____ was collected.

2. There were 8765 day passes sold at the park. How much money was collected for the day passes sold?

   $_____ was collected.

3. How much money was collected today for both ride tickets and day passes?

   $_____ was collected.

4. How many more day passes were sold today than ride tickets?

   _____ more day passes were sold than ride tickets.

5. A group spent $4108.00 on day passes. If each person purchased one day pass, how many people were in their group?

   There were _____ people in their group.

1.

2.

3.

4.

5.

Lesson 1 Addition (whole numbers)

NAME _____

Add the ones. Rename 27 as "2 tens and 7 ones."   Continue adding from right to left.

```
      2
212 104          212 104
323 616          323 616
132 408          132 408
+241 759        +241 759
        7        909 887
```

Add.

	a	b	c	d	e
1.	23 +14	224 +73	312 +5324	43 214 +4 325	41 321 +612 314
2.	16 47 +13	217 316 +142	3317 2154 +1212	21 016 14 527 +51 202	260 316 217 327 +411 342
3.	31 70 14 +52	273 162 253 +210	1131 2262 3473 +1051	41 370 2 151 33 225 +11 118	121 065 302 432 304 144 +41 213
4.	36 75 84 31 +17	633 710 821 502 +221	1123 2651 1762 2873 +1411	11 616 12 573 21 412 40 331 +13 214	232 362 351 171 64 221 71 141 +182 314
5.	34 76 58 67 +73	542 624 852 715 +316	7067 8458 5312 2521 +1214	31 145 14 214 3 142 76 125 +3 214	212 304 321 456 214 672 523 214 +314 235

CHAPTER 1

PRISM MATHEMATICS
Purple Book

Lesson 1
Addition (whole numbers)
19

Lesson 1 Problem Solving

Solve each problem.

1. On Thursday, 1335 books were borrowed from the library. On Friday, 1852 books were borrowed. How many books were borrowed in all?

   _____ books were borrowed.

2. A carpenter ordered pieces of plywood. One box contained 158 pieces, another 232 pieces, and the third 116 pieces. How many pieces were received in all?

   The carpenter received _____ pieces in all.

3. Three new homes were sold last week. The prices were $215 422, $199 554, and $218 432. What were the total sales for the week?

   The total sales were $_____.

4. Joan drove 187 km in one day. She drove 207 km the next day. In all, how far did she drive?

   Joan drove _____ km.

5. Sophia drove 415 km on the first day of her vacation. On the second day, she drove 520 km. How many kilometres did she drive in all?

   Sophia drove _____ km in all.

6. Matthew is going to the school dance on Friday night. He bought a shirt for $31 and a pair of pants for $42. How much did he spend in all?

   Matthew spent $_____.

7. During a three-year period Mrs. Newman drove her car the following distances: 8456 km, 9754 km, and 7652 km. How many kilometres did she drive her car during the three years?

   She drove _____ km.

| 1. |
| 2. |
| 3. |
| 4. |
| 5. |
| 6. |
| 7. |

Lesson 2   Subtraction (whole numbers)

To subtract ones, rename
3 tens and 2 ones as
"2 tens and 12 ones."

$$\begin{array}{r} {}^{\;2\;\,12}\\ 965\,43\cancel{2}\\ -121\,715\\ \hline 7 \end{array}$$

⟶

Continue subtracting from right to left,
renaming as necessary.

$$\begin{array}{r} {}^{4\;\;14\;\;2\;\,12}\\ 96\cancel{5}\,\cancel{4}\cancel{3}\cancel{2}\\ -121\,715\\ \hline 843\,717 \end{array}$$

Subtract.

	a	b	c	d	e
1.	37 −6	327 −16	4325 −214	17 625 −3 214	321 459 −20 123
2.	59 −14	847 −231	6875 −1534	87 654 −14 123	582 785 −131 524
3.	70 −49	968 −159	8752 −4127	78 547 −31 218	495 627 −314 518
4.	97 −78	523 −72	5963 −2172	25 753 −14 182	457 245 −112 158
5.	83 −45	675 −289	5028 −4917	86 743 −21 892	675 247 −321 482
6.	45 −27	607 −299	8207 −3149	74 003 −21 456	900 435 −417 624
7.	81 −27	700 −287	6732 −865	67 524 −29 689	351 257 −165 268

Lesson 2   Problem Solving

Solve each problem.

1. The population of Westerville is 54 552 and the population of Pickerington is 48 964. How many more people live in Westerville than live in Pickerington?

   _____ more people live in Westerville.

2. Violet Elementary School parents and teachers raised $2507 at the Spring Fair. At the Winter Carnival they raised $3465. How much more money did they raise at the Winter Carnival?

   They raised $_____ more at the Winter Carnival.

3. Last year, the cost of a movie ticket at the Palace Theatre was $8. This year, the cost is $9. How much more does a ticket cost this year?

   A ticket costs $_____ more this year.

4. In Newville, 2243 families receive the evening paper and 1875 receive the morning paper. How many more families receive the evening paper?

   _____ more families receive the evening paper.

5. Roy drove 2645 km last week. This week he drove 2847 km. How many kilometres more did he drive this week?

   Roy drove _____ km more this week.

6. Nicholas paid $45 for a book and a CD. The cost of the CD was $15. How much was the book?

   The book cost $_____.

7. There were 316 people at last week's school dance. There were 284 people at this week's dance. How many more people were at last week's dance?

   There were _____ more people last week.

1.
2.
3.
4.
5.
6.
7.

Lesson 3 Multiplication (whole numbers)

```
    4 873
  ×   296
   29 238  ———— 6 × 4873
  438 570  ———— 90 × 4873
  974 600  ———— 200 × 4873
1 442 408   Add.
```

Multiply.

	a	b	c	d	e
1.	63 ×4	432 ×2	679 ×7	2312 ×3	7598 ×8
2.	68 ×20	700 ×34	212 ×43	1720 ×64	2806 ×97
3.	341 ×200	213 ×320	403 ×212	1414 ×312	5875 ×678
4.	700 ×426	646 ×925	925 ×436	9251 ×809	7487 ×869

Lesson 3   Problem Solving

Solve each problem.

1. There were 19 bands in the parade. Each band had 33 members. How many band members were in the parade in all?

   There were _____ band members in all.

2. The farmer shipped 476 bags of potatoes to the market. Each bag had a mass of 26 kg. What was the mass of the potatoes in all?

   The mass of the potatoes was _____ kg.

3. The manager of the local coffee shop ordered 19 boxes of coffee stirrers. Each box contained 165 stirrers. How many coffee stirrers did the manager order?

   The manager ordered _____ stirrers.

4. Mrs. Pinkerman drives 47 km each day. How many kilometres will she drive in five days?

   She will drive _____ km.

5. One apple costs 20¢. How much do 25 apples cost?

   25 apples cost $_____.

6. Ms. Combs bought six boxes of note cards on sale for $7 per box. How much money did she spend?

   She spent $_____.

7. The bus fare from Toronto to Hamilton is $19 for one person. There are seven people in the Davis family. How much will it cost them to make the trip?

   It will cost them $_____.

1.

2.

3.

4.

5.

6.

7.

Lesson 4   Division (whole numbers)

Think

$$312\overline{)66\,831}$$

| $312 \times 1000 = 312\,000$ | Quotient is between 100 and 1000. So its |
| $312 \times 100 = 312\,00$ | first digit will be in the *hundreds* place. |

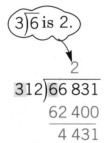

$$\begin{array}{r} 2 \\ 312\overline{)66\,831} \\ 62\,400 \\ \hline 4\,431 \end{array}$$

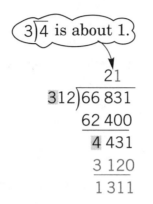

$$\begin{array}{r} 21 \\ 312\overline{)66\,831} \\ 62\,400 \\ \hline 4\,431 \\ 3\,120 \\ \hline 1\,311 \end{array}$$

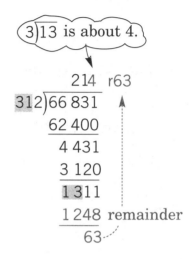

$$\begin{array}{r} 214 \;\; r63 \\ 312\overline{)66\,831} \\ 62\,400 \\ \hline 4\,431 \\ 3\,120 \\ \hline 1\,311 \\ 1\,248 \;\; \text{remainder} \\ \hline 63 \end{array}$$

Divide.

	a	*b*	*c*	*d*	*e*
1.	$9\overline{)687}$	$42\overline{)367}$	$58\overline{)696}$	$123\overline{)975}$	$421\overline{)2354}$
2.	$7\overline{)1425}$	$57\overline{)1457}$	$69\overline{)8345}$	$521\overline{)7295}$	$624\overline{)12\,354}$
3.	$6\overline{)37\,524}$	$83\overline{)12\,576}$	$37\overline{)84\,576}$	$784\overline{)79\,984}$	$379\overline{)97\,542}$

Lesson 4 Problem Solving

Solve each problem.

1. Vinny won $720 in a contest. The money will be paid in 12 equal payments. How much is each payment?

   Each payment is $_____.

2. Emily is decorating for her mother's birthday. She needs to buy 42 balloons. The balloons come in packages of seven. How many packages will she need to buy?

   She will need to buy _____ packages.

3. A group of 152 people want to ride river rafts. Each raft holds eight people. How many rafts are needed so that each person gets one ride?

   _____ rafts are needed.

4. Nicholas and Matthew bought their mother a necklace. The necklace cost $84. They shared the cost equally. How much did each pay?

   Each paid $_____.

5. The school lunch committee will need 180 servings of spaghetti for the school's annual lunch meeting. Each box of spaghetti contains nine servings. How many boxes will be needed?

   _____ boxes of spaghetti will be needed.

6. Kathy is buying juice for the party. She needs 132 servings. If each bottle of juice holds 12 servings, how many bottles must she buy?

   She needs _____ bottles of juice.

7. Christopher and Raymond put 84 candles on their grandmother's birthday cake. There were seven candles in each box. How many boxes of candles did they need?

   They needed _____ boxes of candles.

1.
2.
3.
4.
5.
6.
7.

Lesson 5 Problem Solving

Solve each problem.

1. Luke delivered 225 flyers on Fox Street, 134 on 87th Street, 218 on Hansen Street, and 229 on 89th Street. How many flyers did he deliver?

   He delivered _____ flyers.

2. Wayne Gretzky scored 894 goals during his career. Gordie Howe scored 801. How many more goals did Gretzky score than Howe?

   Gretzky scored _____ more goals.

3. If Ms. Jones drives 350 km each day, how many kilometres will she drive in four days?

   She will drive _____ km.

4. A bricklayer laid 656 bricks in 8 h. Suppose the same number of bricks were laid each hour. How many bricks were laid each hour?

   _____ bricks were laid each hour.

5. The load limit for a small bridge is 3000 kg. Mr. Sims' car has a mass of 1875 kg. How much less than the load limit is the mass of the car?

   The car has a mass of _____ kg less.

6. One week the bakery used 144 sacks of flour. Suppose each sack of flour has a mass of 55 kg. What was the total mass of the flour used?

   _____ kg of flour were used.

7. There are 17 370 items to be packed into boxes of 24 items each. How many boxes will be filled? How many items will be left over?

   _____ boxes will be filled.

   _____ items will be left over.

1.	2.
3.	4.
5.	6.
7.	

Lesson 5 Problem Solving

Solve each problem.

1. The local Plumbers Union has 456 members.
   The local Carpenters Union has 875. How many
   more members does the Carpenters Union have
   than the Plumbers Union?

   There are _____ more members in the
   Carpenters Union.

2. Seven cars can be loaded on a transport truck.
   Each car has a mass of 1875 kg. What is the
   total mass of the cars that can be loaded on the
   truck?

   The total mass is _____ kg.

3. Mr. Cosgrove drove his car 10 462 km last year
   and 11 125 km this year. How many kilometres
   did he drive the car during these two years?

   He drove the car _____ km.

4. There were 1172 women at a banquet. They were
   seated 8 to a table. How many tables were filled?
   How many were at the partially filled table?

   _____ tables were filled.

   _____ women were at the partially filled table.

5. There are 2125 employees at the McKee Plant.
   Each works 35 h a week. What is the total
   number of hours worked by these employees in
   one week?

   The total number of hours is _____.

6. The population of Tomstown is 34 496 and the
   population of Janesburg is 28 574. How much
   greater is the population of Tomstown than the
   population of Janesburg?

   The population is _____ greater.

7. A satellite is orbiting Earth at a speed of
   28 580 km/h. At this rate, how many kilometres
   will the satellite travel in 1 min?

   It will travel _____ km.

1.	2.
3.	4.
5.	6.
7.	

Lesson 6 Addition and Subtraction (decimals)

When adding or subtracting decimals, write the decimals so the decimal points line up. Then, add or subtract as with whole numbers.

```
 26.94        26.940  ⟩  Write these
 45.836       45.836     0s if they
+32          +32.000     help you.
            ─────────
            104.776
```

```
   62.5        62.500  ← Write these
 −43.345     −43.345      0s if they
 ───────     ────────     help you.
              19.155
```

The decimal point in the answer is directly below the other decimal points.

Add or subtract.

	a	b	c	d	e
1.	1.3 +2.6	5 7.6 +3.8	7 4.5 7 +2 1.2	1 8.5 +1 7.3 6	6 7.8 5 7 +2.1 1
2.	4.7 −3.2	6 7.5 −4 3.7	8 7.5 8 −3 4.1	7 5.9 −2 6.6 9	8 7.5 2 −1 2.4 0 3
3.	3.2 4.3 +6.4	5 2.7 −2 6.9	5 3.2 5 1 3.1 +3 1.2 8	6 4.3 −2 5.5 6	1 6.1 0 6 3 4.2 5 +2 1.3
4.	4 7.3 4 −1 3.7 6	1.3 7 2 4.2 3 5 +5.0 5 1	2 5 −1.4 3 5	5.6 0 3 2.7 5 1 +8.8 3 2	3 1.4 2 3 −1 2.8 3
5.	5 7.4 6 3 1.5 9 4 2.3 4 +2.6 7	5.7 0 8 −1.4 3 9	8 3.2 7 5 1 4.2 3 8 8.6 7 5 +3 4.8 7 3	4 8.0 0 3 −1 3.7 4 6	4 7.5 7 8 1 4.4 8 3 7 3.2 4 1 +4 2.9 6 7

Lesson 6 Problem Solving

Solve each problem.

1. The water level of the lake rose 0.85 m during March, 1.30 m during April, and 0.52 m during May. How much did the water level rise during these three months?

   The water level rose _____ m.

2. In problem **1**, how much more did the water level rise during April than during May?

   It rose _____ m more during April.

3. Mr. Tadlock purchased a suit on sale for $97.95 and an overcoat for $87.50. What was the total cost of these articles?

   The total cost was $_____.

4. In problem **3**, how much more did the suit cost than the overcoat?

   The suit cost $_____ more.

5. Last season a certain baseball player had a batting average of .285. This season his batting average is .313. How much has the player's batting average improved?

   The player's average has improved by _____.

6. The thicknesses of three machine parts are 0.514 cm, 0.317 cm, and 0.178 cm. What is the combined thickness of the parts?

   The combined thickness is _____ cm.

7. Ms. Dutcher's lot is 60.57 m long. Mr. Poole's lot is 54.73 m long. How much longer is Ms. Dutcher's lot than Mr. Poole's lot?

   Ms. Dutcher's lot is _____ m longer.

8. Ms. Jolls purchased a dress for $62.95, a pair of shoes for $19, and a purse for $11.49. What was the total amount of these purchases?

   The total amount was $_____.

1.	2.
3.	4.
5.	6.
7.	8.

Lesson 7 Multiplication (decimals)

NAME _____

CHAPTER 1

number of digits to the right of the decimal point

53.1	1	3.24	2	4.21	2	1.72	2
×4	+0	×1.4	+1	×0.47	+2	×0.034	+3
212.4	1	1296		2947		688	
		3240		16840		5160	
		4.536	3	1.9787		0.05848	

Multiply.

	a	b	c	d	e
1.	32.5 ×5	4.57 ×8	672 ×0.4	1678 ×0.07	8.765 ×9
2.	31.4 ×0.09	2.23 ×0.7	417 ×0.009	0.418 ×0.6	167.8 ×0.008
3.	3.14 ×0.17	67.4 ×6.7	5.09 ×0.058	0.724 ×0.46	148.6 ×2.9
4.	65.7 ×0.648	0.584 ×35.6	69.2 ×4.63	7.54 ×60.7	2.408 ×5.69
5.	3.75 ×1.24	3.14 ×0.526	0.957 ×6.18	3.27 ×4.38	2.123 ×4.25

Lesson 7   Problem Solving

Solve each problem.

1. Each case of batteries has a mass of 17.3 kg.
    What is the mass of six cases of batteries?

    The mass is _____ kg.

2. 6.75 truckloads of ore can be processed each
    hour. At that rate, how many truckloads of ore
    can be processed during an 8-h period?

    _____ truckloads of ore can be processed.

3. An article has a mass of 6.47 kg. What would be
    the mass of 24 such articles?

    The mass would be _____ kg.

4. Mr. Swank's car averages 7.8 L of gasoline per
    100 km. How many litres of gasoline would he
    need to drive 1300 km?

    He would need _____ L of gasoline.

5. An industrial machine uses 4.75 L of fuel each
    hour. At that rate, how many litres of fuel will
    be used in 6.5 h?

    _____ L of fuel will be used.

6. What would be the cost of a 6.2-kg roast at
    $5.40 per kilogram?

    The cost would be $_____.

7. Each sheet of paper is 0.043 cm thick. What is
    the combined thickness of 25 sheets?

    It is _____ cm.

8. Brittany runs 1.5 km each day. How far will she
    run in five days?

    She will run _____ km.

1.	2.
3.	4.
5.	6.
7.	8.

Lesson 8 Division (decimals)

shorter way

$0.73\overline{)21.9}$ ⟶ To get a whole number divisor, multiply both 0.73 and 21.9 by ___100___. ⟶

```
      30              30
  73)2190        0.73)21.90
     2190             2190
        0                0

        0                0
        0                0
```

shorter way

$0.059\overline{)0.1357}$ ⟶ To get a whole number divisor, multiply both 0.059 and 0.1357 by _____. ⟶

```
       2.3            2.3
  59)135.7       0.059).135.7
     1180             1180
      177              177
      177              177
        0                0
```

Divide.

	a	b	c	d

1. $0.61\overline{)3.05}$ $9.1\overline{)4.55}$ $0.071\overline{)0.639}$ $1.37\overline{)0.959}$

2. $0.37\overline{)0.999}$ $0.95\overline{)76}$ $0.026\overline{)1.378}$ $16.7\overline{)2.004}$

3. $0.03\overline{)0.798}$ $0.08\overline{)2.008}$ $0.47\overline{)9.729}$ $25.3\overline{)0.92851}$

CHAPTER 1

Lesson 8   Problem Solving

Solve each problem.

1. A rope 40.8 m long is to be cut into four pieces of the same length. How long will each piece be?

   Each piece will be _____ m long.

2. Each can of oil costs $0.92. How many cans of oil can be purchased with $23?

   _____ cans of oil can be purchased.

3. A case of cans has a mass of 9.6 kg. Each can has a mass of 0.6 kg. How many cans are there?

   There are _____ cans in the case.

4. Each sheet of paper is 0.016 cm thick. How many sheets will it take to make a stack of paper 18 cm high?

   It will take _____ sheets.

5. Amy spent $9.60 for meat. A kilogram of meat sells for $2.40. How many kilograms did she buy?

   She bought _____ kg.

6. A machine uses 0.75 L of fuel each hour. At that rate, how long will it take to use 22.5 L of fuel?

   It will take _____ h.

7. Each corn flake has a mass of about 0.08 g. How many flakes will it take to have a mass of 20.4 grams?

   It will take _____ corn flakes.

8. It takes a wheel 0.6 s to make a revolution. What part of a revolution will it make in 0.018 s?

   The wheel will make _____ of a revolution.

1.	2.
3.	4.
5.	6.
7.	8.

CHAPTER 1   PRACTICE TEST
Whole Numbers/Decimals

Add or subtract.

	a	b	c	d
1.	$\begin{array}{r} 7684 \\ 584 \\ +285 \\ \hline \end{array}$	$\begin{array}{r} 79.86 \\ 12.49 \\ +6.91 \\ \hline \end{array}$	$\begin{array}{r} 86\ 714 \\ 56\ 811 \\ +25\ 648 \\ \hline \end{array}$	$\begin{array}{r} 23.846 \\ 2.734 \\ +45.8 \\ \hline \end{array}$
2.	$\begin{array}{r} 89.01 \\ -45.99 \\ \hline \end{array}$	$\begin{array}{r} 76\ 321 \\ -55\ 344 \\ \hline \end{array}$	$\begin{array}{r} 4.612 \\ -1.877 \\ \hline \end{array}$	$\begin{array}{r} 70\ 001 \\ -27\ 689 \\ \hline \end{array}$
3.	$\begin{array}{r} 2312 \\ +5678 \\ \hline \end{array}$	$\begin{array}{r} 12.3 \\ +4.8 \\ \hline \end{array}$	$\begin{array}{r} 16.01 \\ -8.64 \\ \hline \end{array}$	$\begin{array}{r} 257.314 \\ -151.276 \\ \hline \end{array}$

Multiply or divide.

	a	b	c	d
4.	$\begin{array}{r} 648 \\ \times 21 \\ \hline \end{array}$	$\begin{array}{r} 2465 \\ \times 546 \\ \hline \end{array}$	$\begin{array}{r} 46.2 \\ \times 54.1 \\ \hline \end{array}$	$\begin{array}{r} 1.081 \\ \times 0.013 \\ \hline \end{array}$
5.	$\begin{array}{r} 478 \\ \times 478 \\ \hline \end{array}$	$\begin{array}{r} 43.864 \\ \times 0.261 \\ \hline \end{array}$	$67\overline{)15\ 481}$	$99\overline{)485}$
6.	$23\overline{)10\ 764}$	$0.8\overline{)6.32}$	$1.43\overline{)9.867}$	$2.75\overline{)0.33}$

CHAPTER 2   PRETEST
Fractions

Write each fraction in simplest form.

a	b	c	d	e
1. $\dfrac{10}{15} =$	$\dfrac{3}{6} =$	$\dfrac{18}{24} =$	$\dfrac{40}{50} =$	$\dfrac{2}{8} =$

Rename.

2. $\dfrac{1}{2} = \dfrac{}{8}$ $\dfrac{1}{4} = \dfrac{5}{}$ $7 = \dfrac{}{3}$ $4\dfrac{1}{5} = \dfrac{}{5}$ $2\dfrac{7}{8} = \dfrac{}{8}$

Write each sum, difference, product, or quotient in simplest form.

a	b	c	d
3. $\begin{array}{r}\frac{4}{5}\\[4pt]+\frac{3}{5}\\\hline\end{array}$	$\begin{array}{r}1\frac{5}{12}\\[4pt]+4\frac{7}{12}\\\hline\end{array}$	$\begin{array}{r}3\frac{1}{2}\\[4pt]+8\frac{11}{15}\\\hline\end{array}$	$\begin{array}{r}2\frac{2}{3}\\[4pt]4\frac{3}{4}\\[4pt]+3\frac{1}{6}\\\hline\end{array}$
4. $\begin{array}{r}\frac{5}{8}\\[4pt]-\frac{3}{8}\\\hline\end{array}$	$\begin{array}{r}\frac{4}{6}\\[4pt]-\frac{3}{6}\\\hline\end{array}$	$\begin{array}{r}4\frac{3}{4}\\[4pt]-2\frac{1}{3}\\\hline\end{array}$	$\begin{array}{r}7\frac{1}{8}\\[4pt]-3\frac{5}{6}\\\hline\end{array}$

5. $\dfrac{1}{5} \times \dfrac{5}{7} =$ $\dfrac{1}{3} \times \dfrac{6}{7} =$ $1\dfrac{3}{5} \times \dfrac{2}{3} =$ $2\dfrac{2}{5} \times 4\dfrac{3}{8} =$

6. $\dfrac{4}{5} \div \dfrac{5}{4} =$ $3\dfrac{1}{3} \div 4\dfrac{3}{8} =$ $6 \div \dfrac{3}{4} =$ $6\dfrac{1}{4} \div 8\dfrac{1}{3} =$

Lesson 1   Fractions and Mixed Numerals

Study how to change a fraction or mixed numeral to simplest form.

Factors of 6	Factors of 15	Factors of 8	Factors of 10
1, 2, 3, 6	1, 3, 5, 15	1, 2, 4, 8	1, 2, 5, 10

$\frac{6}{15} = \frac{6 \div 3}{15 \div 3}$ Divide 6 and 15 by their greatest common factor.

$= \frac{2}{5}$

$7\frac{8}{10} = 7 + \frac{8}{10}$

$= 7 + \frac{8 \div 2}{10 \div 2}$ Divide 8 and 10 by their greatest common factor.

$= 7 + \frac{4}{5}$ or $7\frac{4}{5}$

$5\overline{)11}$ → $2\frac{1}{5}$ $1 \div 5 = \frac{1}{5}$
$\underline{10}$
1

$3\overline{)17}$ → $5\frac{2}{3}$ $2 \div 3 = \frac{2}{3}$
$\underline{15}$
2

Write each of the following in simplest form.

	a	b	c
1.	$\frac{9}{12}$	$2\frac{2}{4}$	$\frac{13}{5}$
2.	$\frac{2}{8}$	$3\frac{6}{10}$	$\frac{19}{3}$
3.	$\frac{10}{16}$	$7\frac{8}{12}$	$\frac{17}{2}$
4.	$\frac{18}{36}$	$5\frac{15}{20}$	$\frac{12}{8}$
5.	$\frac{15}{45}$	$2\frac{12}{28}$	$\frac{16}{10}$

Lesson 2   Renaming Numbers

$\dfrac{3}{4} = \dfrac{\blacksquare}{8}$

$= \dfrac{3 \times 2}{4 \times 2}$

$= \dfrac{6}{8}$

Multiply both the numerator and the denominator by the same number.

Choose 2 so the new denominator is 8.

$4 = \dfrac{\blacksquare}{8}$

$\dfrac{4}{1} = \dfrac{4 \times 8}{1 \times 8}$

$= \dfrac{32}{8}$

Name the whole number as a fraction whose denominator is 1.

Choose 8 so the new denominator is 8.

$9\dfrac{2}{3} = \dfrac{\blacksquare}{3}$

$9\dfrac{2}{3} = \dfrac{(3 \times 9) + 2}{3}$

$= \dfrac{29}{3}$

Multiply the whole number by the denominator and add the numerator.

Use the same denominator.

$7\dfrac{1}{5} = \dfrac{\blacksquare}{5}$

$7\dfrac{1}{5} = \dfrac{(5 \times 7) + 1}{5}$

$= \dfrac{36}{5}$

Rename.

	a	*b*	*c*	*d*
1.	$\dfrac{1}{2} = \dfrac{\blacksquare}{6}$	$\dfrac{2}{5} = \dfrac{\blacksquare}{15}$	$\dfrac{3}{8} = \dfrac{\blacksquare}{16}$	$\dfrac{5}{6} = \dfrac{\blacksquare}{12}$
2.	$6 = \dfrac{\blacksquare}{4}$	$3 = \dfrac{\blacksquare}{10}$	$7 = \dfrac{\blacksquare}{3}$	$5 = \dfrac{\blacksquare}{2}$
3.	$4\dfrac{1}{2} = \dfrac{\blacksquare}{2}$	$6\dfrac{3}{4} = \dfrac{\blacksquare}{4}$	$2\dfrac{7}{10} = \dfrac{\blacksquare}{10}$	$3\dfrac{5}{6} = \dfrac{\blacksquare}{6}$
4.	$2 = \dfrac{\blacksquare}{12}$	$\dfrac{9}{10} = \dfrac{\blacksquare}{50}$	$1\dfrac{7}{8} = \dfrac{\blacksquare}{8}$	$\dfrac{4}{5} = \dfrac{\blacksquare}{10}$

NAME _____

Lesson 3   Adding and Subtracting Fractions

To add or subtract fractions having different denominators, rename either or both fractions so they have the same denominator. Then add or subtract.

$$\frac{4}{5} = \frac{8}{10}$$
$$+\frac{1}{2} = +\frac{5}{10}$$
$$\frac{13}{10} = 1\frac{3}{10}$$

$$\frac{10}{12} = \frac{10}{12}$$
$$-\frac{1}{3} = -\frac{4}{12}$$
$$\frac{6}{12} = \frac{1}{2}$$

CHAPTER 2

Write each sum or difference in simplest form.

	a	b	c	d
1.	$\frac{2}{5}$ $+\frac{2}{5}$	$\frac{5}{8}$ $+\frac{1}{8}$	$\frac{8}{9}$ $-\frac{7}{9}$	$\frac{7}{8}$ $-\frac{3}{8}$
2.	$\frac{11}{12}$ $-\frac{3}{4}$	$\frac{13}{15}$ $-\frac{2}{3}$	$\frac{1}{2}$ $+\frac{1}{4}$	$\frac{1}{4}$ $+\frac{1}{5}$
3.	$\frac{10}{12}$ $-\frac{1}{3}$	$\frac{1}{3}$ $-\frac{1}{5}$	$\frac{7}{10}$ $+\frac{1}{2}$	$\frac{4}{5}$ $+\frac{2}{4}$
4.	$\frac{4}{5}$ $-\frac{2}{4}$	$\frac{1}{12}$ $+\frac{1}{3}$	$\frac{3}{4}$ $-\frac{1}{2}$	$\frac{5}{8}$ $-\frac{1}{6}$

Lesson 3 Problem Solving

Solve. Write each answer in simplest form.

1. Kelly purchased $\frac{3}{8}$ of a round of gouda cheese and Noah purchased $\frac{3}{8}$ of a round of gouda cheese. How much gouda did they purchase?

   They purchased _____ of a round of gouda.

2. Sara had $\frac{5}{6}$ of a box of raisins before she ate $\frac{1}{6}$ of a box. How much does she have left?

   She has _____ of a box of raisins left.

3. One fourth of the house was painted yesterday and one half was painted today. How much of the house was painted on those two days?

   _____ of the house was painted.

4. Brandon practised his clarinet each day. He spent $\frac{1}{8}$ of his time practising scales and $\frac{5}{8}$ of his time practising new pieces. What fraction of his time did he spend on scales and new pieces?

   _____ of his time was spent on scales and new pieces.

5. Diane bought $\frac{3}{4}$ of a round of gouda cheese and $\frac{1}{2}$ of a round of mozzarella cheese. How much more gouda cheese than mozzarella cheese did she buy?

   She bought _____ of a round more gouda cheese.

6. Eric spent $\frac{1}{4}$ h eating breakfast and $\frac{1}{3}$ h showering and getting dressed. How long did he spend getting ready altogether?

   Eric spent _____ h getting ready.

7. Dan power-walked for $\frac{3}{4}$ h and jogged for $\frac{1}{3}$ h. How long did he exercise in all?

   Dan exercised for _____ h.

1.	2.
3.	4.
5.	6.
7.	

Lesson 4 Adding and Subtracting Mixed Numerals

NAME _____

CHAPTER 2

To add or subtract mixed numerals having different denominators, rename either or both fractions so they have the same denominator. Then add or subtract.

$$2\frac{1}{2} = \ 2\frac{4}{8}$$
$$+3\frac{5}{8} = +3\frac{5}{8}$$
$$5\frac{9}{8} = 6\frac{1}{8}$$

$$4\frac{2}{3} = \ 4\frac{8}{12}$$
$$-1\frac{2}{4} = -1\frac{6}{12}$$
$$3\frac{2}{12} = 3\frac{1}{6}$$

Write each sum or difference in simplest form.

	a	b	c	d
1.	$1\frac{7}{10}$ $-\frac{4}{10}$	$1\frac{4}{7}$ $+\frac{2}{7}$	$2\frac{4}{7}$ $-1\frac{4}{7}$	$2\frac{5}{6}$ $+3\frac{2}{6}$
2.	$2\frac{1}{3}$ $4\frac{1}{6}$ $+5\frac{1}{4}$	$\frac{2}{3}$ $\frac{1}{4}$ $+\frac{1}{2}$	$2\frac{1}{2}$ $4\frac{1}{5}$ $+2\frac{3}{4}$	$8\frac{3}{4}$ $-2\frac{11}{12}$
3.	$3\frac{3}{4}$ $+1\frac{1}{2}$	$8\frac{7}{12}$ $-2\frac{1}{6}$	$4\frac{1}{6}$ $+1\frac{1}{2}$	$9\frac{3}{4}$ $-4\frac{1}{6}$
4.	$4\frac{3}{8}$ $+1\frac{1}{2}$	$8\frac{1}{2}$ $-1\frac{1}{6}$	$3\frac{2}{5}$ $+1\frac{7}{10}$	$9\frac{1}{2}$ $-2\frac{1}{5}$

Lesson 4 Problem Solving

Solve. Write each answer in simplest form.

1. The distance from Chad's house to Ryan's house is $14\frac{1}{2}$ blocks. The distance from Chad's house to Jeff's house is $7\frac{3}{4}$ blocks. How much farther is it from Chad's to Ryan's than from Chad's to Jeff's?

   It is _____ blocks farther.

2. What is the combined distance from problem **1**?

   The combined distance is _____ blocks.

3. Yesterday Anne spent $5\frac{1}{2}$ h in school, $1\frac{3}{4}$ h playing, and $1\frac{1}{4}$ h doing homework. How much time did she spend on these activities?

   She spent _____ h.

4. It is $6\frac{1}{4}$ blocks to the beach and $4\frac{1}{2}$ blocks to the ballpark. How much closer is it to the ballpark than to the beach?

   It is _____ blocks closer to the ballpark.

5. Lauren can run $14\frac{7}{12}$ laps around the track in 1 h. Adam can run $12\frac{3}{4}$ laps in 1 h. How much farther can Lauren run?

   Lauren can run _____ laps farther.

6. What is the combined distance in problem **5**?

   The combined distance is _____ laps.

7. Joan likes to volunteer. Last week she spent $4\frac{2}{3}$ h at a library and $3\frac{1}{4}$ h helping at a school. How much time did she spend last week volunteering?

   Joan spent _____ h volunteering.

8. Carol picked $3\frac{1}{2}$ buckets of strawberries. Each bucket holds $2\frac{1}{2}$ L. How many litres of strawberries did she pick?

   Carol picked _____ L of strawberries.

1.	2.
3.	4.
5.	6.
7.	8.

Lesson 5 Multiplication

$\dfrac{5}{6} \times \dfrac{1}{3} = \dfrac{5 \times 1}{6 \times 3}$ **Multiply numerators.**
Multiply denominators.

$= \dfrac{5}{18}$

$5 \times \dfrac{3}{4} \times \dfrac{1}{2} = \dfrac{5 \times 3 \times 1}{1 \times 4 \times 2}$

$= \underline{\hspace{2cm}}$

$4\dfrac{1}{2} \times 5\dfrac{2}{3} \times 1\dfrac{3}{5} = \dfrac{\overset{3}{\cancel{9}}}{2} \times \dfrac{17}{\underset{1}{\cancel{3}}} \times \dfrac{8}{5}$ Divide a numerator and a denominator by a common factor.

$= \dfrac{\overset{3}{\cancel{9}}}{\underset{1}{\cancel{2}}} \times \dfrac{17}{\underset{1}{\cancel{3}}} \times \dfrac{\overset{4}{\cancel{8}}}{5}$

$= \dfrac{3 \times 17 \times \underline{\hspace{1cm}}}{1 \times \underline{\hspace{1cm}} \times \underline{\hspace{1cm}}}$

$= \underline{\hspace{2cm}}$ or $\underline{\hspace{2cm}}$

CHAPTER 2

Write each product in simplest form.

	a	*b*	*c*	*d*
1.	$\dfrac{3}{5} \times \dfrac{1}{4}$	$\dfrac{2}{3} \times \dfrac{4}{5}$	$\dfrac{1}{3} \times \dfrac{1}{5} \times \dfrac{1}{2}$	$\dfrac{3}{4} \times \dfrac{1}{2} \times \dfrac{3}{5}$
2.	$\dfrac{3}{10} \times \dfrac{2}{5}$	$\dfrac{2}{3} \times \dfrac{7}{8}$	$\dfrac{5}{8} \times \dfrac{3}{10} \times \dfrac{5}{6}$	$\dfrac{7}{12} \times \dfrac{6}{7} \times \dfrac{2}{3}$
3.	$\dfrac{3}{4} \times \dfrac{8}{9}$	$\dfrac{3}{5} \times \dfrac{5}{12}$	$\dfrac{11}{12} \times \dfrac{3}{4} \times \dfrac{8}{11}$	$\dfrac{7}{16} \times \dfrac{4}{5} \times \dfrac{5}{8}$
4.	$1\dfrac{1}{2} \times \dfrac{5}{7}$	$2\dfrac{1}{3} \times \dfrac{5}{12}$	$1\dfrac{7}{8} \times \dfrac{2}{3} \times \dfrac{3}{4}$	$\dfrac{1}{2} \times 3\dfrac{1}{3} \times \dfrac{5}{6}$
5.	$\dfrac{3}{5} \times 3\dfrac{1}{3}$	$\dfrac{5}{6} \times 3\dfrac{1}{2}$	$1\dfrac{1}{2} \times 2\dfrac{1}{3} \times \dfrac{1}{4}$	$\dfrac{2}{3} \times 2\dfrac{1}{2} \times 1\dfrac{3}{4}$
6.	$2\dfrac{2}{3} \times 1\dfrac{3}{4}$	$5\dfrac{1}{2} \times 3\dfrac{1}{6}$	$1\dfrac{2}{3} \times 3\dfrac{1}{2} \times 2\dfrac{1}{4}$	$6\dfrac{1}{2} \times 2\dfrac{1}{3} \times 1\dfrac{3}{5}$

Lesson 5 Problem Solving

Solve each problem. Write each answer in simplest form.

1. The tank on Mr. Kent's lawn mower will hold $\frac{3}{4}$ of a can of gasoline. Suppose the tank is $\frac{1}{2}$ full. How much gasoline is in the tank?

   _____ of a can of gasoline is in the tank.

2. Band practice lasted $1\frac{1}{4}$ h. Two thirds of the time was spent marching. How much time was spent marching?

   _____ h was spent marching.

3. An industrial machine can make $2\frac{1}{2}$ engines an hour. How many engines will be made in $1\frac{3}{4}$ h?

   _____ engines will be made.

4. In Joshua's class, $\frac{1}{4}$ of the students have blond hair. $2\frac{1}{2}$ times that fraction have brown hair. What fraction of the class has brown hair?

   _____ of the class has brown hair.

5. In problem **4**, what fraction of the class has neither brown nor blond hair?

   _____ of the class has neither brown nor blond hair.

6. Steve can run $5\frac{1}{2}$ laps of the track in 12 min. His younger sister can run $\frac{3}{4}$ as far in the same time. How far can Steve's sister run in 12 min?

   She can run _____ laps in 12 min.

7. In problem **6**, Steve ran six 12-min runs during gym class last month. How many laps did he run in all?

   He ran _____ laps in all.

8. The soccer team practises $2\frac{1}{2}$ h on each of five weekday afternoons. How many hours does the team practise each week?

   The team practises _____ h each week.

1.	
2.	
3.	
4.	
5.	
6.	
7.	
8.	

Lesson 6 Division

reciprocals

$$\frac{4}{7} \times \frac{7}{4} = 1$$

reciprocals

$$5 \times \frac{1}{5} = 1$$

reciprocals

$$2\frac{3}{4} \times \frac{4}{11} = 1$$

If two numbers are reciprocals, their product is ___1___.

Multiply by the reciprocal.

$$\frac{3}{8} \div \frac{4}{5} = \frac{3}{8} \times \frac{5}{4}$$
$$= \frac{15}{32}$$

To divide any number, multiply by its reciprocal.

$$6\frac{1}{2} \div \frac{3}{4} = \frac{13}{2} \times \underline{\hspace{1.5cm}}$$
$$= \underline{\hspace{1.5cm}}$$

$$\frac{2}{3} \div 1\frac{1}{2} = \frac{2}{3} \times \underline{\hspace{1.5cm}}$$
$$= \underline{\hspace{1.5cm}}$$

Write each quotient in simplest form.

	a	*b*	*c*	*d*
1.	$\frac{1}{2} \div \frac{3}{4}$	$\frac{7}{8} \div \frac{2}{3}$	$\frac{4}{5} \div \frac{4}{7}$	$\frac{5}{8} \div \frac{7}{10}$
2.	$\frac{4}{5} \div 4$	$8 \div \frac{2}{3}$	$\frac{9}{10} \div 3$	$9 \div \frac{3}{5}$
3.	$1\frac{1}{2} \div \frac{2}{3}$	$3\frac{1}{3} \div \frac{5}{6}$	$2\frac{1}{2} \div \frac{7}{10}$	$4\frac{1}{3} \div \frac{7}{8}$
4.	$\frac{7}{8} \div 2\frac{1}{2}$	$\frac{7}{8} \div 1\frac{3}{4}$	$\frac{5}{6} \div 2\frac{2}{3}$	$\frac{3}{4} \div 1\frac{4}{5}$
5.	$2 \div 1\frac{7}{8}$	$4\frac{1}{2} \div 3$	$6 \div 1\frac{1}{8}$	$3\frac{1}{3} \div 5$
6.	$1\frac{1}{2} \div 2\frac{2}{3}$	$3\frac{1}{4} \div 1\frac{7}{8}$	$4\frac{1}{2} \div 1\frac{1}{2}$	$5\frac{1}{4} \div 1\frac{1}{8}$

Lesson 6 Problem Solving

Solve. Write each answer in simplest form.

1. Football practice lasted $2\frac{1}{2}$ h. An equal amount of time was spent on blocking, tackling, passing, and kicking. How much time was spent on each?

   _____ h was spent on each.

2. Three-fourths of a can of gasoline was poured into four containers. Each container held the same amount. How much gasoline was poured into each container?

   _____ of a can was poured into each container.

3. Suppose a motorboat uses 1 L of fuel in $1\frac{1}{4}$ h. How many litres of fuel will the boat use in 10 h?

   The boat will use _____ L of fuel in 10 h.

4. Due to a heavy rain, the water level on a lake was rising 1 cm every $\frac{2}{3}$ h. How much will the water level rise in $1\frac{1}{3}$ h?

   The water level will rise _____ cm in $\frac{3}{4}$ h.

5. It takes Alyssa $\frac{3}{4}$ h to walk to school and back. How long does it take her to walk one way?

   It takes her _____ h.

6. It takes $\frac{1}{4}$ h for 1 L of a chemical to be filtered. How many litres can be filtered in $2\frac{1}{2}$ h?

   _____ L can be filtered.

7. In problem **6**, how many litres can be filtered in $3\frac{3}{4}$ h?

   _____ L can be filtered.

8. A flight leaves the airport every $1\frac{1}{4}$ min. How many flights will leave each hour?

   _____ flights will leave each hour.

1.
2.
3.
4.
5.
6.
7.
8.

CHAPTER 2 PRACTICE TEST
Fractions

NAME _____

Write each fraction in simplest form.

	a	b	c	d
1.	$\dfrac{6}{15} =$	$\dfrac{14}{85} =$	$\dfrac{3}{12} =$	$\dfrac{3}{30} =$

Rename.

2. $\dfrac{3}{4} = \dfrac{}{20}$ $\dfrac{7}{8} = \dfrac{21}{}$ $5 = \dfrac{}{3}$ $3\dfrac{1}{8} = \dfrac{}{8}$

Write each sum, difference, product, or quotient in simplest form.

3.
$$\begin{array}{r} \frac{1}{7} \\ +\frac{2}{7} \\ \hline \end{array}$$
$$\begin{array}{r} 2\frac{4}{5} \\ +3\frac{9}{10} \\ \hline \end{array}$$
$$\begin{array}{r} 4\frac{2}{3} \\ +3\frac{1}{2} \\ \hline \end{array}$$
$$\begin{array}{r} 3\frac{5}{6} \\ 5\frac{7}{8} \\ +1\frac{3}{4} \\ \hline \end{array}$$

4.
$$\begin{array}{r} \frac{5}{9} \\ -\frac{2}{9} \\ \hline \end{array}$$
$$\begin{array}{r} 2\frac{1}{2} \\ -\frac{1}{4} \\ \hline \end{array}$$
$$\begin{array}{r} 7\frac{2}{3} \\ -1\frac{2}{5} \\ \hline \end{array}$$
$$\begin{array}{r} 4\frac{1}{5} \\ -2\frac{7}{20} \\ \hline \end{array}$$

5. $\dfrac{2}{3} \times \dfrac{3}{4} =$ $\dfrac{5}{7} \times \dfrac{3}{10} =$ $6\dfrac{2}{3} \times \dfrac{1}{5} =$ $3\dfrac{5}{9} \times 3\dfrac{3}{8} =$

6. $\dfrac{3}{8} \div \dfrac{4}{5} =$ $4 \div \dfrac{1}{2} =$ $2\dfrac{2}{3} \div 5\dfrac{5}{7} =$ $8\dfrac{5}{9} \div 1\dfrac{1}{10} =$

CHAPTER 2

PRISM MATHEMATICS
Purple Book

CHAPTER 2 PRACTICE TEST

CHAPTER 3   PRETEST
Pre-Algebra Equations

Solve each equation.

	a	*b*	*c*
1.	$2x = 12$	$5y = 25$	$6z = 96$
2.	$\dfrac{d}{3} = 5$	$\dfrac{e}{6} = 7$	$\dfrac{f}{4} = 13$
3.	$r + 7 = 12$	$s + 3 = 25$	$t + 12 = 20$
4.	$g - 4 = 8$	$h - 5 = 12$	$j - 15 = 15$
5.	$72 = 4m$	$8n = 28 + 28$	$9 = \dfrac{p}{5}$
6.	$18 = a + 6$	$b + 4 = 12 + 3$	$13 = c - 4$
7.	$u - 12 = 23 + 7$	$v + 8 = 8$	$w - 8 = 8$

Lesson 1 Number Phrases   PRE-ALGEBRA

Letters like a, b, n, x, and so on can be used to stand for numbers.

word phrase	number phrase	
Some number a added to 7	$7 + a$	If $a = 5$, then $7 + a = 7 + \underline{\quad 5 \quad}$ or $\underline{\quad 12 \quad}$.
Some number b decreased by 4	$b - 4$	If $b = 6$, then $b - 4 = \underline{\quad 6 \quad} - 4$ or $\underline{\quad 2 \quad}$.
The product of 3 and some number n	$3 \times n$ or $3n$	If $n = 2$, then $3n = 3 \times \underline{\quad 2 \quad}$ or $\underline{\quad 6 \quad}$.
15 divided by some number x	$\frac{15}{x}$ or $15 \div x$	If $x = 3$, then $15 \div x = 15 \div \underline{\qquad}$ or $\underline{\qquad}$.

Write a number phrases for each of the following.

a b

1. Some number c subtracted from 11   _____   Five more than the number b _____

2. A certain number d increased by 12   _____   Some number t divided by 2   _____

3. The product of some number n and 8   _____   Four less than some number x _____

4. Eight divided by some number j _____   The product of $\frac{1}{2}$ and y _____

Complete the following.

5. If $r = 3$, then $12 - r = \underline{\qquad} - \underline{\qquad}$ or $\underline{\qquad}$.

6. If $s = 9$, then $7 + s = \underline{\qquad} + \underline{\qquad}$ or $\underline{\qquad}$.

7. If $t = 3$, then $48 \div t = \underline{\qquad} \div \underline{\qquad}$ or $\underline{\qquad}$.

8. If $u = 72$, then $\frac{1}{4} u = \underline{\qquad} \times \underline{\qquad}$ or $\underline{\qquad}$.

9. If $v = 12$, then $4v = \underline{\qquad} \times \underline{\qquad}$ or $\underline{\qquad}$.

10. If $w = 6$, then $w - 6 = \underline{\qquad} - \underline{\qquad}$ or $\underline{\qquad}$.

11. If $x = 24$, then $\frac{x}{3} = \underline{\qquad} \div \underline{\qquad}$ or $\underline{\qquad}$.

Lesson 2   Writing Equations   PRE-ALGEBRA

An **equation** like $x + 2 = 9$ states that both $x + 2$ and 9 name the same number.

sentence	equation	
The sum of some number and 2 is 9.	$x + 2 = 9$	$x = \underline{7}$ because $\underline{7} + 2 = 9.$
Twelve divided by some number is 6.	$12 \div x = 6$ or $\frac{12}{x} = 6$	$x = \underline{2}$ because $12 \div \underline{} = 6.$
Seven decreased by some number is 5.	$\underline{} - \underset{x}{\underline{}} = \underline{}$	$x = \underline{}$ because $\underline{} - \underline{} = \underline{}.$

Write an equation for each of the following.

a

b

1. Some number a increased by 6 is 20. _____

   A number p decreased by 7 is 15. _____

2. Twenty divided by some number y is 4. _____

   One half of a number t is equal to 14. _____

3. The sum of a certain number b and 7 is 14. _____

   Twelve more than some number v is 18. _____

4. The product of 2 and some number n is 12. _____

   Some number d divided by 3 is equal to 14. _____

Complete the following.

5. $x + 8 = 12$ $x = \underline{}$ because $\underline{} + 8 = 12.$

6. $9r = 45$ $r = \underline{}$ because $9 \times \underline{} = 45.$

7. $6 = \frac{1}{2}d$ $d = \underline{}$ because $6 = \frac{1}{2} \times \underline{}.$

8. $b - 6 = 8$ $b = \underline{}$ because $\underline{} - 6 = 8.$

9. $w \div 3 = 2$ $w = \underline{}$ because $\underline{} \div 3 = 2.$

10. $e + 16 = 18$ $e = \underline{}$ because $\underline{} + 16 = 18.$

11. $35 = 27 + c$ $c = \underline{}$ because $35 = 27 + \underline{}.$

Lesson 3 Solving Equations (division) PRE-ALGEBRA

To solve an equation, you can divide both sides of it by the same non-zero number.

$$4m = 52$$
$$\frac{4m}{4} = \frac{52}{4}$$
$$\frac{\cancel{4}^1 m}{\cancel{4}_1} = \frac{\cancel{52}^{13}}{\cancel{4}_1}$$
$$m = 13$$

To change $4m$ to m,
both sides were divided by _____.

Check
$$4m = 52$$
$$4 \times 13 = 52$$
$$52 = 52$$

$$13y = 100 - 9$$
$$\frac{13y}{13} = \frac{91}{13}$$
$$\frac{\cancel{13}^1 y}{\cancel{13}_1} = \frac{\cancel{91}^7}{\cancel{13}_1}$$
$$y = \_\_\_\_$$

To change $13y$ to y,
both sides were divided by _____.

Solve each equation.

a	b	c
1. $3w = 12$	$3b = 51$	$8m = 100 - 4$
2. $72 = 2a$	$54 = 3c$	$96 - 20 = 4r$
3. $6e = 84$	$25s = 75$	$4d = 75 - 7$
4. $14x = 42$	$75 = 15m$	$3y = 100 - 28$

Study the first problem. Solve problems **2–5** in a similar way.

1. John bought several model kits for $9 each. He spent $36. How many kits did he buy?
   If x stands for the number of kits he bought, then ____9x____ stands for the cost of all the kits.

   Equation: ____$9x = 36$____ $x =$ ____4____

   John bought ____4____ model kits.

   1.

2. A train travels 70 km/h. How long does it take for this train to make a 630-km trip? If x stands for the number of hours for the trip, then _____ stands for the total number of kilometres.

   Equation: _____ $x =$ _____

   It takes _____ h to make the trip.

   2.

3. 3 kg of apples cost $2.34 (234¢). How much does 1 kg of apples cost?
   If x stands for the cost of 1 kg, then _____ stands for the cost of 3 kg.

   Equation: _____ $x =$ _____

   1 kg of apples costs _____ ¢.

   3.

4. Eight loaves of bread cost $7.84 (784¢). How much does one loaf of bread cost?
   If x stands for the cost of one loaf, then _____ stands for the cost of eight loaves.

   Equation: _____ $x =$ _____

   One loaf of bread costs _____ ¢.

   4.

5. A board is 84 cm long. How many metres long is this board?
   If x stands for the number of metres, then _____ stands for the number of centimetres.

   Equation: _____ $x =$ _____

   The board is _____ m long.

   5.

Lesson 4 Solving Equations (multiplication) PRE-ALGEBRA

To solve an equation, you can multiply both sides of it by the same number.

$\dfrac{a}{5} = 35$

$5 \times \dfrac{a}{5} = 5 \times 35$

$\dfrac{\overset{1}{\cancel{5}} \times a}{\cancel{5}_1} = 175$

$a = 175$

Check

$\dfrac{a}{5} = 35$

$\dfrac{175}{5} = 35$

$35 = 35$

$r \div 3 = 11 + 34$

$(r \div 3) \times 3 = 45 \times$ _____

$r =$ _____

To change $\frac{a}{5}$ to a, both sides were multiplied by _____.

To change $r \div 3$ to r, both sides were multiplied by _____.

Solve each equation.

a	b	c
1. $\dfrac{a}{8} = 7$	$\dfrac{b}{13} = 9$	$\dfrac{c}{4} = 6 + 12$
2. $16 = \dfrac{r}{8}$	$8 = s \div 7$	$2 \times 9 = \dfrac{t}{5}$
3. $g \div 17 = 9$	$15 = \dfrac{h}{5}$	$7 \times 6 = \dfrac{j}{3}$
4. $\dfrac{m}{15} = 17$	$23 = \dfrac{n}{28}$	$p \div 19 = 3 \times 9$

Lesson 4 Problem Solving   PRE-ALGEBRA

Study the first problem. Solve problems **2–5** in a similar way.

1. Joseph has $\frac{1}{4}$ the number of points he needs to win. He has 36 points. How many points does he need to win?

If x stands for the number of points needed to win,

then $\underline{\quad \frac{1}{4}x \text{ or } \frac{x}{4} \quad}$ stands for the points he has now.

Equation: $\underline{\quad \frac{1}{4}x = 36 \text{ or } \frac{x}{4} = 36 \quad}$ $x = \underline{\quad 144 \quad}$

Joseph needs $\underline{\quad 144 \quad}$ points to win.

1.

---

2. Mia has $\frac{1}{3}$ the number of points she needs to win. She has 48 points. How many points does she need to win?

If x stands for the total number of points needed to win, then $\underline{\qquad}$ stands for the points she has now.

Equation: $\underline{\qquad\qquad}$ $x = \underline{\qquad}$

Mia needs $\underline{\qquad}$ points to win.

2.

---

3. Three students are absent. This is $\frac{1}{6}$ of the entire class. How many students are in the class?

If x stands for the total number of students, then

$\underline{\qquad}$ stands for the number of students absent.

Equation: $\underline{\qquad\qquad}$ $x = \underline{\qquad}$

There are $\underline{\qquad}$ students in the class.

3.

---

4. Alex drove 120 km and stopped for lunch. He had then travelled $\frac{1}{3}$ the total distance of his trip. What is the total distance of his trip?

If x stands for the total distance, then $\underline{\qquad}$ stands for the distance he has already travelled.

Equation: $\underline{\qquad\qquad}$ $x = \underline{\qquad}$

The total distance of the trip is $\underline{\qquad}$ km.

4.

---

5. Shea solved 12 problems. This was $\frac{1}{5}$ of all she has to solve. How many problems does she have to solve?

Equation: $\underline{\qquad\qquad}$ $x = \underline{\qquad}$

She has $\underline{\qquad}$ problems to solve in all.

5.

Lesson 5   Solving Equations (subtraction)   PRE-ALGEBRA

To solve an equation, you can subtract the same number from both sides of it.

$v + 18 = 47$

$v + 18 - 18 = 47 - 18$

$v + 0 = 29$

$v = 29$

Check

$v + 18 = 47$

$29 + 18 = 47$

$47 = 47$

$c + 6 = 43 + 8$

$c + 6 - $ _____ $ = 51 - $ _____

$c + $ _____ $ = $ _____

$c = $ _____

To change $v + 18$ to v, _____ was subtracted from both sides.

To change $c + 6$ to c, _____ was subtracted from both sides.

Solve each equation.

	a	*b*	*c*
1.	$d + 12 = 48$	$36 + e = 84$	$f + 14 = 18 + 18$
2.	$38 = j + 13$	$27 = 9 + h$	$20 + 34 = 27 + l$
3.	$12 + w = 76$	$114 = x + 38$	$300 - 30 = y + 50$
4.	$200 + 50 = a + 212$	$27 + b = 170 + 3$	$100 - 2 = c + 43$

Lesson 5   Problem Solving   PRE-ALGEBRA

Study the first problem. Solve problems **2–5** in a similar way.

1. A rectangle is 8 m longer than it is wide. If its
   length is 17 m, what is its width?
   If x stands for the number of metres wide, then
   ___$x + 8$___ stands for the number of metres long.

   Equation: ___$x + 8 = 17$___ $x =$ ___9___

   The width of the rectangle is ___9___ m.

2. A rectangle is 27 cm longer than it is wide. If its
   length is 45 cm, what is its width?
   If x stands for the number of centimetres wide,
   then _____ stands for the number of
   centimetres long.

   Equation: _____ $x =$ _____

   The width of the rectangle is _____ cm.

3. Maria's score of 94 is 8 points higher than
   Su-Lin's score. What is Su-Lin's score?
   If x stands for Su-Lin's score, then _____
   stands for Maria's score.

   Equation: _____ $x =$ _____

   Su-Lin's score is _____.

4. The 17 men at work outnumber the women by 5.
   How many women are at work?
   If x stands for the number of women at work,

   then _____ stands for the number of men at
   work.

   Equation: _____ $x =$ _____

   There are _____ women at work.

5. The 48-min trip to work was 19 min longer than
   the trip home from work. How long did it take
   for the trip home?
   If x stands for the number of minutes for the

   trip home, then _____ stands for the trip to
   work.

   Equation: _____ $x =$ _____

   The trip home took _____ min.

1.

2.

3.

4.

5.

Lesson 6 Solving Equations (addition) PRE-ALGEBRA

To solve an equation, you can add the same number to both sides of it.

$t - 3 = 15$

$t - 3 + 3 = 15 + 3$

$t + 0 = 18$

$t = 18$

Check
$t - 3 = 15$
$18 - 3 = 15$
$15 = 15$

$b - 12 = 14 + 3$

$b - 12 +$ _____ $= 17 +$ _____

$b +$ _____ $=$ _____

$b =$ _____

To change $t - 3$ to t, _____ was added to both sides.

To change $b - 12$ to b, _____ was added to both sides.

CHAPTER 3

Solve each equation.

a	b	c
1. $b - 8 = 15$	$x - 14 = 36$	$c - 3 = 28 + 4$
2. $42 = r - 12$	$80 = e - 26$	$20 + 11 = f - 14$
3. $163 = a - 27$	$9 \times 9 = m - 38$	$t - 28 = 102$
4. $117 = w - 83$	$200 - 25 = g - 83$	$h - 75 = 100 + 56$

Lesson 6 Problem Solving   PRE-ALGEBRA

Study the first problem. Solve problems **2–5** in a similar way.

1. The temperature has fallen 12°C since noon. The present temperature is 17°C. What was the noon temperature?
   If x stands for the noon temperature, then
   __$x - 12$__ stands for the present temperature.

   Equation: __$x - 12 = 17$__ $x =$ ____29____

   The noon temperature was ____29____ °C.

   1.

2. The temperature has fallen 7°C since noon. The present temperature is 18°C. What was the noon temperature?
   If x stands for the noon temperature, then
   _____ stands for the present temperature.

   Equation: _____ $x =$ _____

   The noon temperature was _____ °C.

   2.

3. After selling 324 papers, Mr. Merk had 126 papers left. How many papers did he start with?
   If x stands for the number of papers he started with, then _____ stands for the number left.

   Equation: _____ $x =$ _____

   He had _____ papers to start with.

   3.

4. Andrew sold his football for \$15.50 (1550¢). This was 95¢ less than the original cost. What was the original cost?
   If x stands for the original cost, then _____ stands for the amount he sold the football for.

   Equation: _____ $x =$ _____

   The original cost of the football was \$_____.

   4.

5. The width of a rectangle is 37 cm shorter than its length. The width is 75 cm. How long is the rectangle?
   If x stands for the measure of the length, then

   _____ stands for the measure of the width.

   Equation: _____ $x =$ _____

   The rectangle is _____ cm long.

   5.

Lesson 7 Solving Equations Review PRE-ALGEBRA

Solve each equation.

	a	b	c
1.	$4b = 30 + 30$	$13 + 26 = 3u$	$7v = 42 + 42$
2.	$\dfrac{d}{5} = 100 - 40$	$10 - 3 = \dfrac{y}{32}$	$\dfrac{k}{37} = 10 - 8$
3.	$g + 27 = 49 - 4$	$100 - 7 = 39 + x$	$43 = n + 12$
4.	$p - 6 = 3 + 10$	$56 - 3 = k - 42$	$w - 39 = 90 + 3$
5.	$x + 16 = 33 + 12$	$\dfrac{m}{14} = 14 - 4$	$12 + n = 56 + 8$
6.	$7 \times 6 = 3t$	$d + 291 = 400 + 26$	$73 - 8 = n + 5$
7.	$4 + 8 = \dfrac{q}{12}$	$g - 27 = 2 \times 45$	$\dfrac{x}{15} = 20 - 5$

Lesson 7 Problem Solving   PRE-ALGEBRA

Safety Program	
Name	**Points Earned**
Tom	48
Susan	
Bob	
Mallory	
Al	

The bulletin-board chart was torn and some information is missing. Help complete the chart by using the information in the following problems. Write an equation for each problem. Solve the equation. Answer the problem.

1. Tom has earned three times as many points as Susan. How many points has Susan earned?

   Equation: _____ $x =$ _____

   Susan has earned _____ points.

   1. _____

2. Tom has one third the number of points that Bob has. How many points does Bob have?

   Equation: _____ $x =$ _____

   Bob has _____ points.

   2. _____

3. The number of points that Tom has is 27 less than the number of points that Mallory has. How many points does Mallory have?

   Equation: _____ $x =$ _____

   Mallory has _____ points.

   3. _____

4. The number of points that Tom has earned is 27 more than the number of points that Al has earned. How many points has Al earned?

   Equation: _____ $x =$ _____

   Al has earned _____ points.

   4. _____

CHAPTER 3   PRACTICE TEST
Pre-Algebra Equations

Solve each equation.

	a	*b*	*c*
1.	$4m = 40$	$90 = 6n$	$42 - 20 = 2p$
2.	$\dfrac{r}{6} = 7$	$15 = \dfrac{s}{13}$	$\dfrac{t}{2} = 40 + 3$
3.	$a + 9 = 36$	$27 = 6 + b$	$14 + 20 = c + 4$
4.	$x - 9 = 27$	$36 = y - 14$	$z - 6 = 30 + 12$
5.	$42 + 18 = w + 20$	$72 + 18 = \dfrac{x}{6}$	$37 + 12 = y - 18$
6.	$12d = 144$	$17 = \dfrac{e}{3}$	$30m = 3 \times 60$

Write an equation for the problem. Solve.

7. Five workers are absent today. This is one fourth of all workers. How many workers are there?

Equation: _____   There are _____ workers.

CHAPTER 4 PRETEST
Using Pre-Algebra

Complete the following.

	a	b	c

1. $7x + 2x =$ _____ $9y + y =$ _____ $z + 2z =$ _____

2. $6a + 2a =$ _____ $5b + b =$ _____ $c + 2c =$ _____

Solve each equation.

3. $3r + r = 36$ $5s + s = 42$ $t + 3t = 52$

4. $d + d + 8 = 48$ $e + e + 6 = 74$ $f + f - 5 = 95$

5. $u + 2u + 1 = 10$ $v + 3v + 4 = 24$ $w + 5w + 2 = 50$

Solve each problem.

6. Jenna made four times as many widgets as Carmen. They made a total of 60 widgets. How many widgets did Carmen make?

Carmen made _____ widgets.

6.

7. A car averages 72 km per hour. At that rate, how far can the car travel in 3 hours?

The car can travel _____ km.

7.

Lesson 1 Combining Terms

$3a + 2a = a + a + a + a + a$
$\qquad = 5a$

$3b - 2b = b + b + b - b - b$
$\qquad = \underline{\quad 1b \quad}$ or $\underline{\quad b \quad}$

$3a + 2a = (3 + 2)\, a$
$\qquad = 5a$

$3b - 2b = (3 - 2)\, b$
$\qquad = \underline{\quad 1b \quad}$ or $\underline{\quad b \quad}$

Complete the following:

a	b	c
1. $d + 3d = \underline{\quad 4d \quad}$	$5e + 2e = \underline{\qquad}$	$7f + 2f = \underline{\qquad}$
2. $4g - 3g = \underline{\qquad}$	$8h - 4h = \underline{\qquad}$	$5j - j = \underline{\qquad}$
3. $2k + k = \underline{\qquad}$	$5l - 3l = \underline{\qquad}$	$3m + 2m = \underline{\qquad}$
4. $5n + 3n = \underline{\qquad}$	$2p - p = \underline{\qquad}$	$4q - q = \underline{\qquad}$
5. $8r - 2r = \underline{\qquad}$	$5s + 4s = \underline{\qquad}$	$5t + t = \underline{\qquad}$
6. $4u + 3u = \underline{\qquad}$	$9v - v = \underline{\qquad}$	$3w + w = \underline{\qquad}$

Complete the following.

a	b
7. If $a = 5$, then $3a + 2a = \underline{\quad 25 \quad}$.	If $b = 3$, then $5b - 2b = \underline{\qquad}$.
8. If $c = 2$, then $3c + c = \underline{\qquad}$.	If $d = 1$, then $3d - d = \underline{\qquad}$.
9. If $e = 5$, then $2e + 2e = \underline{\qquad}$.	If $f = 4$, then $5f - 4f = \underline{\qquad}$.
10. If $g = 2$, then $g + 3g = \underline{\qquad}$.	If $h = 5$, then $2h - h = \underline{\qquad}$.
11. If $j = 3$, then $2j + 4j = \underline{\qquad}$.	If $k = 3$, then $4k - 3k = \underline{\qquad}$.
12. If $l = 5$, then $3l + 3l = \underline{\qquad}$.	If $m = 1$, then $6m - m = \underline{\qquad}$.

CHAPTER 4

Lesson 2 Solving Equations

$$\begin{aligned}x + 5x &= 18\\6x &= 18\\x &= \frac{18}{6}\\x &= 3\end{aligned}$$

Check

$$\begin{aligned}x + 5x &= 18\\3 + (5 \times 3) &= 18\\3 + 15 &= 18\\18 &= 18\end{aligned}$$

$$\begin{aligned}y + y + 3 &= 27\\2y + 3 &= 27\\2y &= 27 - 3\\2y &= 24\\y &= 24 \div 2\\y &= 12\end{aligned}$$

Check

$$\begin{aligned}y + y + 3 &= 27\\12 + 12 + 3 &= 27\\27 &= 27\end{aligned}$$

If $x + 5x = 18$, then $x =$ _____ and $5x =$ _____.

If $y + y + 3 = 27$, then $y =$ _____

Solve each equation.

a	b	c

1. $4a + a = 25$ $7b + b = 72$ $c + 6c = 49$

2. $d + d + 2 = 22$ $e + e + 8 = 28$ $f + f - 6 = 30$

3. $3g + g = 48$ $h + h - 5 = 25$ $5j + j = 54$

4. $k + k + 4 = 44$ $3l + l = 72$ $m + m - 7 = 19$

5. $n + 8n = 108$ $p + p + 12 = 60$ $2q + q = 72$

Lesson 3   Problem Solving   PRE-ALGEBRA

Larry is twice as old as Marvin. Their combined age is 24 years. How old is each boy?

Check

If x stands for Marvin's age, then

___2x___ stands for Larry's age.

Equation: ___$x + 2x = 24$___

Marvin is ___8___ years old.

Larry is ___16___ years old.

$x + 2x = 24$

$3x = 24$

$x = 24 \div 3$

$x = 8$

Since $x = 8$,

$2x = 2 \times 8$ or 16.

$x + 2x = 24$

$8 + (2 \times 8) = 24$

$8 + 16 = 24$

$24 = 24$

CHAPTER 4

Write an equation for each problem. Solve each problem.

1. An office has 28 workers. There are three times as many men as women. How many women are there? How many men are there?

   Equation: _____

   There are _____ women and _____ men.

   1.

2. During the summer Kim worked four times as many days as Lana. They worked a total of 75 days. How many days did each work?

   Equation: _____

   Lana worked _____ days. Kim worked

   _____ days.

   2.

3. A truck has a mass of 4200 kg. The mass of the truck body is six times that of the engine. What is the mass of the engine? What is the mass of the truck body?

   Equation: _____

   The mass of the engine is _____ kg and the

   mass of the truck body is _____ kg.

   3.

4. Jair is three times as old as Sue. Their combined age is 52. How old is each person?

   Equation: _____

   Sue is _____ years old. Jair is _____ years old.

   4.

Lesson 4 Problem Solving   PRE-ALGEBRA

In an election between two girls, 75 votes were cast. Bianca received 5 more votes than Jaime. How many votes did each girl receive?

Check

If x stands for the number of votes for Jaime, then __$x + 5$__ stands for the number of votes for Bianca.

Equation: __$x + (x + 5) = 75$__

Jaime received __35__ votes.

Bianca received __40__ votes.

$$x + (x + 5) = 75$$
$$2x + 5 = 75$$
$$2x = 75 - 5$$
$$2x = 70$$
$$x = 35$$

Since $x = 35$,
$x + 5 = 35 + 5$ or 40.

$$x + (x + 5) = 75$$
$$35 + 35 + 5 = 75$$
$$75 = 75$$

Write an equation for each problem. Solve each problem.

1. Paul made 7 more gadgets than Jeremy. Together they made 55 gadgets. How many did each man make?

   Equation: _____

   Paul made _____ gadgets and Jeremy made _____.

   1.

2. Two pairs of shoes cost $58. One pair costs $6 more than the other. How much did each pair cost?

   Equation: _____

   One pair cost $_____ and the other cost $_____.

   2.

3. Yoko's mass is 8 kg more than Tara's mass. Their combined mass is 92 kg. What is each girl's mass?

   Equation: _____

   Tara's mass is _____ kg and Yoko's mass is _____ kg.

   3.

4. Lisa has 12 more cases to unload than Mick does. They have a total of 150 cases to unload. How many cases does each have to unload?

   Equation: _____

   Mick has _____ cases and Lisa has _____ cases.

   4.

Lesson 5 Problem Solving   PRE-ALGEBRA

Max has two boards that have a combined length of 16 m. One board is 1 m longer than twice the length of the other. What is the length of each board?

Check

If x stands for the length of the shorter board, then __$2x + 1$__ stands for the length of the longer board.

Equation: ____$x + (2x + 1) = 16$____

The shorter board is ____5____ m long.

The longer board is ____11____ m long.

$$x + (2x + 1) = 16$$
$$3x + 1 = 16$$
$$3x = 16 - 1$$
$$3x = 15$$
$$x = 5$$

Since $x = 5$,
$2x + 1 = (2 \times 5) + 1$ or 11.

$$x + (2x + 1) = 16$$
$$5 + (2 \times 5) + 1 = 16$$
$$5 + 10 + 1 = 16$$
$$16 = 16$$

CHAPTER 4

Write an equation for each problem. Solve each problem.

1. Mark and Bill have a combined mass of 85 kg. Mark's mass is 20 kg less than twice Bill's mass. What is each boy's mass?

    Equation: _____

    Bill's mass is _____ kg.

    Mark's mass is _____ kg.

    1.

2. Cara and Amber have saved $43. Amber has saved $3 more than three times the amount Cara has saved. How much money has each girl saved?

    Equation: _____

    Cara has saved $_____.

    Amber has saved $_____.

    2.

3. A carpenter cut a board that was 5 m long into two pieces. The longer piece is 1 m longer than three times the length of the shorter piece. What is the length of each piece?

    Equation: _____

    The shorter piece is _____ m long.

    The longer piece is _____ m long.

    3.

Lesson 5 Problem Solving   PRE-ALGEBRA

Write an equation for each problem. Solve each problem.

1. Elise said that Box A is 2 kg heavier than Box D. She also said that together these boxes have a mass of 16 kg. What is the mass of each box?

   Equation: _____

   Box A's mass is _____ kg.

   Box D's mass is _____ kg.

2. Box C is twice as heavy as Box A. Together their mass is 27 kg. What is the mass of each box?

   Equation: _____

   Box A's mass is _____ kg.

   Box C's mass is _____ kg.

3. Box B's mass is 1 kg more than twice the mass of Box D. They have a combined mass of 22 kg. What is the mass of each box?

   Equation: _____

   Box B's mass is _____ kg.

   Box D's mass is _____ kg.

4. Elise's mass is 1 kg more than Mark's. Their total mass is 97 kg. What is the mass of each person?

   Equation: _____

   Mark's mass is _____ kg.

   Elise's mass is _____ kg.

1.

2.

3.

4.

Lesson 6   Problem Solving

PRE-ALGEBRA

$$\text{distance} = \text{rate} \times \text{time}$$
$$d = r \times t$$

A robin flew 171 km in 3 hours.
At what speed did the robin fly?

Equation: _____ $171 = r \times 3$ _____

The robin flew _____ 57 _____ km per hour.

$$d = r \times t$$
$$171 = r \times 3$$
$$\frac{171}{3} = r$$
$$57 = r$$

Write an equation for each problem. Solve each problem.

1. At 450 km per hour, how far can a plane fly in 5 h?

   Equation: _____

   The plane can fly _____ km in 5 h.

   1.

2. The Willards want to travel 744 km in 12 h. They plan to travel the same distance each hour. At what speed would they travel?

   Equation: _____

   They would travel _____ km per hour.

   2.

3. A ship averages 25 knots per hour. How far can the ship travel in 2 days?

   Equation: _____

   The ship can travel _____ knots in 2 days.

   3.

4. At what speed would a plane have to fly in order to travel 780 km in 2 h?

   Equation: _____

   It would fly at _____ km per hour.

   4.

5. At 204.8 km per hour, how far can a race car travel in 4 h?

   Equation: _____

   It can travel _____ km in 4 h.

   5.

Lesson 6 Problem Solving   PRE-ALGEBRA

For all levers, $w \times d = W \times D$.

w

W

d

D

6 cm

D cm

10 g

12 g

fulcrum

To balance the lever (or scale), how far from the fulcrum must the 12-gram mass be placed?

Check

$$w \times d = W \times D \qquad w \times d = W \times D$$
$$10 \times 6 = 12 \times D \qquad 10 \times 6 = 12 \times 5$$
$$\frac{60}{12} = D \qquad\qquad 60 = 60$$
$$5 = D$$

The 12-g mass must be placed _____ cm from the fulcrum.

Write an equation for each problem. Solve each problem.

1. A 60-kg boy sits 2 m from the fulcrum of a seesaw. How far from the fulcrum should a 40-kg girl sit so the seesaw is balanced?

    Equation: _____

    She should sit _____ m from the fulcrum.

2. How much mass would have to be applied at point A so that the lever is balanced?

    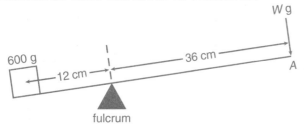

    600 g

    12 cm

    36 cm

    W g

    A

    fulcrum

    Equation: _____

    _____ g would have to be applied at point A.

3. What mass is needed at point S on the scale so that the scale is balanced?

    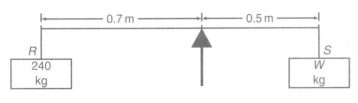

    0.7 m

    0.5 m

    R

    240 kg

    S

    W kg

    Equation: _____

    _____ kg are needed at point S.

1.

2.

3.

CHAPTER 4 PRACTICE TEST
Using Pre-Algebra

Solve each problem.

1. Maggie worked three times as many hours as Ann. They worked a total of 32 h. How many hours did Ann work?

    Equation: _____

    Ann worked _____ h.

    1.

2. An eraser and a pencil cost 87¢. The pencil cost 9¢ more than the eraser. How much did the pencil cost?

    Equation: _____

    The pencil cost _____ ¢.

    2.

3. Dane and Jim earned 215 points in a contest. Dane earned 5 more than twice as many points as Jim. How many points did each boy earn?

    Equation: _____

    Jim earned _____ points.

    Dane earned _____ points.

    3.

4. Darla scored twice as many points as the combined scores of Gina and Hikaru. Darla scored 88 points. Gina scored 20 points. How many points did Hikaru score?

    Hikaru scored _____ points.

    4.

5. At 51 km per hour, how far can a car travel in 3 h?

    It can travel _____ km in 3 h.

    5.

6. To balance the lever, how far from the fulcrum must the 40-kg mass be placed?

    It must be _____ m from the fulcrum.

    6.

CHAPTER 5   PRETEST
Ratio, Rate, Proportion, and Percent

Circle each proportion below.

a	b
1. $\frac{3}{16} = \frac{6}{24}$	$\frac{7}{8} = \frac{28}{32}$
2. $\frac{8}{20} = \frac{4}{5}$	$\frac{2}{3} = \frac{10}{15}$
3. $\frac{7}{9} = \frac{21}{27}$	$\frac{24}{15} = \frac{8}{5}$

Solve each of the following.

4. $\frac{n}{3} = \frac{9}{27}$	$\frac{3}{5} = \frac{15}{n}$
5. $\frac{5}{6} = \frac{n}{36}$	$\frac{n}{8} = \frac{3}{6}$
6. $\frac{8}{24} = \frac{n}{15}$	$\frac{n}{10} = \frac{9}{15}$
7. $\frac{10}{25} = \frac{8}{n}$	$\frac{42}{n} = \frac{3}{4}$

Complete the following.

a	b
8. _____ is 12% of 36.	7 is _____ % of 16.
9. $\frac{1}{2}$ is 50% of _____.	45 is 75% of _____.
10. $\frac{2}{5}$ is _____% of $\frac{1}{2}$.	_____ is 30% of 200.
11. 3.6 is 80% of _____.	1.8 is _____% of 2.4.
12. _____ is 6.7% of 83.	135 is _____% of 90.

Lesson 1   Ratio

A **ratio** is a comparison of the numbers of two sets of like objects.
A **rate** is a comparison of the numbers of two sets of different objects.

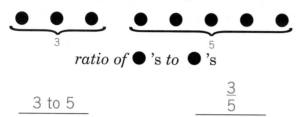

ratio of ● *'s to* ● *'s*

3 to 5 $\frac{3}{5}$

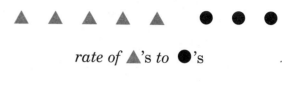

rate of ▲*'s to* ●*'s*

5 to 3   _____

Express the ratio or the rate of the number of items in the first set to the number of items in the second set in two ways as shown.

		a	*b*
1. {○, □}	{*, △, □}	2 to 3	$\frac{2}{3}$
2. {Jim, John}	{Jo, Sue, Ann, Kay}	_____	_____
3. {1, 2, 3, 4}	{a, b, c}	_____	_____
4. {Bob, Dick, Al}	{1st, 2nd, 3rd}	_____	_____
5. {m, n, o, p, q}	{w, x, y, z}	_____	_____

Express each of the following as a ratio or a rate in two ways as shown.

	a	*b*
6. 7 runs in 9 innings	7 to 9	$\frac{7}{9}$
7. 5 boys to 6 girls	_____	_____
8. 3 teachers for 72 students	_____	_____
9. 5 pages in 20 minutes	_____	_____
10. 5 touchdowns in 4 games	_____	_____
11. 11 chairs to 2 tables	_____	_____
12. 6 goals for 9 shots	_____	_____

Lesson 2 Proportions (recognizing)

NAME _____

A **proportion** expresses the equality of two ratios.

$\frac{2}{3} = \frac{4}{6}$ __is__ a proportion because $2 \times 6 = 3 \times 4$ is __true__.

$\frac{5}{8} = \frac{3}{4}$ __is not__ a proportion because $5 \times 4 = 8 \times 3$ is __false__.

$\frac{4}{5} = \frac{7}{8}$ _____ a proportion because $4 \times 8 = 5 \times 7$ is _____.

$\frac{3}{4} = \frac{9}{12}$ _____ a proportion because $3 \times 12 = 4 \times 9$ is _____.

Circle each proportion below.

a .... b

1. $\frac{2}{3} = \frac{8}{12}$ .... $\frac{1}{4} = \frac{2}{9}$

2. $\frac{5}{8} = \frac{11}{16}$ .... $\frac{5}{6} = \frac{20}{24}$

3. $\frac{1}{6} = \frac{2}{12}$ .... $\frac{14}{16} = \frac{7}{8}$

4. $\frac{5}{12} = \frac{15}{36}$ .... $\frac{8}{3} = \frac{15}{6}$

5. $\frac{7}{20} = \frac{15}{40}$ .... $\frac{9}{24} = \frac{1}{3}$

6. $\frac{1}{3} = \frac{6}{18}$ .... $\frac{15}{24} = \frac{5}{8}$

7. $\frac{7}{12} = \frac{9}{16}$ .... $\frac{4}{5} = \frac{10}{12}$

8. $\frac{9}{10} = \frac{90}{100}$ .... $\frac{8}{10} = \frac{4}{5}$

9. $\frac{4}{12} = \frac{5}{16}$ .... $\frac{4}{3} = \frac{5}{4}$

10. $\frac{12}{25} = \frac{48}{100}$ .... $\frac{125}{1000} = \frac{1}{8}$

Lesson 3   Proportions   PRE-ALGEBRA

Study how the proportions below are solved.

$$\frac{5}{8} = \frac{15}{n}$$

$5 \times n = 8 \times 15$

$5n = 120$

$n = \underline{\ 24\ }$

$$\frac{2}{3} = \frac{n}{24}$$

$2 \times 24 = 3 \times n$

$48 = 3n$

$\underline{\ \ \ \ } = n$

$$\frac{5}{n} = \frac{6}{24}$$

$5 \times 24 = n \times 6$

$120 = 6n$

$\underline{\ \ \ \ } = n$

$$\frac{n}{6} = \frac{20}{24}$$

$n \times 24 = 6 \times 20$

$24n = 120$

$n = \underline{\ \ \ \ }$

Solve each of the following.

	a	*b*	*c*
1.	$\frac{2}{3} = \frac{n}{18}$	$\frac{3}{5} = \frac{n}{25}$	$\frac{3}{4} = \frac{n}{100}$
2.	$\frac{1}{4} = \frac{2}{n}$	$\frac{5}{6} = \frac{10}{n}$	$\frac{7}{8} = \frac{42}{n}$
3.	$\frac{n}{6} = \frac{2}{3}$	$\frac{n}{8} = \frac{21}{24}$	$\frac{n}{3} = \frac{24}{36}$
4.	$\frac{8}{n} = \frac{1}{2}$	$\frac{5}{n} = \frac{20}{28}$	$\frac{4}{n} = \frac{80}{100}$
5.	$\frac{n}{2} = \frac{12}{8}$	$\frac{5}{8} = \frac{n}{1000}$	$\frac{3}{4} = \frac{36}{n}$

Lesson 4 Proportions   PRE-ALGEBRA

A train can travel 120 km in 2 h. At that rate, how far can the train travel in 3 hours?

Let *n* represent the number of kilometres travelled in 3 h. Then the following proportions can be obtained by thinking as follows.

Compare the number of hours to the number of kilometres travelled.	Compare the number of kilometres travelled to the number of hours.	Compare the first number of hours to the second and the first number of kilometres to the second.	Compare the second number of hours to the first and the second number of kilometres to the first.
$\dfrac{2}{120} = \dfrac{3}{n}$	$\dfrac{120}{2} = \dfrac{n}{3}$	$\dfrac{2}{3} = \dfrac{120}{n}$	$\dfrac{3}{2} = \dfrac{n}{120}$
$2n = 360$	$360 = 2n$	$2n = 360$	$360 = 2n$
$n =$ _____	_____ $= n$	$n =$ _____	_____ $= n$

Use a proportion to solve each problem.

1. If eight cases of merchandise cost $60, what would 12 cases cost?

   12 cases would cost $_____.

2. 2 kg of apples can be purchased for 98¢. At this rate, what would 1 kg of apples cost?

   1 kg of apples would cost _____¢.

3. Caitlin delivered 450 flyers in 3 h. At this rate, how many flyers can she deliver in 4 h?

   She can deliver _____ flyers in 4 h.

4. In his last game the Rams' quarterback threw 18 passes and completed 10. At this rate, how many passes will he complete if he throws 27 passes in a game?

   He will complete _____ passes.

5. Mrs. Svage used 3 L of paint to cover 30 m². At this rate, how much paint will be needed to cover 40 m²?

   _____ L will be needed.

1.

2.

3.

4.

5.

Lesson 5 Scale Drawings

In a **scale drawing,** the dimensions of the object are in proportion to the actual object. The scale is the ratio of the drawing size to the actual size of the object.

Find the missing information.

scale: 3 cm: 1 km
drawing length: ?
actual length: 4.5 km

Set up a proportion to find the length.

scale $\longrightarrow$ $\dfrac{3}{1} = \dfrac{n}{4.5}$ $\dfrac{\text{drawing length}}{\text{actual length}}$

$3 \times 4.5 = 1 \times n$

$13.5 = n$

The length of the drawing is 13.5 cm.

scale: ? cm: ? m
drawing length: 6 cm
actual length: 12 m

Set up a ratio to find the scale.

$\dfrac{6 \text{ cm}}{12 \text{ m}}$ $\dfrac{\text{drawing length}}{\text{actual length}}$

$\dfrac{1 \text{ cm}}{2 \text{ m}}$

The scale is 1 cm: 2 m.

CHAPTER 5

Find the missing information.

	a	b

1. scale: _____
   drawing length: 5 cm
   actual length: 20 m

scale: 2 cm: 5 m
drawing length: _____
actual length: 35 m

2. scale: 3 cm: 2 m
   drawing length: 13.5 cm
   actual length: _____

scale: 1.5 cm: 5 m
drawing length: _____
actual length: 100 m

3. scale: _____
   drawing length: 2.5 cm
   actual length: 40 km

scale: 1 m: 0.5 km
drawing length: 4 m
actual length: _____

4. scale: 2 cm: 3 km
   drawing length: 3 cm
   actual length: _____

scale: _____
drawing length: 1 mm
actual length: 3.5 m

Lesson 5 Problem Solving

Solve each problem.

1. Mr. Jonas made a scale drawing of an addition that he is making to his house. The scale he used is 1 cm: 3 m. The length of the addition is 12 m. What is the length of the addition on the drawing?

   The length of the addition on the drawing is

   _____ cm.

1.

2. Elizabeth is designing a flower garden for her community. The garden will be 9 m wide and 13.5 m long. The drawing has a width of 5 cm. She includes in the drawing a key for the scale that is 1.25 cm long. What actual distance does the key for the scale represent?

   The drawing of Elizabeth's garden is scaled as

   _____.

2.

3. Use the scale from problem 2 to find the length of Elizabeth's garden in the drawing.

   Elizabeth's drawing has a length of

   _____ cm.

3.

4. Mrs. Finney is a sculptor of famous people. She uses a 1 cm: 2 cm scale. She is making a sculpture of the mayor of her city. The finished sculpture is 13.75 cm from the base of the neck to the tip of the head. What is the actual height of his head from the base of his neck to the tip of his head?

   The mayor's head from the base of his neck to the tip of his head is _____ cm.

4.

5. The actual size of an artifact is 3 cm by 5.5 cm. In the archive files a drawing that measures 9 cm by 16.5 cm shows every detail of its design. Is the ratio that represents this scale drawing greater than 1, equal to 1, or less than 1?

   The scale for the archived drawing is

   _____.

5.

Lesson 6 Problem Solving   PRE-ALGEBRA

As **A** revolves twice,
B revolves once.

As **C** revolves 4 times,
D revolves 14 times.

As **E** revolves 4 times,
F revolves 3 times.

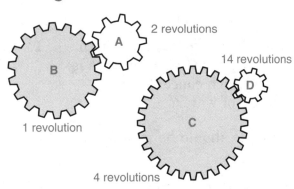
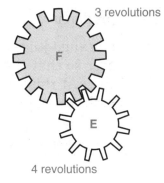

Use a proportion to solve each problem.

1. When gear **A** has completed six revolutions, how many revolutions will gear **B** have made?

   Gear **B** will have made _____ revolutions.

   1.

2. While gear **B** is making 30 revolutions, how many revolutions will gear **A** make?

   Gear **A** will make _____ revolutions.

   2.

3. When gear **C** has completed 12 revolutions, how many revolutions will gear **D** have made?

   Gear **D** will have made _____ revolutions.

   3.

4. While gear **D** is making 84 revolutions, how many revolutions will gear **C** make?

   Gear **C** will make _____ revolutions.

   4.

5. When gear **E** has completed 56 revolutions, how many revolutions will gear **F** have made?

   Gear **F** will have made _____ revolutions.

   5.

6. While gear **F** is making 90 revolutions, how many revolutions will gear **E** make?

   Gear **E** will make _____ revolutions.

   6.

7. When gear **E** has completed 76 revolutions, how many revolutions will gear **F** have made?

   Gear **F** will have made _____ revolutions.

   7.

Lesson 6   Problem Solving   PRE-ALGEBRA

Use a proportion to solve each problem.

1. An orange-juice concentrate is to be mixed with water so that the ratio of water to concentrate is 3 to 1. At this rate, how much concentrate should be mixed with 6 L of water?

   _____ L of concentrate should be mixed with 6 L of water.

   1.

2. A shoe store sells 4 pairs of black shoes for every 7 pairs of brown shoes. There were 4900 pairs of brown shoes sold last year. How many pairs of black shoes were sold?

   _____ pairs of black shoes were sold.

   2.

3. At the Kolbus Building, 3 out of every 7 employees use public transportation. There are 9800 employees at the building. How many use public transportation?

   _____ use public transportation.

   3.

4. The ratio of box seats at the hockey arena to general-admission seats is 2 to 7. There are 2500 box seats. How many general-admission seats are there?

   There are _____ general-admission seats.

   4.

5. At the snack bar, 7 hot dogs are sold for every 10 hamburgers sold. At this rate, how many hot dogs will be sold if 90 hamburgers are sold?

   _____ hot dogs will be sold.

   5.

6. Jacob delivered 90 flyers in 30 min. At this rate, how long will it take him to deliver 135 flyers?

   It will take him _____ min.

   6.

7. At the airport, four planes land every 8 min. At this rate, how many planes will land in 1 h?

   _____ planes will land in 1 h.

   7.

Lesson 7   Percent   PRE-ALGEBRA

If n stands for a number, then $n\%$ stands for the ratio of n to 100 or $\frac{n}{100}$.

$1\% = \dfrac{1}{100}$ or $\underline{0.01}$ $37\% = \dfrac{37}{100}$ or $\underline{0.37}$ $125\% = \dfrac{125}{100}$ or $\underline{1.25}$

$5\% = \underline{\hphantom{xx}}$ or $\underline{\hphantom{xx}}$ $53\% = \underline{\hphantom{xx}}$ or $\underline{\hphantom{xx}}$ $149\% = \underline{\hphantom{xx}}$ or $\underline{\hphantom{xx}}$

Complete the following.

	percent	fraction	decimal
1.	3%		
2.	27%		
3.	121%		
4.	7%		
5.	39%		
6.	141%		
7.	9%		
8.	11%		
9.	167%		
10.	57%		
11.	251%		
12.	69%		
13.	391%		
14.	87%		

CHAPTER 5

Lesson 8   Fractions and Percent

Study how to change a fraction to a percent.

$$\frac{4}{5} = \frac{n}{100}$$

$400 = 5n$

$80 = n$

$$\frac{4}{5} = \underline{80\%}$$

$$\frac{1}{8} = \frac{n}{100}$$

$100 = 8n$

$12\frac{1}{2} = n$

$$\frac{1}{8} = \underline{12\frac{1}{2}} \%$$

Study how to change a percent to a fraction or mixed numeral.

$$175\% = \frac{175}{100}$$

$$= \frac{7}{4} \text{ or } \underline{1\frac{3}{4}}$$

$$3\frac{1}{2}\% = \frac{3\frac{1}{2}}{100}$$

$$= 3\frac{1}{2} \times \frac{1}{100}$$

$$= \frac{7}{2} \times \frac{1}{100}$$

$$= \frac{7}{200}$$

Complete the following.

	a	b
1.	$\frac{1}{4}$ = _____%	$\frac{3}{8}$ = _____%
2.	$\frac{1}{10}$ = _____%	$\frac{3}{4}$ = _____%
3.	$\frac{1}{2}$ = _____%	$\frac{5}{8}$ = _____%
4.	$\frac{7}{10}$ = _____%	$\frac{2}{5}$ = _____%
5.	$\frac{4}{5}$ = _____%	$\frac{7}{8}$ = _____%

Change each of the following to a fraction or mixed numeral in simplest form.

6. 10% = _____ 80% = _____

7. 160% = _____ $12\frac{1}{2}\%$ = _____

8. 250% = _____ $62\frac{1}{2}\%$ = _____

9. 20% = _____ 16% = _____

10. 125% = _____ $37\frac{1}{2}\%$ = _____

Lesson 9 Decimals and Percent

NAME _____

Study how to change a decimal to a percent.

$$0.3 = 0.30 = \frac{30}{100} = \underline{\quad 30 \quad}\%$$

$$1.24 = \frac{124}{100} = \underline{\quad 124 \quad}\%$$

$$0.375 = \frac{37.5}{100} = \underline{\quad 37.5 \quad}\%$$

$$1.6 = 1.60 = \frac{160}{100} = \underline{\quad\quad}\%$$

$$0.59 = \frac{59}{100} = \underline{\quad\quad}\%$$

$$2.125 = \frac{212.5}{100} = \underline{\quad\quad}\%$$

Study how to change a percent to a decimal.

$$17.6\% = \frac{17.6}{100} = \underline{\quad 0.176 \quad}$$

$$7.25\% = \frac{7.25}{100} = \underline{\quad 0.0725 \quad}$$

$$16\frac{3}{4}\% = 16.75\% = \frac{16.75}{100} = \underline{\quad 0.1675 \quad}$$

$$8.4\% = \frac{8.4}{100} = \underline{\quad\quad}$$

$$9.69\% = \frac{9.69}{100} = \underline{\quad\quad}$$

$$37\frac{1}{2}\% = 37.5\% = \frac{37.5}{100} = \underline{\quad\quad}$$

Complete the following.

a

	decimal	percent
1.	0.2	_____
2.	1.9	_____
3.	0.02	_____
4.	0.36	_____
5.	1.47	_____
6.	0.067	_____
7.	0.123	_____
8.	1.625	_____

b

percent	decimal
52%	_____
148%	_____
5.4%	_____
8.75%	_____
183.75%	_____
$9\frac{1}{2}\%$	_____
$7\frac{1}{4}\%$	_____
$8\frac{3}{4}\%$	_____

NAME _____

Lesson 10 Fractions, Decimals, and Percent

Change each fraction to a percent. Change each percent to a fraction or mixed numeral in simplest form.

	a	b

1. $\frac{1}{8} =$ _____% 　　30% = _____

2. 80% = _____ 　　$\frac{1}{5} =$ _____%

3. $\frac{3}{5} =$ _____% 　　120% = _____

4. $87\frac{1}{2}\% =$ _____ 　　$\frac{3}{4} =$ _____%

5. $\frac{1}{10} =$ _____% 　　150% = _____

6. $31\frac{1}{4}\% =$ _____ 　　$\frac{9}{10} =$ _____%

7. $\frac{4}{25} =$ _____% 　　64% = _____

8. 110% = _____ 　　$\frac{9}{20} =$ _____%

Change each decimal to a percent. Change each percent to a decimal.

9. 0.5 = _____% 　　4% = _____

10. 17.7% = _____ 　　1.1 = _____%

11. 0.67 = _____% 　　6.625% = _____

12. 8.46% = _____ 　　1.58 = _____%

13. 0.125 = _____% 　　4.075% = _____

14. 6.007% = _____ 　　0.312 = _____%

15. $6\frac{1}{4}\% =$ _____ 　　$9\frac{3}{4}\% =$ _____

16. $7\frac{3}{4}\% =$ _____ 　　$5\frac{1}{2}\% =$ _____

Lesson 11   Comparing and Ordering

When comparing percents, fractions, and decimals, use inequality symbols or the equal symbol to show the relationship.

> The **inequality symbols** that show order are
>
> > greater than   ≥ greater than or equal to
>
> < less than   ≤ less than or equal to

Replace the _____ with <, >, or = in the following number sentences.

0.60 _____ $\frac{6}{100}$ $\frac{1}{3}$ _____ 30%   15% _____ 0.165

To make comparing easier, rewrite the numbers so that each is in the same format.

0.60 ___>___ 0.06 $33\frac{1}{3}$% ___>___ 30%   0.15 ___<___ 0.165

Replace the _____ with <, >, or = in the following number sentences.

	a	*b*	*c*
1.	0.07 _____ $\frac{2}{3}$	$\frac{1}{3}$ _____ 0.33	85% _____ 8.5
2.	$\frac{4}{5}$ _____ 20%	12% _____ 0.012	15% _____ $\frac{1}{15}$
3.	80% _____ $\frac{3}{5}$	$\frac{6}{7}$ _____ 85%	2.5 _____ $\frac{5}{2}$
4.	0.14% _____ $\frac{14}{10}$	0.082 _____ 80%	$\frac{7}{11}$ _____ 0.64

Write the numbers from least to greatest.

	a	*b*
5.	$\frac{1}{2}$, 0.55, 45%; _____ < _____ < _____	90%, 0.99, 1; _____ < _____ < _____

Write the numbers from greatest to least.

	a	*b*
6.	$\frac{3}{4}$, 7.5, 68%; _____ > _____ > _____	0.115, 11%, $\frac{1}{11}$; _____ > _____ > _____

CHAPTER 5

Lesson 11 Problem Solving

Solve each problem.

1. Jim ate $\frac{3}{5}$ of a large pizza from a pizzeria. Sonny ate 75% of a large pizza from the same pizzeria. Who ate the largest portion of pizza?

   _____ ate the most pizza.

   1.

2. Sarah, Johannah, and Trista collect postcards. They each have the same number of postcards in their collections. They decided to compare how many each had from New Brunswick. Sarah said, "half of my collection is from New Brunswick." Trista said, "$\frac{5}{8}$ of my collection is from New Brunswick." Then Johannah proclaimed, "I have you both beat, 62% of my collection is from New Brunswick." Is Johannah's statement true or false? List the girls in order from the one who has the greatest number of New Brunswick postcards to the one who has the fewest New Brunswick postcards.

   Johannah's statement is _____.

   From greatest to fewest, the number of New Brunswick postcards is _____.

   2.

3. Mr. Morrison owned 5 hectares (ha) of land. He decided to distribute the property among his three children. The oldest child received the deed to $\frac{3}{8}$ of his land. The middle child was given $\frac{1}{3}$. The youngest child received about 30% of the land. Write the size of each child's land as a decimal. Decide if the size of land received matched each child's order in the family.

   The oldest child received _____ of the land.

   The middle child received about _____ of the land.

   The youngest child received _____ of the land.

   The largest parcel of land was given to the _____ child and the smallest parcel of land was given to the _____ child.

   3.

Lesson 12   Percent of a Number

What number is $16\frac{1}{2}$% of 90?

$$n = 16\frac{1}{2}\% \times 90$$
$$= 0.165 \times 90$$
$$= \underline{}$$

$\underline{}$ is $16\frac{1}{2}$% of 90.

What number is 135% of 83?

$$n = 135\% \times 83$$
$$= 1.35 \times 83$$
$$= \underline{}$$

$\underline{}$ is 135% of 83.

Complete the following.

	a	*b*
1.	_____ is 40% of 20.	_____ is 32% of 15.
2.	_____ is 120% of 80.	_____ is 62% of 48.
3.	_____ is 33% of 69.	_____ is 150% of 38.
4.	_____ is $62\frac{1}{2}$% of 840.	_____ is 6.7% of 83.
5.	_____ is 50% of $\frac{3}{8}$.	_____ is 7.8% of 65.
6.	_____ is 85% of 480.	_____ is 25% of 23.6.
7.	_____ is $37\frac{1}{2}$% of 64.	_____ is 175% of 40.
8.	_____ is 6% of 112.	_____ is 9.6% of 480.
9.	_____ is 80% of 540.	_____ is 12.5% of 49.8.
10.	_____ is 8% of 180.	_____ is 130% of 96.

CHAPTER 5

Lesson 12 Problem Solving   PRE-ALGEBRA

Solve each problem.

1. Of the building permits issued, 85% were for single-family dwellings. There were 760 permits issued. How many were for single-family dwellings?

   _____ were for single-family dwellings.

2. Leona answered all the questions on a test. She had 90% of them correct. There were 40 questions in all. How many did she have correct?

   She had _____ correct.

3. Of the 45 seats on the bus, 60% are filled. How many seats are filled?

   _____ seats are filled.

4. An oil tank will hold 250 L. The tank is 80% full. How many litres of oil are in the tank?

   _____ L of oil are in the tank.

5. A contractor is to remove 600 m³ of earth. So far, 70% of the work has been done. How many cubic metres of earth have been removed?

   _____ m³ of earth have been removed.

6. Mrs. Hughes bought a mixture of grass seed that contained 75% bluegrass seed. She purchased 2.5 kg of grass seed in all. How many kilograms of bluegrass seed did she get?

   She got _____ kg of bluegrass seed.

7. Mr. Jones' car gets 6.6 km per litre of fuel efficiency. He can improve his fuel efficiency by 15% by getting a tune-up. By how much will his fuel efficiency improve with a tune-up?

   His fuel efficiency will improve by _____ km per litre.

1.

2.

3.

4.

5.

6.

7.

Lesson 13   Percent of a Number

NAME _____

PRE-ALGEBRA

25 is what percent of 40?

$$25 = n\% \times 40$$
$$25 = \frac{n}{100} \times 40$$
$$25 = \frac{40n}{100}$$
$$2500 = 40n$$
$$\underline{\quad 62.5 \quad} = n$$

25 is _____% of 40.

$\frac{3}{8}$ is what percent of $\frac{1}{2}$?

$$\frac{3}{8} = n\% \times \frac{1}{2}$$
$$\frac{3}{8} = \frac{n}{100} \times \frac{1}{2}$$
$$\frac{3}{8} = \frac{n}{200}$$
$$600 = 8n$$
$$\underline{\quad 75 \quad} = n$$

$\frac{3}{8}$ is _____% of $\frac{1}{2}$.

Complete the following.

a

1. 32 is _____% of 64.

2. 88 is _____% of 80.

3. $\frac{3}{8}$ is _____% of $\frac{3}{4}$.

4. $18\frac{3}{4}$ is _____% of 75.

5. 50 is _____% of 80.

6. $\frac{2}{3}$ is _____% of $\frac{5}{6}$.

7. 78 is _____% of 104.

8. 0.72 is _____% of 0.48.

9. $8\frac{1}{3}$ is _____% of $33\frac{1}{3}$.

10. $6\frac{1}{4}$ is _____% of 50.

b

40 is _____% of 50.

67 is _____% of 67.

0.8 is _____% of 3.2.

96 is _____% of 120.

1.6 is _____% of 6.4.

19 is _____% of 76.

19 is _____% of 95.

24 is _____% of 40.

64 is _____% of 80.

0.69 is _____% of 2.76.

PRISM MATHEMATICS
Purple Book

Lesson 13
Percent of a Number

89

Lesson 13 Problem Solving   PRE-ALGEBRA

Solve each problem.

1. Last season a baseball player hit 48 home runs. So far this season he has hit 30 home runs. The number of home runs he has hit so far this season is what percent of the number of home runs he hit last season?

   The number he has hit this season is _____% of the number he hit last season.

   1.

2. In April, 175 cases of toy cars were sold. In May, 125 cases were sold. April's sales were what percent of May's sales?

   April's sales were _____% of May's sales.

   2.

3. The down payment on a bike is $15. The bike costs $75. The down payment is what percent of the cost?

   The down payment is _____% of the cost.

   3.

4. On a spelling test, Janice spelled 17 words correctly. There were 20 words on the test. What percent of the words did she spell correctly?

   She spelled _____% correctly.

   4.

5. The Andersons are planning to take a 960-km trip. They will travel 840 km by car. What percent of the distance will they travel by car?

   They will travel _____% of the distance by car.

   5.

6. During hockey practice, Lea attempted 30 penalty shots and made 21. What percent of these penalty shots did she make?

   She made _____% of the shots.

   6.

7. Emily's mass is 54 kg, and Marta's mass is 36 kg. Emily's mass is what percent of Marta's mass?

   Emily's mass is _____% of Marta's mass.

   7.

Lesson 14   Percent of a Number

32 is 16% of what number?

$$32 = 16\% \times n$$
$$32 = \frac{16}{100} \times n$$
$$32 = \frac{16n}{100}$$
$$3200 = 16n$$
$$\underline{200} = n$$

32 is 16% of _____.

1.4 is 5.6% of what number?

$$1.4 = 5.6\% \times n$$
$$1.4 = \frac{5.6}{100} \times n$$
$$1.4 = \frac{5.6n}{100}$$
$$140 = 5.6n$$
$$\underline{25} = n$$

1.4 is 5.6% of _____.

Complete the following.

	a	*b*
1.	37 is 20% of _____.	92 is 50% of _____.
2.	3.4 is 25% of _____.	60 is 150% of _____.
3.	60 is 60% of _____.	9 is 30% of _____.
4.	50 is 40% of _____.	78 is 60% of _____.
5.	264 is 6% of _____.	84 is 12% of _____.
6.	18 is 75% of _____.	2.6 is 50% of _____.
7.	8.7 is 30% of _____.	72 is 80% of _____.
8.	9 is 100% of _____.	1.3 is 65% of _____.
9.	144 is 24% of _____.	2.16 is 3.6% of _____.
10.	192 is 75% of _____.	12.8 is 6.4% of _____.

CHAPTER 5

Lesson 14 Problem Solving   PRE-ALGEBRA

Solve each problem.

1. Mr. Buccola has a tree that is 15 m tall. He estimates that the tree is 75% as tall now as it will be when fully grown. How tall will the tree be when fully grown?

   The tree will be _____ m tall.

2. There are 35 boys on the school football team. This number represents 5% of the school's total enrollment. What is the school's total enrollment?

   The school's total enrollment is _____.

3. Jessica has read 120 pages of a library book. This is 40% of the book. How many pages are there in the book?

   There are _____ pages in the book.

4. When operating at 75% capacity, a factory can produce 360 cases of nails each day. How many cases of nails can be produced each day when the factory is operating at full capacity?

   _____ cases can be produced each day.

5. Brianna received 212 votes for class secretary. This was 53% of the total number of votes cast. How many votes were cast?

   _____ votes were cast.

6. Kristen has earned 75% of the points she needs for a prize. She has earned 660 points. How many points are needed to win a prize?

   _____ points are needed.

7. Emma can throw a baseball 8 m. This is 80% as far as her older brother can throw the ball. How far can her older brother throw the ball?

   Her older brother can throw the ball _____ m.

1.

2.

3.

4.

5.

6.

7.

Lesson 15 Percent PRE-ALGEBRA

Complete the following.

	a		b

1. _____ is 40% of 30.   73 is _____% of 365.

2. 26 is _____% of 50.   24 is 60% of _____.

3. 39 is 52% of _____.   _____ is 25% of 76.

4. 37 is _____% of 50.   _____ is 60% of 360.

5. 18 is 25% of _____.   69 is _____% of 276.

6. _____ is 24% of 96.   8 is 16% of _____.

7. 0.7 is _____% of 1.4.   _____ is 50% of 98.4.

8. 3.9 is 75% of _____.   0.09 is _____% of 0.25.

9. _____ is 6.8% of 720.   0.95 is 1.9% of _____.

10. 64 is 125% of _____.   _____ is 100% of 986.

11. 175 is _____% of 125.   98 is 150% of _____.

12. _____ is 120% of 720.   275 is _____% of 125.

13. $\frac{1}{3}$ is _____% of $\frac{5}{6}$.   30 is 75% of _____.

14. _____ is 60% of 1000.   1 is _____% of 1.

15. 15 is 50% of _____.   _____ is 75% of 2.

16. _____ is 25% of 4.   73 is 25% of _____.

CHAPTER 5

Lesson 15 Problem Solving   PRE-ALGEBRA

Solve each problem.

1. There are 850 students at a school. Of these, 36% are in grade 8. How many students are in the grade 8?

   _____ students are in grade 8.

   1. _____

2. Mail was delivered to 171 out of the 180 houses on Saylor Street. To what percent of the houses on Saylor Street was mail delivered?

   Mail was delivered to _____% of the houses.

   2. _____

3. A savings bond costs $18.75 and can be redeemed at maturity for $25. The cost of the bond is what percent of its value at maturity?

   Its cost is _____% of its value at maturity.

   3. _____

4. Mrs. Wilson sold merchandise to 25% of the clients she contacted. She sold to six clients. How many clients did she contact?

   She contacted _____ clients.

   4. _____

5. A store sold 185 bicycles last month. Of those, 60% were girls' bicycles. How many girls' bicycles were sold?

   _____ girls' bicycles were sold.

   5. _____

6. Of the library books turned in today, 95% were turned in on time. There were 285 books turned in on time. What was the total number of books turned in?

   There were _____ books turned in.

   6. _____

7. The enrollment at Pleasant Street School is 110% of last year's enrollment. The enrollment last year was 390. What is the enrollment this year?

   The enrollment this year is _____.

   7. _____

CHAPTER 5   PRACTICE TEST
Ratio, Rate, Proportion, and Percent

NAME _____

Express each of the following as a ratio or a rate in two ways as shown.

	a	b
1. 8 goals in 3 games	8 to 3	$\frac{8}{3}$
2. 5 policemen to 4 firemen	_____	_____
3. 4 planes in 30 minutes	_____	_____
4. 5 quarts for 9 boys	_____	_____

Solve the following.

	a	b
5.	$\dfrac{n}{3} = \dfrac{12}{36}$	$\dfrac{4}{n} = \dfrac{16}{20}$
6.	$\dfrac{8}{9} = \dfrac{n}{45}$	$\dfrac{7}{8} = \dfrac{49}{n}$
7.	$\dfrac{18}{24} = \dfrac{n}{16}$	$\dfrac{n}{12} = \dfrac{4}{16}$

Complete the following.

	a	b
8.	_____ is 35% of 64.	11 is _____% of 55.
9.	18 is _____% of 25.	30 is 7.5% of _____.
10.	$1\frac{3}{4}$ is _____% of $2\frac{1}{2}$.	_____ is $12\frac{1}{2}$% of 27.
11.	_____ is 150% of 180.	2.4 is _____% of 9.6.

CHAPTER 6 PRETEST
Simple/Compound Interest

Complete the following for simple interest.

	principal	rate	time	interest
1.	$320	7%	1 year	
2.	$300	$5\frac{1}{2}$%	$\frac{1}{2}$ year	
3.	$800	10%		$80
4.	$500		$\frac{1}{4}$ year	$10
5.		16%	2 years	$192
6.	$26 000		4 years	$9360

Interest is to be compounded in each account below. Find the total amount that will be in each account after the period of time indicated.

	principal	rate	time	compounded	total amount
7.	$200	6%	2 years	annually	
8.	$100	5%	3 years	annually	
9.	$300	8%	$1\frac{1}{2}$ years	semiannually	
10.	$400	5%	1 year	quarterly	

Lesson 1 Simple Interest   PRE-ALGEBRA

If the rate of interest is 12% a year, what will the interest be on a $300 loan for $1\frac{1}{2}$ years?

$$\text{\textit{interest} = \textit{principal} × \textit{rate} × \textit{time}} \text{ (in years)}$$

$$
\begin{aligned}
i \quad &= \quad p \quad × \quad r \quad × \quad t \\
&= \quad 300 \quad × \quad 0.12 \quad × \quad \frac{3}{2} \\
&= \quad\quad\quad 36 \quad\quad × \quad \frac{3}{2} \\
&= \quad\quad\quad\quad\quad 54
\end{aligned}
$$

The interest will be $_____.

If the rate of interest is $9\frac{1}{2}$% a year, what will the interest be on a $100 loan for 2 years?

$$
\begin{aligned}
i \quad &= \quad p \quad × \quad r \quad × \quad t \\
&= \quad \underline{} \quad × \quad \underline{} \quad × \quad \underline{} \\
&= \quad \underline{} \quad × \quad \underline{} \\
&= \quad \underline{}
\end{aligned}
$$

The interest will be $_____.

Find the interest for each loan described below.

	principal	rate	time	interest
1.	$250	10%	2 years	
2.	$400	12%	2 years	
3.	$550	8%	$1\frac{1}{4}$ years	
4.	$650	$11\frac{1}{2}$%	3 years	
5.	$600	16%	3 years	
6.	$500	$11\frac{1}{4}$%	1 year	
7.	$1500	15%	$1\frac{1}{3}$ years	
8.	$1000	$12\frac{1}{2}$%	3 years	
9.	$2890	14%	$2\frac{1}{2}$ years	
10.	$2600	9%	$2\frac{1}{2}$ years	

Lesson 1 Problem Solving PRE-ALGEBRA

Solve each problem.

1. Mr. Wilkinson borrowed $600 for $1\frac{1}{2}$ years. He is to pay 9% annual interest. How much interest is he to pay?

    He will pay $_____ interest.

    1.

2. Hillary had $350 in a savings account for $\frac{1}{2}$ year. Interest was paid at an annual rate of 5%. How much interest did she receive?

    She received $_____ interest.

    2.

3. Suppose you deposit $700 in a savings account at $5\frac{1}{2}$% interest. How much interest will you receive in one year?

    You will receive $_____.

    3.

4. The Tremco Company borrowed $10 000 at 12% annual interest for a 1-year period. How much interest did the company have to pay? What was the total amount (principal + interest) the company needed to repay the loan?

    The company had to pay $_____ interest.

    The total amount needed was $_____.

    4.

5. Ian borrowed $700 for 1 year. Interest on the first $300 of the loan was 18%, and interest on the remainder of the loan was 12%. How much interest did he pay?

    He paid $_____ interest.

    5.

6. Molly's mother borrowed $460 at 10% annual interest. What would be the interest if the loan were repaid after $\frac{1}{2}$ year? What would the interest be if the loan were repaid after $\frac{3}{4}$ year?

    The interest would be $_____ for $\frac{1}{2}$ year.

    The interest would be $_____ for $\frac{3}{4}$ year.

    6.

Lesson 2 Simple Interest   PRE-ALGEBRA

$36 interest is paid in 2 years at a flat rate of 9%. Find the principal.

$$i = p \times r \times t$$
$$36 = p \times 0.09 \times 2$$
$$36 = 0.18p$$
$$\frac{36}{0.18} = p$$
$$\underline{\quad 200 \quad} = p$$

The principal is $\underline{\;200.00\;}$.

$16 interest is paid in 2 years on $100 principal. Find the rate.

$$i = p \times r \times t$$
$$16 = 100 \times r \times 2$$
$$16 = 200r$$
$$\frac{16}{200} = r$$
$$\underline{\quad 0.08 \quad} = r$$

The rate is _____ %.

$50 interest is paid on $200 principal at a rate of 10%. Find the time.

$$i = p \times r \times t$$
$$50 = 200 \times 0.10 \times t$$
$$50 = 20t$$
$$\frac{50}{20} = t$$
$$\underline{\quad 2.5 \quad} = t$$

The time is _____ years.

Complete the following.

	principal	rate	time	interest
1.		7%	3 years	$21
2.	$325		$1\frac{1}{2}$ years	$39
3.	$375	10%		$18.75
4.	$780	15%	2 years	
5.	$1200	9%		$216
6.	$1400		$1\frac{1}{2}$ years	$168
7.		$8\frac{1}{2}$%	$1\frac{1}{2}$ years	$446.25
8.	$8000		$2\frac{1}{2}$ years	$1500
9.	$18\ 050	12%		$6498
10.	$25\ 000	15%	3 years	

CHAPTER 6

Lesson 2 Problem Solving PRE-ALGEBRA

Solve each problem.

1. Mrs. Vernon paid $72 interest for a 2-year loan at 9% annual interest. How much money did she borrow?

   She borrowed $_____.

2. Matthew paid $63 interest for a $350 loan for $1\frac{1}{2}$ years. What was the rate of interest?

   The rate of interest was _____%.

3. Suppose you borrow $600 at 10% interest. What period of time would you have the money if the interest is $30?

   The period of time would be _____ year.

4. Albertito had $740 in a savings account at 5% interest. The money was in the account for $\frac{1}{4}$ year. How much interest did he receive? Suppose he withdrew the principal and interest after $\frac{1}{4}$ year. How much money would he withdraw from the account?

   He received $_____ interest.

   He would withdraw $_____ from the account.

5. How much must you deposit at $5\frac{1}{2}$% annual interest in order to earn $33 in 1 year?

   You would need $_____ in the account.

6. The interest on a $300 loan for 2 years is $90. What rate of interest is charged?

   The rate of interest is _____%.

7. How much must you have on deposit at $6\frac{1}{2}$% of annual interest in order to earn $221 in a year?

   You would have to deposit $_____.

1.

2.

3.

4.

5.

6.

7.

Lesson 3 Compound Interest

Interest paid on the original principal and the interest already earned is called **compound interest**.

Bev had $400 in a savings account for 3 years that paid 6% interest compounded annually. What was the total amount in her account at the end of the third year?

At the end of 1 year:

interest = 400 × 0.06 × 1 = 24.00 or $24

↓

new principal = 400 + 24 = 424 or $424

At the end of 2 years:

interest = 424 × 0.06 × 1 = 25.44 or $25.44

↓

new principal = 424 + 25.44 = 449.44 or $449.44

At the end of 3 years:

interest = 449.44 × 0.06 × 1 = 26.9664 or $26.97

↓

total amount = __449.44__ + __26.97__ = __476.41__ or $_____

Assume interest is compounded annually. Find the total amount for each of the following.

	principal	rate	time	total amount
1.	$500	6%	2 years	
2.	$700	$5\frac{1}{2}$%	2 years	
3.	$800	5%	3 years	
4.	$800	$6\frac{1}{2}$%	3 years	
5.	$200	9%	3 years	
6.	$1000	8%	2 years	

CHAPTER 6

Lesson 3   Problem Solving

Solve each problem.

1. Heidi had $600 in a savings account for 2 years. Interest was paid at the rate of 6% compounded annually. What was the total amount in her account at the end of 2 years?

   The total amount was $_____.

2. Travis deposited $400 in an account that pays 5% interest compounded annually. What will be the total amount in his account after 2 years? After 3 years?

   It will be $_____ after 2 years.

   It will be $_____ after 3 years.

3. Aubrey deposited $300 in an account that pays 7% interest compounded annually. Tori deposited $300 in an account at an annual rate of 7% (simple interest). After 3 years what will be the total amount in Aubrey's account? In Tori's account?

   Aubrey's account will have $_____.

   Tori's account will have $_____.

4. Ms. Sanchez has $500 in her savings account, which pays 5% interest compounded annually. What will be the value of the account after 3 years?

   The value will be $_____.

5. Landon deposited $300 at 6% interest compounded annually. Elisa deposited $200 at $6\frac{1}{2}$% interest compounded annually. Who will have the greater account after 3 years? How much greater will it be?

   _____ will have the greater account.

   It will be $_____ greater.

	1.
	2.
	3.
	4.
	5.

Lesson 4 Compound Interest

Interest may be paid annually (each year), semiannually (twice a year), quarterly (four times a year), monthly (every month), or daily (every day).

Ed had $100 in an account for $1\frac{1}{2}$ years that paid 6% interest compounded semiannually. What was the total amount in his account at the end of $1\frac{1}{2}$ years?

At the end of $\frac{1}{2}$ year:

$$\text{interest} = 100 \times 0.06 \times \tfrac{1}{2} = 3.00 \text{ or } \$3$$

$$\text{new principal} = 100 + 3 = 103 \text{ or } \$103$$

At the end of 1 year:

$$\text{interest} = 103 \times 0.06 \times \tfrac{1}{2} = 3.09 \text{ or } \$3.09$$

$$\text{new principal} = 103 + 3.09 = 106.09 \text{ or } \$106.09$$

At the end of $1\frac{1}{2}$ years:

$$\text{interest} = 106.09 \times 0.06 \times \tfrac{1}{2} = 3.1827 \text{ or } \$3.18$$

$$\text{total amount} = \underline{\hspace{1.5cm}} + \underline{\hspace{1.5cm}} = \underline{\hspace{1.5cm}} \text{ or } \$\underline{\hspace{1.5cm}}$$

Find the total amount for each of the following.

	principal	rate	time	compounded	total amount
1.	$200	6%	$1\frac{1}{2}$ years	semiannually	
2.	$300	5%	2 years	semiannually	
3.	$100	5%	1 year	quarterly	
4.	$400	7%	$\frac{3}{4}$ year	quarterly	
5.	$500	8%	4 months	monthly	
6.	$600	9%	$\frac{1}{4}$ year	monthly	

Lesson 4   Problem Solving

Solve each problem.

1. Mrs. Fauler had $600 in a savings account that paid 5% interest compounded semiannually. What was the value of her account after $1\frac{1}{2}$ years?

   The value was $_____.

   1.

2. How much interest would $3000 earn in two years at 7% interest compounded semiannually?

   It would earn $_____ interest.

   2.

3. Suppose $100 were deposited in each savings account with rates of interest as follows:
       Account **A**—6% compounded annually
       Account **B**—6% compounded semiannually
       Account **C**—6% compounded quarterly
   What would be the value of each account after 1 year?

   $_____ will be in account **A**.

   $_____ will be in account **B**.

   $_____ will be in account **C**.

   3.

4. Assume $200 was deposited in a 2-year account at 9%. How much more interest would be in the account if the interest were compounded annually rather than computed as simple interest?

   There would be $_____ more in the account.

   4.

5. Account **A** has $500 at 8% interest compounded quarterly. Account **B** has $500 at 8% interest compounded semiannually. Which account will have a greater amount of money after 1 year? How much more?

   Account _____ will have more money.

   It will have $_____ more.

   5.

CHAPTER 6   PRACTICE TEST
Simple/Compound Interest

Complete the following for simple interest.

	principal	rate	time	interest
1.	$150	15%	3 years	
2.	$700	$8\frac{1}{2}\%$	2 years	
3.	$645		$\frac{1}{4}$ year	$19.35
4.	$540	10%		$135.00
5.		$9\frac{1}{2}\%$	2 years	$729.60
6.	$1800		2 years	$540.00

Interest is to be compounded in each account below. Find the total amount that will be in each account after the period of time indicated.

	principal	rate	time	compounded	total amount
7.	$300	7%	2 years	annually	
8.	$600	5%	3 years	annually	
9.	$500	6%	2 years	semiannually	
10.	$400	9%	$\frac{1}{4}$ year	monthly	

CHAPTER 7   PRETEST
Metric Measurement

Circle the unit you would use to measure each of the following:

1. capacity of a tank   *metre*   *litre*   *gram*

2. length of a string   *centimetre*   *centilitre*   *centigram*

3. weight of an ant   *millimetre*   *millilitre*   *milligram*

Write *1000; 0.01;* or *0.001* to make each sentence true.

4. The prefix *milli* means _____.

5. The prefix *kilo* means _____.

6. The prefix *centi* means _____.

Measure each line segment to the nearest unit indicated.

7. _____ cm   ▬▬▬▬▬▬▬▬▬

8. _____ mm   ▬▬▬▬▬▬▬▬▬▬

Complete the following:

a	*b*
9. 1 m = _____ km	100 mm = _____ cm
10. 2 L = _____ mL	2 kg = _____ g
11. 0.5 g = _____ mg	300 cm = _____ m
12. 1.4 kL = _____ L	0.05 km = _____ m

Lesson 1   Metric Prefixes

A **metre** is a unit of *length*.

A **litre** is a unit of *capacity*.

A **gram** is a unit of *mass*.

Kilo means 1000.   *Kilometre* means __1000__ m.

Hecto means 100.   *Hectolitre* means __100__ L.

Deca means 10.   *Decagram* means __10__ g.

Deci means 0.1.   *Decimetre* means _____ m.

Centi means 0.01.   *Centilitre* means _____ L.

Milli means 0.001.   *Milligram* means _____ g.

The most commonly used prefixes are *kilo, centi,* and *milli.*

CHAPTER 7

Tell whether the following would be measured in *metres, litres,* or *grams.*

a

1. amount of juice in a glass _____

2. distance a baseball is thrown _____

3. amount of fuel in a truck _____

b

mass of a pencil _____

length of a bus _____

mass of a bird _____

Complete the following as shown.

4. Kilolitre means ____1000 L____.

5. Centigram means _____.

6. Millilitre means _____.

Kilogram means _____.

Centimetre means _____.

Millimetre means _____.

Name two things that could be measured with each of the following.

7. metres   _____   _____

8. litres   _____   _____

9. grams   _____   _____

Lesson 2 Length

To name a unit of length other than the metre, a *prefix* is attached to the word *metre*. This prefix denotes the relationship of that particular unit to the metre.

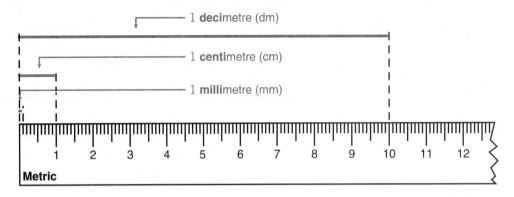

1 mm = __0.001__ m   1 dm = _____ m

1 cm = _____ m   1 **kilo**metre (km) = 1000 m

In each pair of measurements below, circle the measurement for the greater length.

	a	*b*	*c*
1.	1 km ; 1 dm	1 dm ; 1 cm	1 km ; 1 mm
2.	1 mm ; 1 dm	1 cm ; 1 km	1 cm ; 1 mm

Complete the following.

	a	*b*	*c*
3.	1 m = _____ cm	1 m = _____ mm	1 m = _____ dm
4.	0.01 m = _____ cm	0.001 m = _____ mm	0.1 m = _____ dm
5.	1000 m = _____ km	1 m = _____ km	0.001 km = _____ m

Lesson 3   Units of Length

To change from	to millimetres, multiply by	to centimetres, multiply by	to metres, multiply by	to kilometres, multiply by
millimetres		0.1	0.001	0.000 001
centimetres	10		0.01	0.00 001
metres	1000	100		0.001
kilometres	1 000 000	100 000	1000	

Using the table makes it easy to complete exercises like the following.

$8.43 \text{ km} = \underline{\quad ? \quad} \text{ m}$ $75 \text{ mm} = \underline{\quad ? \quad} \text{ cm}$

$1 \text{ km} = 1000 \text{ m}$ $1 \text{ mm} = 0.1 \text{ cm}$

$8.43 \text{ km} = (8.43 \times 1000) \text{ m}$ $75 \text{ mm} = (75 \times 0.1) \text{ cm}$

$8.43 \text{ km} = \underline{\quad 8430 \quad} \text{ m}$ $75 \text{ mm} = \underline{\qquad} \text{ cm}$

Complete.

a   *b*

1. $5 \text{ km} = \underline{\qquad} \text{ m}$ $0.452 \text{ km} = \underline{\qquad} \text{ m}$

2. $38 \text{ m} = \underline{\qquad} \text{ km}$ $948 \text{ m} = \underline{\qquad} \text{ km}$

3. $7.5 \text{ m} = \underline{\qquad} \text{ cm}$ $80 \text{ m} = \underline{\qquad} \text{ cm}$

4. $4 \text{ cm} = \underline{\qquad} \text{ m}$ $75 \text{ cm} = \underline{\qquad} \text{ m}$

5. $92 \text{ cm} = \underline{\qquad} \text{ mm}$ $4.86 \text{ cm} = \underline{\qquad} \text{ mm}$

6. $92 \text{ mm} = \underline{\qquad} \text{ cm}$ $7 \text{ mm} = \underline{\qquad} \text{ cm}$

7. $0.5 \text{ m} = \underline{\qquad} \text{ mm}$ $0.003 \text{ m} = \underline{\qquad} \text{ mm}$

8. $92 \text{ mm} = \underline{\qquad} \text{ m}$ $3600 \text{ mm} = \underline{\qquad} \text{ m}$

9. A city block is about 200 m long. How long is a city block in kilometres? _____

10. How long would five city blocks be in metres? _____   In kilometres? _____

Lesson 4 Capacity

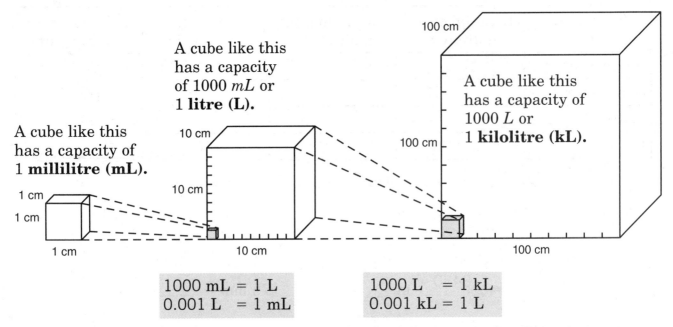

A cube like this has a capacity of 1 **millilitre (mL)**.

A cube like this has a capacity of 1000 *mL* or 1 **litre (L)**.

A cube like this has a capacity of 1000 *L* or 1 **kilolitre (kL)**.

1000 mL = 1 L
0.001 L = 1 mL

1000 L   = 1 kL
0.001 kL = 1 L

Underline the measurement for the greater amount.

	a	*b*
1.	10 L, 10 kL	100 mL, 1 kL
2.	0.1 kL, 1000 L	10 mL, 1 L
3.	1000 L, 10 000 mL	0.001 kL, 1 mL
4.	500 L, 1 kL	700 mL, 1 L

Complete the following.

5. 1 L = _____ mL   0.1 L = _____ mL

6. 1 kL = _____ L   0.01 kL = _____ L

7. 0.001 kL = _____ L   1000 mL = _____ L

8. 100 L = _____ kL   10 kL = _____ L

Lesson 5 Units of Capacity

1.2 kL = _____?_____ L   54 L = _____?_____ kL

1 kL = 1000 L   1 L = 0.001 kL

1.2 kL = (1.2 × 1000) L   54 L = (54 × 0.001) kL

1.2 kL = __1200__ L   54 L = _____ kL

Complete the following.

	a		*b*
1.	6.4 L = _____ mL	6000 mL = _____ L
2.	25 kL = _____ L	752 L = _____ kL
3.	78 L = _____ mL	529 mL = _____ L
4.	0.986 kL = _____ L	42 L = _____ kL
5.	7.5 L = _____ mL	7.5 mL = _____ L
6.	7.5 kL = _____ L	7.5 L = _____ kL

 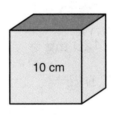

1 L of water will fill a cube
with side length 10 cm.

1 mL of water will fill a cube
with side length 1 cm.

Would you use millilitres or litres to measure each of the following?

7. a dose of cough medicine   L   mL

8. water in an aquarium   L   mL

9. perfume in a bottle   L   mL

Lesson 6 Units of Mass

NAME _____

  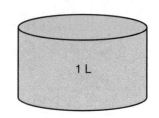

An aspirin tablet has a mass of about 350 **milligrams (mg).**

1 mL of water has a mass of 1 **gram (g).**

1 L of water has a mass of 1 **kilogram (kg).**

| 1000 mg = 1 g | 1000 g = 1 kg |
| 0.001 g = 1 mg | 0.001 kg = 1 g |

65 g = ___?___ mg   250 g = ___?___ kg

1 g = 1000 mg   1 g = 0.001 kg

65 g = (65 × 1000) mg   250 g = (250 × 0.001) kg

65 g = __65 000__ mg   250 g = _____ kg

Complete the following.

         a   *b*

1. 26 g = _____ mg   6.2 g = _____ mg

2. 75.2 mg = _____ g   2420 mg = _____ g

3. 89 kg = _____ g   7.5 kg = _____ g

4. 835 g = _____ kg   5.6 g = _____ kg

5. 60.5 g = _____ mg   60.5 g = _____ kg

6. A teaspoon holds about 5 mL of water. What is the mass of 5 mL in grams? In milligrams?

   It's mass is _____ g.

   It's mass is _____ mg.

6.

7. A nickel has a mass of about 5 g. What is the mass of 200 nickels in grams? In kilograms?

   200 nickels have a mass of about _____ g.

   200 nickels have a mass of about _____ kg.

7.

Lesson 7   Problem Solving

Solve each problem.

1. A pitcher contained 1.2 L of milk. You used 250 mL of milk from the pitcher. How many millilitres of milk are left in the pitcher?

   _____ mL are left.

2. Megan says she is 1.6 m tall. Nicole says she is 162 cm tall. Who is taller? How many centimetres taller?

   _____ is _____ cm taller.

3. A jet flew 1 km on 15 L of fuel. How many kilolitres of fuel are needed for the jet to fly 3000 km?

   The jet would need _____ kL of fuel.

4. 2 L of grape juice will fill eight glasses of the same size. What is the capacity of each glass in millilitres?

   Each glass has a capacity of _____ mL.

5. Tim bought 6 kg of meat for $25.20. What was the cost per kilogram?

   The cost was $_____ per kilogram.

6. During a contest, Frog A jumped 59.3 cm. Frog B jumped 590 mm. Which frog jumped farther? How many centimetres farther?

   Frog _____ jumped _____ cm farther.

7. Ben drove 158 km. Ali drove 230 km. How much farther than Ben did Ali drive?

   She drove _____ km farther.

1.

2.

3.

4.

5.

6.

7.

Lesson 8 Temperature

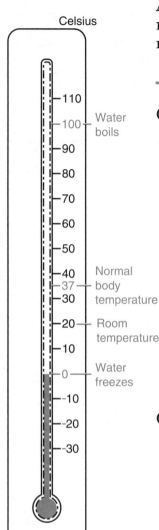

A thermometer measures temperature. This thermometer reads 0°C. Temperatures below 0°C are written with a negative sign: −5°C.

Complete each of the following.

1. What is room temperature? _____°C

2. At what temperature does water freeze? _____°C

3. How many degrees warmer is room temperature than the temperature at which water freezes? _____°C

4. At what temperature does water boil? _____°C

5. What is normal body temperature? _____°C

6. How many degrees warmer is the temperature at which water boils than normal body temperature?   _____°C

Circle the correct answer.

7.	swimming weather	15°C	28°C
8.	snow-skiing weather	10°C	−5°C
9.	waterskiing weather	27°C	86°C
10.	shirt-sleeve weather	10°C	30°C
11.	water would be frozen	28°C	−2°C
12.	water would be boiling	112°C	85°C

What outdoor activity might be appropriate for each temperature given below?

13. 25°C _____

14. 0°C _____

CHAPTER 7   PRACTICE TEST
Metric Measurement

Measure each line segment to the nearest unit as indicated.

1. _____ cm

2. _____ mm

Complete the following.

a	b
3. 25 cm = _____ mm	35 m = _____ cm
4. 6 km = _____ m	7 m = _____ km
5. 260 cm = _____ m	600 mm = _____ m
6. 7.5 m = _____ mm	2.5 mm = _____ cm
7. 12 L = _____ mL	13.5 mL = _____ L
8. 5.4 kL = _____ L	1200 L = _____ kL
9. 0.045 L = _____ mL	260 L = _____ kL
10. 58 kg = _____ g	400 g = _____ kg
11. 3000 mg = _____ g	3.8 kg = _____ g
12. 0.6 g = _____ mg	50 mg = _____ g

13. Water freezes at _____°C.

14. Water boils at _____°C.

Solve each problem.

15. There are 5.5 kL of water in a tank. If 3200 L of water are used, how many litres will be in the tank? How many kilolitres is that?

    There will be _____ L in the tank.

    That is _____ kL.

16. Chloe jumped 1.45 m. Evan jumped 138 cm. Who jumped farther? How much farther?

    _____ jumped _____ cm farther.

15.

16.

CHAPTER 8   PRETEST
More Metric Measurement and Estimation

Complete the following.

	a	*b*
1.	40 mm = _____ cm	4 cm = _____ mm
2.	48 h = _____ days	5 m = _____ cm
3.	3 h = _____ min	5 kg = _____ g
4.	2000 L = _____ kL	5 min 4 s= _____ s
5.	4000 g = _____ kg	3 kL = _____ L
6.	8000 mL = _____ L	7 g = _____ mg

Add, subtract, or multiply.

	a	*b*	*c*
7.	8 h 3 min +2 h 4 min	3 min 49 s −1 min 27 s	2 kg ×4
8.	5 min 2 s +2 min 2 s	5 h 2 min −2 h 3 min	1 kg ×7

Round as indicated.

	a *nearest ten*	*b* *nearest hundred*	*c* *nearest thousand*
9. 8324	_____	_____	_____
10. 74 485	_____	_____	_____

Lesson 1 Units of Length

1m = 100 cm
1m = 1000 mm
1cm = 10 mm

6 cm = ___?___ mm

1 cm = 10 mm
6 cm = (6 × 10) mm
6 m = __60__ mm

40 mm = ___?___ cm

10 mm = 1 cm
40 mm = (40 ÷ 10) cm

40 mm = _____ cm

_____

4 m = ___?___ cm

1 m = 100 cm

4 m = (4 × 100) cm
4 m = _____ cm

Complete the following.

	a	*b*
1.	50 mm = _____ cm	5 cm = _____ mm
2.	7 cm = _____ mm	6 m = _____ cm
3.	400 cm = _____ mm	2 m = _____ mm
4.	5 m = _____ cm	12 cm = _____ mm
5.	7000 mm = _____ m	5 m = _____ cm
6.	7 m = _____ mm	4 cm = _____ mm
7.	100 mm = _____ cm	6 m = _____ mm
8.	3000 mm = _____ m	3 m = _____ cm
9.	3 cm = _____ mm	8 cm = _____ mm
10.	20 mm = _____ cm	2 cm = _____ mm
11.	5 m = _____ mm	1 m = _____ mm

CHAPTER 8

Lesson 1 Problem Solving

Solve each problem.

1. The Higgins' fence is 200 cm high. What is the
   height of the fence in metres?

   The height of the fence is _____ cm.

2. Mr. Baxter is 2 m tall. How many centimetres
   tall is he?

   He is _____ cm tall.

3. Kasey purchased 2 m of ribbon. How many
   millimetres of ribbon did she purchase?

   She purchased _____ mm of ribbon.

4. A football field is 59 m wide. What is the width
   of the field in centimetres?

   The width of the field is _____ cm.

5. Zach threw a baseball 5000 cm. How many
   metres did he throw the baseball?

   He threw the baseball _____ m.

6. Mr. Kelly's lot is 20 m wide. What is the width of
   the lot in centimetres?

   The width of the lot is _____ cm.

7. Logan has a piece of wire 3000 mm long. What is
   the length of the wire in metres?

   The length of the wire is _____ m.

8. When the high-jump bar is set at 200 cm, what
   is the height of the bar in millimetres?

   The height is _____ mm.

9. Mrs. Avilla's garage door is 3 m wide. What is
   the width of the door in millimetres?

   The width of the door is _____ mm.

1.
2.
3.
4.
5.
6.
7.
8.
9.

Lesson 2 Units of Capacity, Time, Mass

1000 mL = 1 L	60 s = 1 min	1000 mg = 1 g
1000 L = 1 kL	60 min = 1 h	1000 g = 1 kg
	24 h = 1 day	1000 kg = 1 t

300 s = _____?_____ min

1 min = 60 s
300 s = (300 ÷ 60) min

300 s = _____ min

5 kg = _____?_____ g

1 kg = 1000 g
5 kg = (5 × 1000) g
5 kg = _____ g

Complete the following.

a   b

1. $5\frac{1}{2}$ min = _____ s   2 min 14 s = _____ s

2. 3000 g = _____ kg   3 h 40 min = _____ min

3. 5000 L = _____ kL   5 kL = _____ L

4. $3\frac{1}{2}$ h = _____ min   3 L = _____ mL

5. 3 t = _____ kg   2 L = _____ mL

6. 3000 mL = _____ L   6 kg = _____ g

7. 72 min = _____ h   3 min 51 s = _____ s

8. 2000 mL = _____ L   10 g = _____ mg

9. 96 h = _____ days   5 h 16 min = _____ min

10. 4 g = _____ mg   2 h 15 min = _____ min

11. 3 days = _____ h   3 kL = _____ L

CHAPTER 8

Lesson 2   Problem Solving

Solve each problem.

1. It took Jeremy 3 min 25 s to run around the block. How many seconds did it take him to run around the block?

   It took him _____ s.

   1.

2. The capacity of a container is 2 kL. What is the capacity of the container in litres?

   The capacity is _____ L.

   2.

3. Last month 64 000 mL of milk were delivered to the Collins' house. How many litres of milk was that?

   That was _____ L of milk.

   3.

4. Mrs. Johnson purchased a 2-kg can of shortening. How many grams of shortening did she purchase?

   She purchased _____ g of shortening.

   4.

5. Mr. Singer showed his class a film that lasted 120 min. How many hours did the film last?

   The film lasted _____ h.

   5.

6. The cooling system of Mr. Bigg's car has a capacity of 8 L. What is the capacity of the cooling system in millilitres?

   The capacity is _____ mL.

   6.

7. The Smith's baby had a mass of 4 kg at birth. What was the mass of the baby in grams?

   The baby's mass was _____ g.

   7.

8. An elephant at the zoo has a mass of 2 t. What is the mass of the elephant in kilograms?

   The elephant has a mass of _____ kg.

   8.

Lesson 3 Adding Time

NAME _____

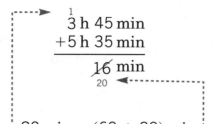

$$\begin{array}{r} 3\,h\ 45\,min \\ +5\,h\ 35\,min \\ \hline 80\,min \end{array}$$

(45 + 35) min = _____ min

80 min = (60 + 20) min
    =   1 h 20 min

(1 + 3 + 5) h = _____ h

Complete the following.

	a	b
1.	75 min = 1 h _____ min	73 s = 1 min _____ s
2.	90 s = 1 min _____ s	71 s = 1 min _____ s
3.	79 min = 1 h _____ min	100 min = 1 h _____ min
4.	75 min = 1 h _____ min	95 s = 1 min _____ s

Find each sum.

	a	b	c	d
5.	7 min 1 s +2 min 1 s	3 min 14 s +2 min 29 s	3 h 1 min +2 h 2 min	7 h 20 min +2 h 15 min
6.	3 h 4 min +2 h 7 min	8 min 7 s +2 min 3 s	3 h 21 min +2 h 16 min	5 h 30 min +3 h 30 min
7.	3 h 40 min +2 h 40 min	7 h 34 min +5 h 49 min	9 min 7 s +3 min 6 s	5 h 32 min +2 h 45 min
8.	3 h 35 min +6 h 30 min	5 h 40 min +1 h 25 min	1 min 17 s +4 min 53 s	3 h 30 min +2 h 45 min
9.	9 min 35 s +2 min 25 s	7 h 11 min +1 h 49 min	3 h 30 min +2 h 30 min	9 min 20 s +3 min 40 s

PRISM MATHEMATICS
Purple Book

Lesson 3
Adding Time

121

Lesson 3   Problem Solving

Solve each problem.

1. The first feature at the Rex Theatre lasts
   1 h 45 min. The second lasts 1 h 36 min. The
   features are shown one after the other. How
   long will the double feature last?

   It will last _____ h _____ min.

2. Aaron took 3 min 45 s to solve the first part of a
   puzzle and 6 min 25 min to solve the second
   part. How long did it take him to solve the whole
   puzzle?

   It took Aaron _____ min _____ s to solve
   the whole puzzle.

3. Lee ran the first leg of a two-person relay in
   6 min 20 s, and Elmer ran the second leg in 5 min
   55 s. How long did it take the boys to run the
   relay?

   It took them _____ min _____ s.

4. It took Del 1 h 45 min to clean the garage and
   4 h 45 min to clean the house. How much time
   did Del spend cleaning in all?

   Del spent _____ h _____ min cleaning
   in all.

5. Margaret did the crossword puzzle in 6 min 35 s
   and the word-search puzzle in 4 min 50 s. How
   much time did Margaret spend on the two
   puzzles?

   Margaret spent _____ min _____ s on the
   puzzles.

6. Mrs. Little took 3 min 30 s to fill her car with
   gasoline and 2 min 55 s to pay for the gasoline.
   How long did she spend at the gas station?

   Mrs. Little spent _____ min _____ s at
   the gas station.

7. Tyler's sister ran the first kilometre of a 2-km
   race in 4 min 35 s. She ran the second kilometre
   in 4 min 53 s. What was her time for the race?

   Her time was _____ min _____ s.

1.
2.
3.
4.
5.
6.
7.

Lesson 4   Subtracting Time

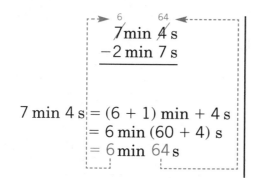

$$7 \min 4 s = (6 + 1) \min + 4 s$$
$$= 6 \min (60 + 4) s$$
$$= 6 \min 64 s$$

$$
\begin{array}{r}
\overset{6}{\cancel{7}}\min\ \overset{64}{\cancel{4}} s \\
-2 \min\ 7 s \\
\hline
57 s
\end{array}
$$

$$(64 - 7) s = \rule{2cm}{0.4pt} s$$

$$
\begin{array}{r}
\overset{6}{\cancel{7}}\min\ \overset{64}{\cancel{4}} s \\
-2 \min\ 7 s \\
\hline
4 \min 57 s
\end{array}
$$

$$(6 - 2) \min = \rule{2cm}{0.4pt} \min$$

Complete the following.

	a	b
1.	15 min 4 s = 14 min _____ s	4 h 3 min = 3 h _____ min
2.	7 h 2 min = 6 h _____ min	6 min 2 s = 5 min _____ s
3.	5 h 1 min = 4 h _____ min	2 min 45 s = 1 min _____ s
4.	4 h 3 min = 3 h _____ min	3 h 1 min = 2 h _____ min

Find each difference.

	a	b	c	d
5.	9 min 7 s −3 min 6 s	7 h 14 min −3 h 9 min	3 h 45 min −2 h 19 min	5 min 3 s −1 min 2 s
6.	16 h 9 min −9 h 9 min	8 min 2 s −3 min 1 s	6 h 1 min −3 h 1 min	8 min 27 s −5 min 16 s
7.	15 min 7 s −12 min 9 s	2 h 1 min −1 h 1 min	5 h 19 min −3 h 45 min	8 min 4 s −2 min 9 s
8.	3 h 15 min −1 h 30 min	8 min 20 s −5 min 40 s	16 h 25 min −8 h 55 min	9 min 6 s −2 min 8 s
9.	6 min 0 s −2 min 51 s	8 h −4 h 15 min	8 min −4 min 11 s	7 h −2 h 30 min

Lesson 4 Problem Solving

Solve each problem.

1. A frozen ham took 7 h 30 min to thaw in the fridge, and a small frozen turkey took 16 h 15 min. How much longer did the turkey take to thaw than the ham?

    The turkey took _____ h _____ min longer to thaw.

2. The first game of a doubleheader lasted 2 h 48 min. The second game lasted 3 h 19 min. How much longer did the second game last than the first?

    The second game lasted _____ min longer.

3. Abby ran four laps of the track in 4 min 45 s. Renée ran four laps in 5 min 10 s. How much longer did it take Renée to run the four laps?

    It took Renée _____ min _____ s longer.

4. Of Heather's 9-h workday, 5 h 45 min were spent packing crates. How much time did she have left for other tasks?

    She had _____ h _____ min left.

5. It took Sonya 4 h 30 min to paint the living room and 1 h 45 min to paint the bathroom. How long did she paint in all?

    She painted for _____ h _____ min.

6. The Ace Factory operates 3 h 30 min in the morning and 4 h 15 min in the afternoon. How much longer does the factory operate in the afternoon than in the morning?

    It operates _____ min longer in the afternoon.

7. Katie took 4 min 35 s to run 1 km. Her boyfriend took 5 min 45 s to run 1 km. How much longer did Katie's boyfriend take to run 1 km?

    It took Katie's boyfriend _____ h _____ min longer.

1.
2.
3.
4.
5.
6.
7.

Lesson 5   Multiplying Measures

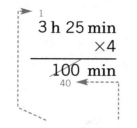

3 h 25 min
×4
_____
100 min

3 h 25 min
×4
_____
100 min
40

3 h 25 min
×4
_____
13 h 100 min
40

(4 × 25) min = _____ min | 100 min = _____ h _____ min | [(4 × 3) + 1] h = _____ h

---

Find each product.

	a	*b*	*c*
1.	4 cm ×4	3 min 12 s ×4	3 kL ×3
2.	3 h 20 min ×3	5 kg ×5	7 m ×2
3.	55 cm ×9	65 L ×7	2.5 kg ×6
4.	37 g ×9	106 m ×6	9 min 36 s ×5
5.	3 m ×8	5 min 20 s ×6	300 mg ×3
6.	2 kg ×5	1 h 10 min ×6	60 L ×3
7.	2.5 km ×8	4.5 m ×6	7.1 kg ×9

CHAPTER 8

Lesson 5 Problem Solving

Solve each problem.

1. Six tables are to be placed end to end. Each table is 128 cm. What will be the total length of the tables?

   The total length will be _____ cm.

2. It takes 2 min 15 s to assemble a doodad. How long will it take to assemble three doodads?

   It will take _____ min _____ s.

3. Each doodad has a mass of 1.6 kg. There are six doodads in each case. How much will the mass of the doodads in a case be?

   They will have a mass of _____ kg.

4. A laundry purchased five large bottles of detergent. Each bottle contained 2 L. How much detergent was purchased?

   _____ L of detergent were purchased.

5. Mr. Mitchell purchased eight boards. Each board was 2.5 m long. What was the total length of the boards he purchased?

   The total length was _____ m.

6. Nine cases of art supplies are to be shipped. Each case has a mass of 4 kg. How much will the mass of the shipment be?

   It will have a mass of _____ kg.

7. Each shift at the Kempf Factory lasts 7 h 30 min. There are nine shifts each week. How long does the factory operate each week?

   The factory operates _____ h _____ min each week.

1.
2.
3.
4.
5.
6.
7.

Lesson 6 Measurement

Complete the following.

	a		*b*
1.	2 h = _____ min		3 cm = _____ mm
2.	5 kg = _____ g		2 kg = _____ g
3.	700 L = _____ kL		3 min 38 s = _____ s
4.	70 mm = _____ cm		4 L = _____ mL
5.	240 s = _____ min		5 m = _____ cm

Add, subtract, or multiply.

	a	*b*	*c*
6.	3 h 7 min +5 h 4 min	4 min 14 s −2 min 7 s	7.2 L ×3
7.	16 h 25 min +4 h 35 min	6.2 cm ×5	6 h −2 h 3 min

Solve each of the following.

8. Freda slept for 8 h 30 min last night. Francis slept for 11 h 15 min last night. How much longer did Francis sleep than Freda?

Francis slept for _____ h _____ min longer than Freda.

8.

9. It is 112 m from home plate to the right-field fence at the foul pole. What is this distance in centimetres?

It is _____ cm.

9.

Lesson 7 Rounding Numbers

Round 32 to the nearest ten.

32 is nearer 30 than 40.

32 rounded to the nearest

ten is ___30___.

Round 75 to the nearest ten.

75 is as near 70 as 80.
In such cases, use the
greater multiple of ten.

75 rounded to the nearest

ten is ___80___.

Round 4769 to the nearest hundred.

4769 is nearer 4800 than 4700.

4769 rounded to the nearest hundred

is _____.

Round 4500 to the nearest thousand.

4500 is as near 4000 as 5000.
In such cases, use the *greater
multiple* of one thousand.

4500 rounded to the nearest

thousand is _____.

Round to the nearest ten.

	a	*b*	*c*
1.	28 _____	73 _____	85 _____
2.	244 _____	477 _____	655 _____
3.	1696 _____	2792 _____	8245 _____

Round to the nearest hundred.

4.	321 _____	479 _____	550 _____
5.	1459 _____	2628 _____	1650 _____
6.	24 136 _____	35 282 _____	47 350 _____

Round to the nearest thousand.

7.	4325 _____	6782 _____	7500 _____
8.	5943 _____	8399 _____	8500 _____
9.	16 482 _____	27 501 _____	43 500 _____

Lesson 8 Estimating Sums and Differences

	estimated sum	actual sum

Estimate the sum of 744 and 378.

```
 744 —— to the nearest hundred ——►   700      744
+378 —— to the nearest hundred ——►  +400     +378
                                    ─────     ─────
                                     1100      1122
```

To estimate the sum of 6375 and 8678, round 6375 to _____ and 8678 to _____.

The estimated sum would be 6000 + 9000 or _____.

Estimate the difference between 6232 and 2948.

	estimated difference	actual difference

```
 6232 —— to the nearest thousand ——►   6000      6232
-2948 —— to the nearest thousand ——►  -3000     -2948
                                      ─────      ─────
                                       3000       3284
```

To estimate the difference between 38 735 and 12 675, round 38 735 to _____ and

12 675 to _____. The estimated difference would be 40 000 − 10 000 or _____.

Estimate each sum or difference. Then find each sum or difference.

	a estimate	*b* estimate	*c* estimate
1.	739 +435	678 −245	743 +825
2.	7254 −1326	1375 +6427	2795 −1246
3.	7524 +3542	6852 −4526	7689 +3824
4.	25 243 −12 675	76 425 +23 142	95 245 −58 624

Lesson 9 Estimating Products

Study how to estimate the product of 187 and 63.

		estimated product	*actual product*

187 —— to the nearest hundred ——→ 200

×63 —— to the nearest ten ——→ ×60

                                      12 000

actual product

  187
×63
____
  561
11 220
_____
11 781

To estimate 86 × 224, round 86 to _____ and 224 to _____.

The estimated product would be 90 × 200 or _____.

_____

Write the estimated product on each _____. Then find each product.

	a	*b*	*c*
1.	72 ×38 _____	91 ×57 _____	55 ×65 _____
2.	69 ×48 _____	56 ×78 _____	75 ×66 _____
3.	84 ×63 _____	93 ×43 _____	74 ×45 _____
4.	125 ×78 _____	469 ×36 _____	724 ×63 _____
5.	427 ×43 _____	825 ×73 _____	974 ×47 _____

CHAPTER 8   PRACTICE TEST
More Metric Measurement and Estimation

Complete the following.

	a	*b*
1.	3 cm = _____ mm	3 m = _____ cm
2.	90 min = _____ h	4 kg = _____ g
3.	5 kg = _____ g	2 h 27 min = _____ min
4.	96 h = _____ days	3 cm = _____ mm
5.	3 kL = _____ L	3 L = _____ mL

Add, subtract, or multiply.

6.	3 min 6 s +2 min 8 s	8 h 6 min −2 h 4 min	2 min 14 s ×3

7.	6 h 30 min −4 h 45 min	3.3 m ×4	6 h 50 min +2 h 48 min

Round as indicated.

	a *nearest ten*	*b* *nearest hundred*	*c* *nearest thousand*
8. 4773	_____	_____	_____
9. 63 575	_____	_____	_____

Write an estimate for each exercise. Then find the answer.

10.	7129 +4516	9046 −3978	296 ×78

CHAPTER 8

CHAPTER 9   PRETEST
Geometry

a	b	c	d	e	f

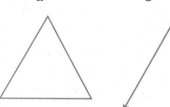  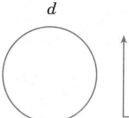 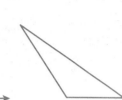

g	h	i	j	k	l

 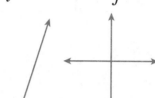 

On the _____ before each name below, write the letter(s) of the figures(s) it describes above.

a	b	c
1. _____ ray	_____ line segment	_____ isosceles triangle
2. _____ line	_____ obtuse angle	_____ obtuse triangle
3. _____ circle	_____ right triangle	_____ perpendicular lines
4. _____ acute angle	_____ parallel lines	_____ equilateral triangle
5. _____ right angle	_____ acute triangle	_____ scalene triangle

Use a protractor to find the measure of each angle below.

a	b
6. _____ °	_____ °

NAME _____

Lesson 1   Lines, Line Segments, and Rays

Line *BC* or $\overleftrightarrow{BC}$

Any two points on a line can be used to name that line. Do $\overleftrightarrow{BC}$ and $\overleftrightarrow{CB}$ name the same line? _____

_____

Line segment *JK* or $\overline{JK}$

$\overline{JK}$ consists of all points on the line between and including *endpoints J* and *K*. Do $\overline{JK}$ and $\overline{JK}$ name the same line segment? _____

_____

Ray *PQ* or $\overrightarrow{PQ}$

$\overrightarrow{PQ}$ consists of endpoint *P* and all points on $\overrightarrow{PQ}$ that are on the same side of *P* as *Q*. Do $\overrightarrow{PQ}$ and $\overrightarrow{QP}$ name the same ray? _____

_____

Complete the following as shown.

1. E •————————• D   line *ED* or *DE* $\overleftrightarrow{ED}$ or $\overleftrightarrow{DE}$
    Endpoints: __None__

2. G •————————• F   ray *FG* $\overrightarrow{FG}$
    Endpoint: __F__

3. L •————————• M   line segment *LM* or *ML* $\overline{LM}$ or $\overline{ML}$
    Endpoints: __L and M__

4. R ... S   _____   _____
    Endpoint(s): _____

5. X ... Y   _____   _____
    Endpoint(s): _____

6. T •————————• V   _____   _____
    Endpoint(s): _____

7. A •————————• C   _____   _____
    Endpoint(s): _____

8. W •————————• Z   _____   _____
    Endpoint(s): _____

9. H ... N   _____   _____
    Endpoint(s): _____

Lesson 2 Circles

By placing the compass point at point *P*, you can locate all the points in a plane (never-ending flat surface) that are the same distance from point *P*.

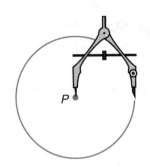

A **circle** is a set of points in a plane such that each point is the same distance from some given point called the *centre*.

You can name a circle by naming its centre. Circle *P* is shown at the left.

A **radius** of a circle is a line segment from the centre of the circle to a point on the circle.

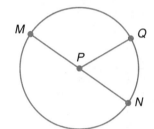

$\overline{PM}$ is a radius of circle *P*. Name two more radii of circle *P*. _____

A **diameter** of a circle is a line segment that has its endpoints on the circle and passes through the centre of the circle.

Name a diameter of circle *P*. _____

Name the centre, a radius, and a diameter of each circle.

1.
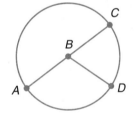

centre	radius	diameter
_____	_____	_____

2.
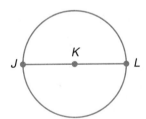

_____ _____ _____

Write *True* or *False* after each statement.

3. All radii of the same circle have the same length. _____

4. All diameters of the same circle have the same length. _____

5. The length of a diameter of a circle is twice the length of a radius. _____

Lesson 3 Angles

An **angle** is formed by two rays that have a common endpoint.

Study how angle *ACB* (denoted ∠*ACB*) is constructed below.

Step 1

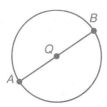

Draw circle *Q* and diameter *AB*.

Step 2

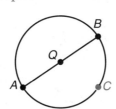

Select point *C* anywhere on circle *Q*.

Step 3

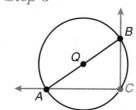

Draw $\overrightarrow{CA}$ and $\overrightarrow{CB}$.

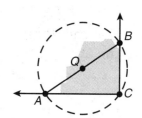

Compare ∠*ACB* with a corner of a page of this book.

Angles such as ∠*ACB* are called **right angles.**

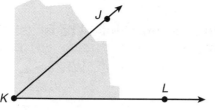

Does ∠*JKL* appear to be larger or smaller than a right angle? _____

Angles like ∠*JKL* are called **acute angles.**

Does ∠*PQR* appear to be larger or smaller than a right angle? _____

Angles like ∠*PQR* are called **obtuse angles.**

Compare each angle with a model of a right angle. Then describe each angle by writing either *acute, obtuse,* or *right* on each _____.

a   *b*   *c*

1.

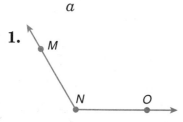

_____ angle

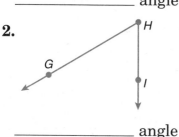

_____ angle

2.

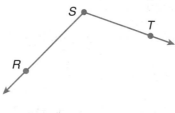

_____ angle

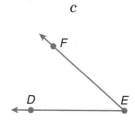

_____ angle

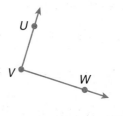

_____ angle

CHAPTER 9

Lesson 4 Angle Measurement

NAME _____

To use a protractor to measure an angle:

a. Place the centre of the protractor at the vertex of the angle.

b. Align one side of the angle with the base of the protractor so that the other side of the angle intersects the curved edge of the protractor.

c. Use the scale starting at 0 and read the measure of the angle where the other side of the angle intersects the curved edge of the protractor.

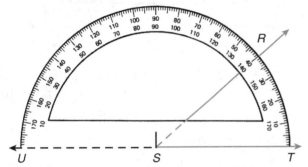

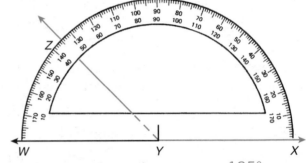

The measurement of ∠*TSR* is ___40°___.
40° is read 40 *degrees*.
The measurement of ∠*USR* is ___140°___.

The measurement of ∠*XYZ* is ___135°___.

The measurement of ∠*WYZ* is _____.

Use a protractor to measure each angle below.

a   *b*   *c*

1.

_____ °

_____ °

_____ °

2.

_____ °

_____ °

_____ °

Lesson 5 Angle Measurement

Use a protractor to measure each angle in the figure below.

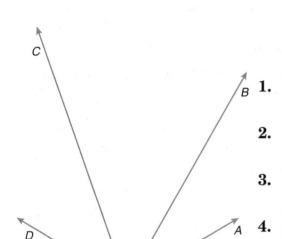

	a	
	angle	**measurement**
1.	∠AFB	_____
2.	∠BFC	_____
3.	∠CFD	_____
4.	∠DFE	_____
5.	∠AFC	_____

b	
angle	**measurement**
∠BFD	_____
∠CFE	_____
∠AFD	_____
∠BFE	_____
∠AFE	_____

Use a protractor to draw angles having the measurements given below.

	a	*b*	*c*
6.	75°	90°	30°
7.	120°	60°	135°

Lesson 6 Congruent Angles

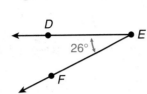

Two angles that have the same size are called **congruent angles.**

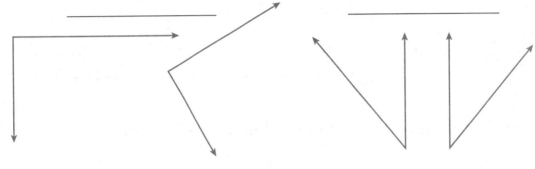

The measurement of ∠PQR is 26°.

The measurement of ∠DEF is 26°.

∠PQR ≅ ∠DEF (read ∠PQR *is congruent to* ∠DEF)

For each exercise, measure both angles. Write *congruent* if the angles are congruent. Write *not congruent* if the angles are not congruent.

a   b

1. _____   _____

2. _____   _____

Find the measurement for each angle below. Then draw an angle congruent to each angle.

3.

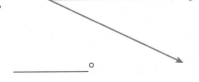 _____°

 _____°

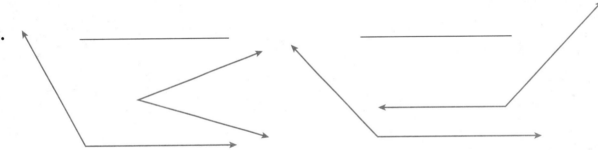

Lesson 7 Parallel and Perpendicular Lines

parallel lines

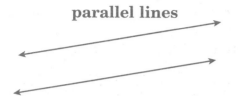

Parallel lines are always the same distance apart. They will never intersect, even if extended.

perpendicular lines

Perpendicular lines form right angles.

Write *parallel* if the lines are parallel. Write *perpendicular* if the lines are perpendicular. Write *neither* if the lines are neither parallel nor perpendicular.

	a	b	c

1. _____ _____ _____

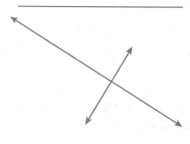  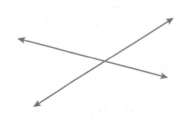

2. _____ _____ _____

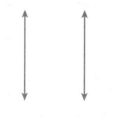 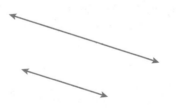 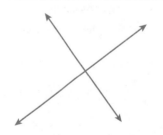

3. _____ _____ _____

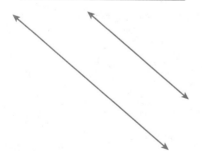 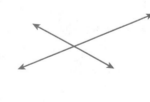 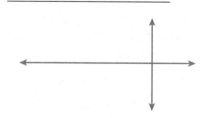

CHAPTER 9

Lesson 8 Triangles

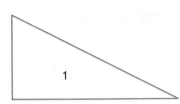
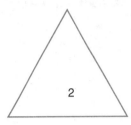
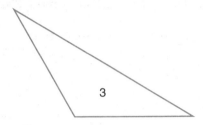

Compare the angles of each triangle with a model of a right angle.

An **acute triangle** contains all acute angles.

Which triangle above is an acute triangle?

_____

A **right triangle** contains one right angle.

Which triangle above is a right triangle?

_____

An **obtuse triangle** contains one obtuse angle.

Which triangle above is an obtuse triangle?

_____

Use a ruler to compare the lengths of the sides of each triangle.

A **scalene triangle** has no sides the same length.

Which triangle above is a scalene triangle?

_____

An **isosceles triangle** has two or more sides the same length.

Which triangles above are isosceles triangles?

_____

An **equilateral triangle** has all three sides the same length.

Which triangle above is an equilateral triangle? _____

Compare the angles of each triangle below with a model of a right angle. Then describe each triangle as being either *acute*, *obtuse*, or *right*.

1.

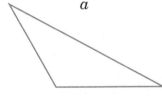
a

b

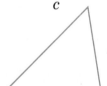
c

_____ triangle   _____ triangle   _____ triangle

2. Compare the lengths of the sides of each triangle. Then describe each triangle as being either *scalene*, *isosceles*, or *equilateral*.

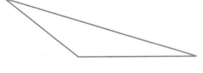

_____ triangle   _____ triangle   _____ triangle

CHAPTER 9 PRACTICE TEST
Geometry

Use the figures below to answer the questions that follow.

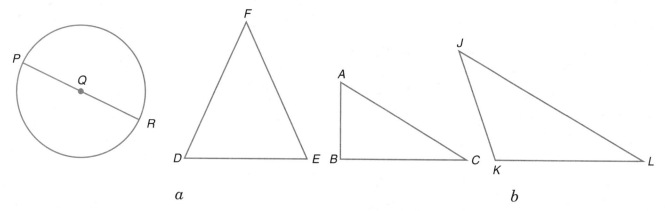

a b

1. Name a radius of circle *Q*. _____   Name a diameter of circle *Q*. _____
2. Which figure is a right triangle?   Which figure is an isosceles triangle?

    _____   _____

3. Which figures are scalene triangles?   Which figure is an obtuse triangle?

    _____   _____

Use a protractor to measure each angle. Then describe each angle by writing *acute, obtuse,* or *right.*

| *a* | *b* | *c* |

4. _____° , _____   _____° , _____   _____° , _____

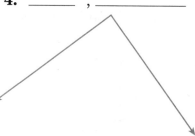 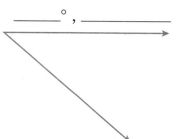 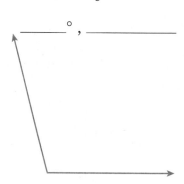

Tell whether each pair of lines is *parallel* or *perpendicular.*

5. _____   _____   _____

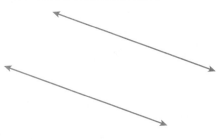 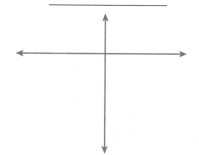

CHAPTER 10 PRETEST
Similar Triangles

Find the length of the side shown in colour in each pair of similar triangles below.

1.

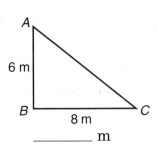

_____ m

2.

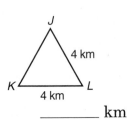

_____ km

3.

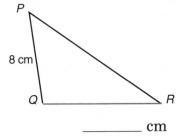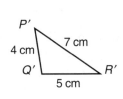

_____ cm

Use the Pythagorean Theorem and the table on page **149** to help you find the length of each side shown in colour below.

a

b

4.

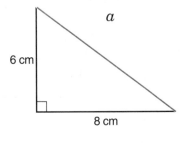

_____ cm

_____ m

5.

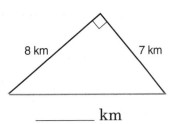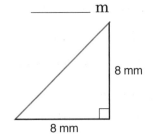

_____ km

_____ mm

Lesson 1 Similar Triangles

When this photo was enlarged, the size of the angles did not change.

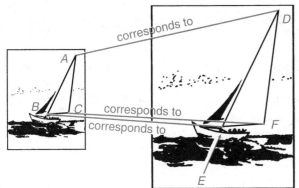

$\angle C \cong \angle F$

$\angle A \cong \angle D$

$\angle B \cong \angle E$

Did the lengths of the sides change? _____

Are the two triangles the same size? _____

$\triangle ABC$ is similar to $\triangle DEF$.

or

$\triangle ABC \sim \triangle DEF$

> Two triangles are similar if their corresponding angles are congruent.

One triangle in each pair below is labelled with symbols like D' (read *D prime*) and J' (read *J prime*). This makes it easy to tell that D corresponds to D' and J corresponds to J', and so on. Complete the following.

a   *b*

1.
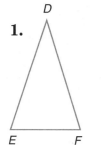

$\angle D \cong \angle D'$

$\angle E \cong \angle E'$

$\angle F \cong \angle F'$

$\triangle DEF \sim \triangle$ _____

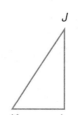

$\angle J' \cong \angle J$

$\angle K' \cong \angle K$

$\angle L' \cong \angle L$

$\triangle J'K'L' \sim \triangle$ _____

2.

$\triangle PQR \sim \triangle P'Q'R'$

$\angle P \cong \angle$ _____

$\angle Q \cong \angle$ _____

$\angle R \cong \angle$ _____

$\triangle MNO \sim \triangle M'N'O'$

$\angle M \cong \angle$ _____

$\angle N \cong \angle$ _____

$\angle O \cong \angle$ _____

Write *True* or *False* after each statement below.

3. Two triangles that are similar must be the same size.   _____

4. Two triangles that are similar have the same shape.   _____

5. Two triangles that are similar have corresponding
angles that are congruent.   _____

6. All right triangles are similar.   _____

CHAPTER 10

Lesson 2 Similar Triangles

NAME _____

$\triangle ABC \sim \triangle A'B'C'$

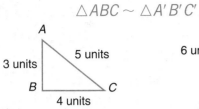 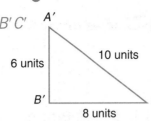

Side AB corresponds to side $A'B'$.

Side BC corresponds to side _____.

Side _____ corresponds to side $C'A'$.

If AB denotes the measure of side AB, $A'B'$ the measure of side $A'B'$, and so on, the ratios of the measures of corresponding sides can be expressed as follows.

$$\frac{AB}{A'B'} = \underline{\frac{3}{6}} = \underline{\frac{1}{2}} \qquad \frac{BC}{B'C'} = \underline{\frac{4}{8}} = \underline{\qquad} \qquad \frac{CA}{C'A'} = \underline{\qquad} = \underline{\qquad}$$

> **If two triangles are similar, the ratios of the measures of their corresponding sides are equal.**

For each pair of similar triangles, complete the following to show that the ratios of the measures of corresponding sides are equal.

1.

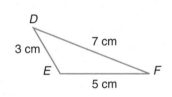 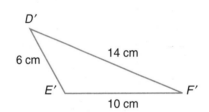

$\dfrac{DE}{D'E'} = \underline{\qquad} = \underline{\qquad}$

$\dfrac{EF}{E'F'} = \underline{\qquad} = \underline{\qquad}$

$\dfrac{FD}{F'D'} = \underline{\qquad} = \underline{\qquad}$

2.

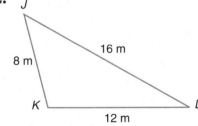 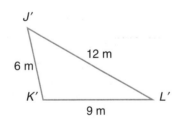

$\dfrac{JK}{J'K'} = \underline{\qquad} = \underline{\qquad}$

$\dfrac{KL}{K'L'} = \underline{\qquad} = \underline{\qquad}$

$\dfrac{LJ}{L'J'} = \underline{\qquad} = \underline{\qquad}$

3.

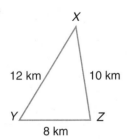 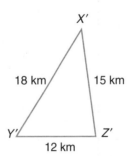

$\dfrac{XY}{X'Y'} = \underline{\qquad} = \underline{\qquad}$

$\dfrac{YZ}{Y'Z'} = \underline{\qquad} = \underline{\qquad}$

$\dfrac{ZX}{Z'X'} = \underline{\qquad} = \underline{\qquad}$

Lesson 3 Similar Triangles

PRE-ALGEBRA

A 5-m post casts a shadow 8 m long while a nearby flagpole casts a shadow 48 m long.
What is the height of the flagpole?

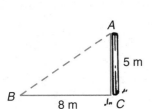

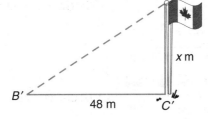

$$\frac{BC}{B'C'} = \frac{CA}{C'A'}$$

$$\frac{8}{48} = \frac{5}{x}$$

$$8 \times x = 48 \times 5$$

$$\underline{30} = x$$

The height of the flagpole is _____ m.

Find the length of the side shown in colour in each pair of similar triangles below.

| a | b |

1.

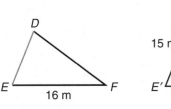

_____ m

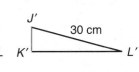

_____ cm

2.

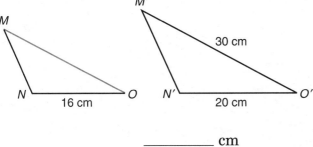

_____ cm

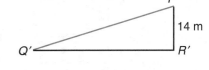

_____ m

3.

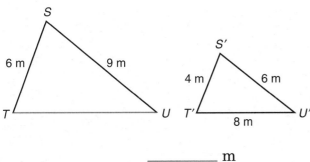

_____ m

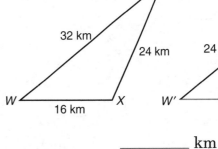

_____ km

Lesson 3 Problem Solving   PRE-ALGEBRA

Solve each problem.

1. A tree 8 m high casts a 4-m shadow. At the same time, a nearby building casts a 16-m shadow. What is the height of the building?

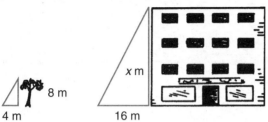

The height of the building is _____ m.

2. If $\triangle CAB \sim \triangle EDC$, what is the length of the pond shown below?

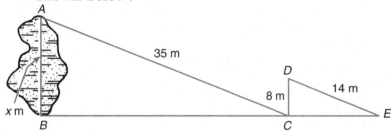

The length of the pond is _____ m.

3. $\triangle JKL \sim \triangle PQL$, what is the height of the building shown below?

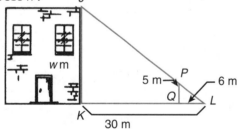

The height of the building is _____ m.

4. A pole 8 m high casts a shadow 6 m long. At the same time, a TV tower casts a shadow 30 m long. How high is the TV tower?

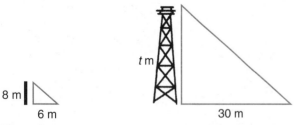

The TV tower is _____ m high.

1.

2.

3.

4.

Lesson 4   Squares and Square Roots

6^2 is read 6 *squared*.

6^2 means 6×6.

$6^2 =$ ___6___ $\times$ ___6___ $=$ ___36___

$9^2 =$ ___9___ $\times$ ___9___ $=$ _____

$3^2 =$ _____ $\times$ _____ $=$ _____

$\sqrt{36}$ is read *the square root of 36*.

$\sqrt{36}$ is some positive number a so that $a \times a = 36$.

$\sqrt{36} = \sqrt{\underline{\quad 6 \quad} \times \underline{\quad 6 \quad}} =$ ___6___

$\sqrt{81} = \sqrt{\underline{\quad 9 \quad} \times \underline{\quad 9 \quad}} =$ _____

$\sqrt{9} = \sqrt{\underline{\quad\quad} \times \underline{\quad\quad}} =$ _____

Complete the following.

a

1. $5^2 =$ _____ $\times$ _____ $=$ _____

2. $8^2 =$ _____ $\times$ _____ $=$ _____

3. $2^2 =$ _____ $\times$ _____ $=$ _____

4. $10^2 =$ _____ $\times$ _____ $=$ _____

5. $4^2 =$ _____ $\times$ _____ $=$ _____

6. $12^2 =$ _____ $\times$ _____ $=$ _____

7. $20^2 =$ _____ $\times$ _____ $=$ _____

8. $11^2 =$ _____ $\times$ _____ $=$ _____

9. $19^2 =$ _____ $\times$ _____ $=$ _____

10. $25^2 =$ _____ $\times$ _____ $=$ _____

11. $31^2 =$ _____ $\times$ _____ $=$ _____

12. $43^2 =$ _____ $\times$ _____ $=$ _____

13. $50^2 =$ _____ $\times$ _____ $=$ _____

b

$\sqrt{25} = \sqrt{\underline{\quad\quad} \times \underline{\quad\quad}} =$ _____

$\sqrt{64} = \sqrt{\underline{\quad\quad} \times \underline{\quad\quad}} =$ _____

$\sqrt{4} = \sqrt{\underline{\quad\quad} \times \underline{\quad\quad}} =$ _____

$\sqrt{100} = \sqrt{\underline{\quad\quad} \times \underline{\quad\quad}} =$ _____

$\sqrt{16} = \sqrt{\underline{\quad\quad} \times \underline{\quad\quad}} =$ _____

$\sqrt{144} = \sqrt{\underline{\quad\quad} \times \underline{\quad\quad}} =$ _____

$\sqrt{400} = \sqrt{\underline{\quad\quad} \times \underline{\quad\quad}} =$ _____

$\sqrt{121} = \sqrt{\underline{\quad\quad} \times \underline{\quad\quad}} =$ _____

$\sqrt{361} = \sqrt{\underline{\quad\quad} \times \underline{\quad\quad}} =$ _____

$\sqrt{625} = \sqrt{\underline{\quad\quad} \times \underline{\quad\quad}} =$ _____

$\sqrt{961} = \sqrt{\underline{\quad\quad} \times \underline{\quad\quad}} =$ _____

$\sqrt{1849} = \sqrt{\underline{\quad\quad} \times \underline{\quad\quad}} =$ _____

$\sqrt{2500} = \sqrt{\underline{\quad\quad} \times \underline{\quad\quad}} =$ _____

CHAPTER 10

NAME _____

Lesson 5   Squares and Square Roots (table)

Study how the table is used to find the square and the square root of a number n. ($\doteq$ is read *is approximately equal to*.)

n	n^2	$\sqrt{n}$
1	1	1.00
2	4	1.41
3	9	1.73
4	16	2.00
5	25	2.24
6	36	2.45
7	49	2.65
8	64	2.83
9	81	3.00

If $n = 2$, then $2^2 =$ ___4___ and $\sqrt{2} \doteq$ ___1.41___.

If $n = 4$, then $4^2 =$ ___16___ and $\sqrt{4} =$ ___2.00 or 2___.

If $n = 7$, then $7^2 =$ _____ and $\sqrt{7} \doteq$ _____.

If $n = 9$, then $9^2 =$ _____ and $\sqrt{9} \doteq$ ___ or ___.

Use the table on page **149** to help you complete the following.

1. If $n = 18$, then $18^2 =$ _____ and $\sqrt{18} \doteq$ _____.

2. If $n = 25$, then $25^2 =$ _____ and $\sqrt{25} =$ _____.

3. If $n = 45$, then $45^2 =$ _____ and $\sqrt{45} \doteq$ _____.

4. If $n = 64$, then $64^2 =$ _____ and $\sqrt{64} =$ _____.

5. If $n = 83$, then $83^2 =$ _____ and $\sqrt{83} \doteq$ _____.

6. If $n = 75$, then $75^2 =$ _____ and $\sqrt{75} \doteq$ _____.

7. If $n = 90$, then $90^2 =$ _____ and $\sqrt{90} \doteq$ _____.

8. If $n = 104$, then $104^2 =$ _____ and $\sqrt{104} \doteq$ _____.

9. If $n = 135$, then $135^2 =$ _____ and $\sqrt{135} \doteq$ _____.

10. If $n = 147$, then $147^2 =$ _____ and $\sqrt{147} \doteq$ _____.

11. If $n = 150$, then $150^2 =$ _____ and $\sqrt{150} \doteq$ _____.

Lesson 6   Squares and Square Roots (table)

Table of Squares and Square Roots								
n	n^2	$\sqrt{n}$	n	n^2	$\sqrt{n}$	n	n^2	$\sqrt{n}$
1	1	1.00	51	2 601	7.14	101	10 201	10.05
2	4	1.41	52	2 704	7.21	102	10 404	10.10
3	9	1.73	53	2 809	7.28	103	10 609	10.15
4	16	2.00	54	2 916	7.35	104	10 816	10.20
5	25	2.24	55	3 025	7.42	105	11 025	10.25
6	36	2.45	56	3 136	7.48	106	11 236	10.30
7	49	2.65	57	3 249	7.55	107	11 449	10.34
8	64	2.83	58	3 364	7.62	108	11 664	10.39
9	81	3.00	59	3 481	7.68	109	11 881	10.44
10	100	3.16	60	3 600	7.75	110	12 100	10.49
11	121	3.32	61	3 721	7.81	111	12 321	10.54
12	144	3.46	62	3 844	7.87	112	12 544	10.58
13	169	3.61	63	3 969	7.94	113	12 769	10.63
14	196	3.74	64	4 096	8.00	114	12 996	10.68
15	225	3.87	65	4 225	8.06	115	13 225	10.72
16	256	4.00	66	4 356	8.12	116	13 456	10.77
17	289	4.12	67	4 489	8.19	117	13 689	10.82
18	324	4.24	68	4 624	8.25	118	13 924	10.86
19	361	4.36	69	4 761	8.31	119	14 161	10.91
20	400	4.47	70	4 900	8.37	120	14 400	10.95
21	441	4.58	71	5 041	8.43	121	14 641	11.00
22	484	4.69	72	5 184	8.49	122	14 884	11.05
23	529	4.80	73	5 329	8.54	123	15 129	11.09
24	576	4.90	74	5 476	8.60	124	15 376	11.14
25	625	5.00	75	5 625	8.66	125	15 625	11.18
26	676	5.10	76	5 776	8.72	126	15 876	11.22
27	729	5.20	77	5 929	8.77	127	16 129	11.27
28	784	5.29	78	6 084	8.83	128	16 384	11.31
29	841	5.39	79	6 241	8.89	129	16 641	11.36
30	900	5.48	80	6 400	8.94	130	16 900	11.40
31	961	5.57	81	6 561	9.00	131	17 161	11.45
32	1 024	5.66	82	6 724	9.06	132	17 424	11.49
33	1 089	5.74	83	6 889	9.11	133	17 689	11.53
34	1 156	5.83	84	7 056	9.17	134	17 956	11.58
35	1 225	5.92	85	7 225	9.22	135	18 225	11.62
36	1 296	6.00	86	7 396	9.27	136	18 496	11.66
37	1 369	6.08	87	7 569	9.33	137	18 769	11.70
38	1 444	6.16	88	7 744	9.38	138	19 044	11.75
39	1 521	6.24	89	7 921	9.43	139	19 321	11.79
40	1 600	6.32	90	8 100	9.49	140	19 600	11.83
41	1 681	6.40	91	8 281	9.54	141	19 881	11.87
42	1 764	6.48	92	8 464	9.59	142	20 164	11.92
43	1 849	6.56	93	8 649	9.64	143	20 449	11.96
44	1 936	6.63	94	8 836	9.70	144	20 736	12.00
45	2 025	6.71	95	9 025	9.75	145	21 025	12.04
46	2 116	6.78	96	9 216	9.80	146	21 316	12.08
47	2 209	6.86	97	9 409	9.85	147	21 609	12.12
48	2 304	6.93	98	9 604	9.90	148	21 904	12.17
49	2 401	7.00	99	9 801	9.95	149	22 201	12.21
50	2 500	7.07	100	10 000	10.00	150	22 500	12.25

CHAPTER 10

Lesson 6   Square Roots

Study how the table on page **149** can be used to find the square root of a number greater than 150.

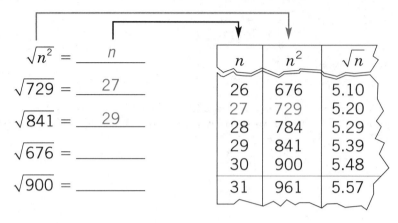

$$\sqrt{n^2} = \underline{\quad n \quad}$$

$$\sqrt{729} = \underline{\quad 27 \quad}$$

$$\sqrt{841} = \underline{\quad 29 \quad}$$

$$\sqrt{676} = \underline{\qquad\quad}$$

$$\sqrt{900} = \underline{\qquad\quad}$$

n	n^2	$\sqrt{n}$
26	676	5.10
27	729	5.20
28	784	5.29
29	841	5.39
30	900	5.48
31	961	5.57

Use the table on page **149** to help you complete each of the following.

	a	*b*	*c*
1.	$\sqrt{169} = \underline{\qquad}$	$\sqrt{529} = \underline{\qquad}$	$\sqrt{784} = \underline{\qquad}$
2.	$\sqrt{256} = \underline{\qquad}$	$\sqrt{361} = \underline{\qquad}$	$\sqrt{961} = \underline{\qquad}$
3.	$\sqrt{1225} = \underline{\qquad}$	$\sqrt{2209} = \underline{\qquad}$	$\sqrt{3969} = \underline{\qquad}$
4.	$\sqrt{1681} = \underline{\qquad}$	$\sqrt{3136} = \underline{\qquad}$	$\sqrt{4761} = \underline{\qquad}$
5.	$\sqrt{5329} = \underline{\qquad}$	$\sqrt{6084} = \underline{\qquad}$	$\sqrt{6889} = \underline{\qquad}$
6.	$\sqrt{7921} = \underline{\qquad}$	$\sqrt{8649} = \underline{\qquad}$	$\sqrt{9604} = \underline{\qquad}$
7.	$\sqrt{10\ 201} = \underline{\qquad}$	$\sqrt{11\ 025} = \underline{\qquad}$	$\sqrt{11\ 449} = \underline{\qquad}$
8.	$\sqrt{12\ 544} = \underline{\qquad}$	$\sqrt{17\ 424} = \underline{\qquad}$	$\sqrt{22\ 201} = \underline{\qquad}$
9.	$\sqrt{4900} = \underline{\qquad}$	$\sqrt{1849} = \underline{\qquad}$	$\sqrt{16\ 900} = \underline{\qquad}$
10.	$\sqrt{10\ 000} = \underline{\qquad}$	$\sqrt{12\ 100} = \underline{\qquad}$	$\sqrt{2500} = \underline{\qquad}$
11.	$\sqrt{8464} = \underline{\qquad}$	$\sqrt{19\ 321} = \underline{\qquad}$	$\sqrt{13\ 924} = \underline{\qquad}$
12.	$\sqrt{8281} = \underline{\qquad}$	$\sqrt{18\ 225} = \underline{\qquad}$	$\sqrt{21\ 316} = \underline{\qquad}$

Lesson 7 The Pythagorean Theorem   PRE-ALGEBRA

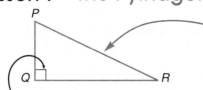

⌐ means a right angle.

In a right triangle the side opposite the right angle is called the **hypotenuse.**

Which side is the hypotenuse in $\triangle PQR$? _____

Pythagorean Theorem: The square of the measure of the hypotenuse of a right triangle is equal to the sum of the squares of the measures of the other two sides.

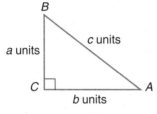

$$c^2 = a^2 + b^2 \text{ or } c^2 = b^2 + a^2$$

Find c if $a = 3$ and $b = 4$.
$$c^2 = a^2 + b^2$$
$$c^2 = 3^2 + 4^2$$
$$c^2 = 9 + 16 \text{ or } 25$$
$$\sqrt{c^2} = \sqrt{25}$$

$$c = _____$$

Use $\triangle ABC$ above and the table on page **149** to help you complete the following.

1. If $a = 6$ and $b = 8$, then $c =$ _____.

2. If $a = 7$ and $b = 24$, then $c =$ _____.

3. If $a = 5$ and $b = 7$, then $c \doteq$ _____.

4. If $a = 7$ and $b = 9$, then $c \doteq$ _____.

5. If $a = 5$ and $b = 12$, then $c =$ _____.

6. If $a = 8$ and $b = 8$, then $c \doteq$ _____.

7. If $a = 8$ and $b = 15$, then $c =$ _____.

8. If $a = 3$ and $b = 8$, then $c \doteq$ _____.

9. If $a = 20$ and $b = 21$, then $c =$ _____.

10. If $a = 12$ and $b = 2$, then $c \doteq$ _____.

11. If $a = 45$ and $b = 28$, then $c =$ _____.

CHAPTER 10

Lesson 7 Problem Solving   PRE-ALGEBRA

Use the Pythagorean Theorem and the table on page **149** to help you solve each of the following.

1. The foot of a ladder is placed 5 m from a building. The top of the ladder rests 12 m up on the building. How long is the ladder?

    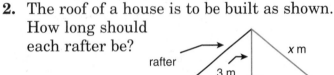

    The ladder is _____ m long.

2. The roof of a house is to be built as shown. How long should each rafter be?

    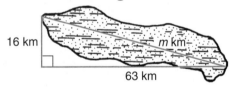

    Each rafter should be _____ m long.

3. A ship left port and sailed 5 km east and then 7 km north. How far was the ship from the port then?

    The ship was about _____ km from the port.

4. What is the length of the lake shown below?

    The length is _____ km.

5. An inclined ramp rises 5 m over a horizontal distance of 11 m. What is the length of the ramp?

    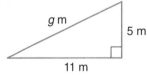

    The length is _____ m.

1.

2.

3.

4.

5.

Lesson 8   Using the Pythagorean Theorem   PRE-ALGEBRA

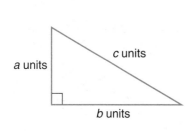

a units

c units

b units

Find a if $c = 17$ and $b = 15$.

$$c^2 = a^2 + b^2$$
$$17^2 = a^2 + 15^2$$
$$289 = a^2 + 225$$
$$289 - 225 = a^2 + 225 - 225$$
$$64 = a^2$$
$$\sqrt{64} = \sqrt{a^2}$$
$$\underline{8} = a$$

Find b if $c = 13$ and $a = 12$.

$$c^2 = b^2 + a^2$$
$$13^2 = b^2 + 12^2$$
$$169 = b^2 + 144$$
$$169 - 144 = b^2 + 144 - 144$$
$$25 = b^2$$
$$\sqrt{25} = \sqrt{b^2}$$
$$\underline{} = b$$

Use the triangle above and the table on page **149** to help you complete the following.

1. If $c = 25$ and $a = 24$, then $b =$ _____.

2. If $c = 41$ and $b = 40$, then $a =$ _____.

3. If $c = 61$ and $a = 60$, then $b =$ _____.

4. If $c = 25$ and $b = 22$, then $a \doteq$ _____.

5. If $c = 26$ and $a = 24$, then $b =$ _____.

6. If $c = 20$ and $b = 17$, then $a \doteq$ _____.

7. If $c = 89$ and $a = 80$, then $b =$ _____.

8. If $c = 65$ and $b = 63$, then $a =$ _____.

9. If $c = 72$ and $a = 71$, then $b \doteq$ _____.

10. If $c = 73$ and $b = 48$, then $a =$ _____.

11. If $c = 38$ and $a = 36$, then $b \doteq$ _____.

12. If $c = 85$ and $b = 36$, then $a =$ _____.

CHAPTER 10

Lesson 8 Problem Solving   PRE-ALGEBRA

Use the Pythagorean Theorem and the table on page **149** to help you solve each of the following.

1. Suppose the foot of a 12-m ladder was placed 4 m from the building. How high up on the building would the top of the ladder reach?

   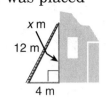

   The ladder will reach about _____ m.

   1.

2. A ship is 24 km east of port. How far north must the ship sail to reach a point that is 25 km from the port?

   The ship must sail _____ km north.

   2.

3. A telephone pole is braced by a guy wire as shown. How high up on the pole is the wire fastened?

   The wire is fastened _____ m above the ground.

   3.

4. How far is it across the pond shown below?

   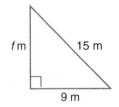

   It is _____ m across the pond.

   4.

5. Alstown, Donville, and Maxburg are located as shown below. How many kilometres is it from Alstown to Maxburg?

   Donville
   13 km
   6 km
   Alstown
   v km
   Maxburg

   It is about _____ km from Alstown to Maxburg.

   5.

6. A sail is shaped as shown. How high is the sail?

   f m   15 m

   9 m

   The sail is _____ m high.

   6.

Lesson 9   Similar Right Triangles   PRE-ALGEBRA

Study how the Pythagorean Theorem and the ratios of similar triangles are used to find the measure of $\overline{AB}$, the measure of $\overline{A'C'}$, and the measure of $\overline{B'C'}$.

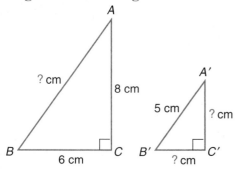

right $\triangle ABC \sim$ right $\triangle A'B'C'$

Step 1

Use $c^2 = a^2 + b^2$ to find the measure of $\overline{AB}$.

$$c^2 = a^2 + b^2$$
$$c^2 = 6^2 + 8^2$$
$$c^2 = 100$$
$$c = 10$$
$$AB = \underline{}10$$

Step 2

Use the measure of $\overline{AB}$ from *Step 1* and find the measure of $\overline{A'C'}$ and $\overline{B'C'}$.

$$\frac{AB}{A'B'} = \frac{AC}{A'C'} \qquad \frac{AB}{A'B'} = \frac{BC}{B'C'}$$

$$\frac{10}{5} = \frac{8}{A'C'} \qquad \frac{10}{5} = \frac{6}{B'C'}$$

$$A'C' = \underline{}4 \qquad B'C' = \underline{}3$$

$\overline{AB}$ is _____ cm long. $\overline{A'C'}$ is _____ cm long. $\overline{B'C'}$ is _____ cm long.

Find the length of each side shown in colour in each pair of similar right triangles below. You may use the table on page **149** if necessary.

1.

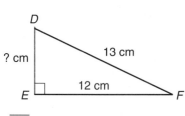
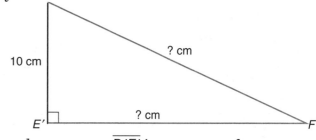

$\overline{DE}$ is _____ cm long. $\overline{E'F'}$ is _____ cm long. $\overline{D'F'}$ is _____ cm long.

2.

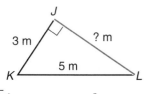
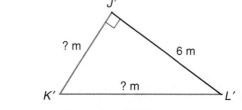

$\overline{JL}$ is _____ m long. $\overline{J'K'}$ is _____ m long. $\overline{K'L'}$ is _____ m long.

3.

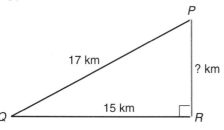
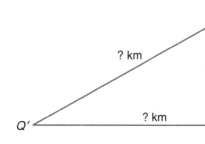

$\overline{PR}$ is _____ km long. $\overline{Q'R'}$ is _____ km long. $\overline{Q'P'}$ is _____ km long.

CHAPTER 10

Lesson 9   Problem Solving   PRE-ALGEBRA

Solve each problem. If necessary, use the table on page **149**.

1. If $\triangle ABD \sim \triangle ECD$, how far is it from the pier to the island? From the boathouse to the campsite? From the lodge to the campsite?

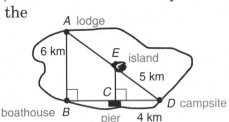

It is _____ km from the pier to the island.

It is _____ km from the boathouse to the campsite.

It is _____ km from the lodge to the campsite.

2. A cellphone tower is steadied by guy wires as shown. If $\triangle JKL \sim \triangle MKN$, what are the lengths of the guy wires? How high is the upper guy wire fastened above the ground?

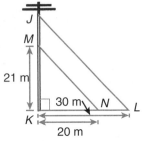

The shorter wire is _____ m long.

The longer wire is _____ m long.

The upper guy wire is fastened _____ m above the ground.

3. Two inclined ramps are shaped as shown below and $\triangle PQR \sim \triangle XYZ$. What is the length of $\overline{QR}$? What is the height of each ramp?

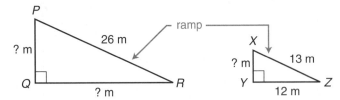

The length of the taller ramp is _____ m.

The height of the shorter ramp is _____ m.

The height of the taller ramp is _____ m.

1.

2.

3.

CHAPTER 10 PRACTICE TEST
Similar Triangles

Use the similar triangles below to help you complete the following.

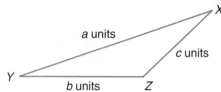

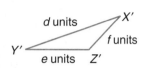

$$\frac{a}{d} = \frac{b}{e} = \frac{c}{f}$$

1. If $a = 6$, $d = 9$, and $b = 8$, then $e =$ _____.

2. If $b = 24$, $e = 12$, and $c = 16$, then $f =$ _____.

3. If $c = 8$, $f = 4$, and $e = 6$, then $b =$ _____.

4. If $e = 9$, $b = 3$, and $d = 6$, then $a =$ _____.

Use the triangle below and the table on page **149** to help you complete the following.

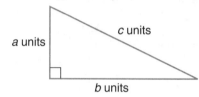

$$c^2 = a^2 + b^2 \text{ or } c^2 = b^2 + a^2$$

5. If $a = 8$ and $b = 6$, then $c =$ _____.

6. If $a = 16$ and $c = 65$, then $b =$ _____.

7. If $b = 20$ and $c = 23$, then $a \doteq$ _____.

8. If $a = 9$ and $b = 8$, then $c \doteq$ _____.

Solve each of the following.

9. A post and a flagpole cast shadows as shown below. What is the height of the flagpole?

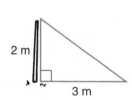

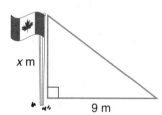

The height of the flagpole is _____ m.

10. A windowpane is 18 cm by 18 cm. What is the distance between opposite corners of the windowpane?

The distance is about _____ cm.

CHAPTER 11 PRETEST
Perimeter, Area, and Volume

Find the perimeter and area of each figure.

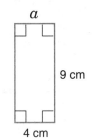

a

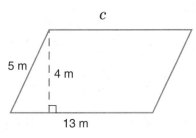

b   *c*

perimeter: _____ cm   _____ cm   _____ m

area: _____ cm²   _____ cm²   _____ m²

Complete the table below. Use 3.14 for π. Find the approximate circumference and area.

diameter	radius	circumference	area
2. 12 cm	_____ cm	about _____ cm	about _____ cm²
3. _____ mm	3 mm	about _____ mm	about _____ mm²

Find the surface area of each figure. Use 3.14 for π.

a   *b*   *c*

4.

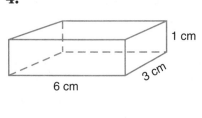

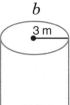

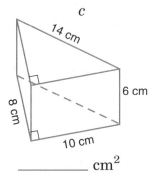

_____ cm²   about _____ m²   _____ cm²

Find the volume of each figure. Use 3.14 for π.

5.

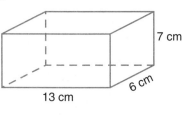

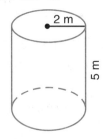

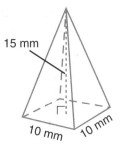

_____ cm³   about _____ m³   _____ mm³

Lesson 1 Perimeter   PRE-ALGEBRA

The perimeter measure (P) of a figure is equal to the sum of the measures of its sides.

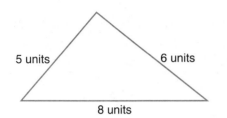

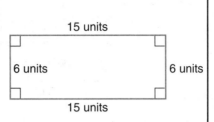

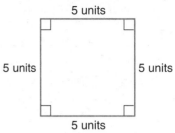

Find P if $a = 5$, $b = 6$, and $c = 8$.

$$P = a + b + c$$
$$= 5 + 8 + 6$$
$$= \underline{\quad 19 \quad}$$

The perimeter is $\underline{19}$ units.

Find P if $l = 15$ and $w = 6$.

$$P = l + w + l + w$$
$$= 2(l + w)$$
$$= 2(15 + 6)$$
$$= 2 \times 21 \text{ or } \underline{\quad\quad}$$

The perimeter is ___ units.

Find P if $s = 5$.

$$P = s + s + s + s$$
$$= 4s$$
$$= 4 \times 5$$
$$= \underline{\quad\quad}$$

The perimeter is ___ units.

Find the perimeter of each figure below.

	a	b	c

1.

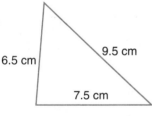

_____ cm

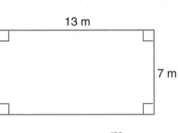

_____ m

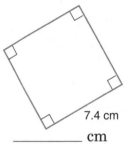

_____ cm

2.

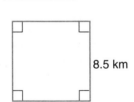

_____ km

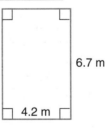

_____ m

7 mm 8 mm 9 mm 8 mm 10 mm

_____ mm

3.

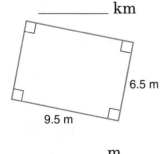

_____ m

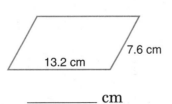

_____ cm

_____ m

CHAPTER 11

Lesson 2   Circumference   PRE-ALGEBRA

The ratio of the measure of the circumference to the measure of a diameter is the same for all circles. The symbol π stands for this ratio. π is approximately equal to 3.14.

The circumference measure (C) of a circle is equal to π times the measure of a diameter (d) of the circle. $C = \pi d$	The measure of a diameter (d) is twice the measure of a radius (r). Hence, $C = \pi d$ can be changed to $C = \pi(2r)$ or $C = 2\pi r$.

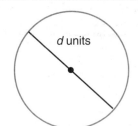

Find C if $d = 7$.

$C = \pi d$

$\doteq 3.14 \times 7$

$\doteq$ _____21.98_____

The circumference is about _____ units.

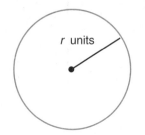

Find C if $r = 6$.

$C = 2\pi r$

$\doteq 2 \times 3.14 \times 6$

$\doteq$ _____

The circumference is about _____ units.

Find the approximate circumference of each circle below. Use 3.14 for π.

        a   *b*   *c*

1.

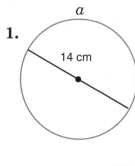
14 cm

2.8 m

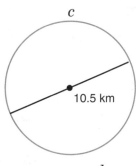
10.5 km

_____ cm   _____ m   _____ km

Find the approximate circumference of each circle described below. Use 3.14 for π.

	a			*b*	
	diameter	**approximate circumference**		**radius**	**approximate circumference**
2.	6 m	_____ m		21 mm	_____ mm
3.	15 cm	_____ cm		6.7 cm	_____ cm
4.	6.8 km	_____ km		48 cm	_____ cm
5.	81 mm	_____ mm		37 mm	_____ mm
6.	27 mm	_____ mm		9.6 m	_____ m
7.	4.2 m	_____ m		4 km	_____ km

Lesson 3 Area of a Rectangle

The area measure (A) of a rectangle is equal to the product of the measure of its length (*l*) and the measure of its width (*w*). $A = l \times w$ or $A = lw$

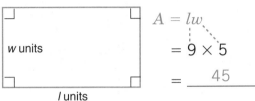

Find A if $l = 9$ and $w = 5$.

$A = lw$

$= 9 \times 5$

$= \underline{\quad 45 \quad}$

The area is _____ square units.

Find A if $s = 3$.

$A = s \times s$ or s^2

$= 3 \times 3$

$= \underline{\qquad}$

The area is _____ square units.

Find the area of each rectangle below.

a

b

c

1.

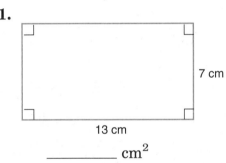

7 cm

13 cm

_____ cm^2

8.5 km

_____ km^2

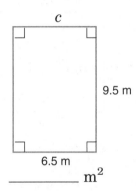

9.5 m

6.5 m

_____ m^2

Find the area of each rectangle described below.

	length	width	area
2.	33 cm	27 cm	_____ cm^2
3.	5.3 m	3.5 m	_____ m^2
4.	3.8 km	2 km	_____ km^2
5.	6.7 m	6.7 m	_____ m^2
6.	9.2 cm	7.7 cm	_____ cm^2
7.	18 m	4.6 m	_____ m^2
8.	3.6 km	3.6 km	_____ km^2
9.	9.5 cm	6.6 cm	_____ cm^2

CHAPTER 11

Lesson 4 Area of a Triangle

PRE-ALGEBRA

The area measure (A) of a triangle is equal to $\frac{1}{2}$ the product of the measure of its base (b) and the measure of its height (h). $\qquad A = \frac{1}{2}bh \quad$ or $\quad A = 0.5bh$

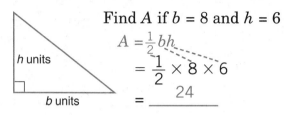

Find A if $b = 8$ and $h = 6$

$$A = \frac{1}{2}bh$$
$$= \frac{1}{2} \times 8 \times 6$$
$$= \underline{\quad 24 \quad}$$

The area is _____ square units.

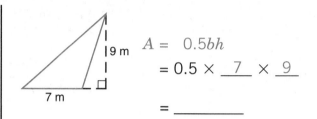

$$A = 0.5bh$$
$$= 0.5 \times \underline{\ 7\ } \times \underline{\ 9\ }$$
$$= \underline{\qquad}$$

The area is _____ m².

Find the area of each triangle below.

a	b	c

1.

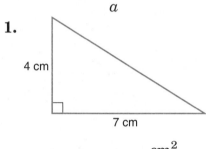

4 cm

7 cm

_____ cm²

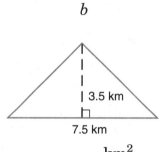

3.5 km

7.5 km

_____ km²

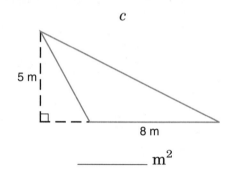

5 m

8 m

_____ m²

Find the area of each triangle described below.

	base	height	area
2.	15 m	9 m	_____ m²
3.	$3\frac{1}{2}$ mm	$6\frac{1}{2}$ mm	_____ mm²
4.	7.4 cm	6.5 cm	_____ cm²
5.	$11\frac{1}{2}$ m	7 m	_____ m²
6.	154 mm	37 mm	_____ mm²
7.	85 cm	35 cm	_____ cm²
8.	18.8 m	7.5 m	_____ m²
9.	9.5 km	6.6 km	_____ km²

Lesson 5 Area of a Circle   PRE-ALGEBRA

The area measure (A) of a circle is equal to the product of π and the square of the measure of a radius (r^2) of the circle. $A = \pi r^2$

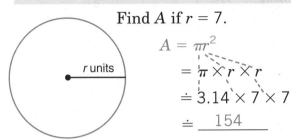

Find A if $r = 7$.

$A = \pi r^2$

$= \pi \times r \times r$

$\doteq 3.14 \times 7 \times 7$

$\doteq \underline{\quad 154 \quad}$

The area is about _____ square units.

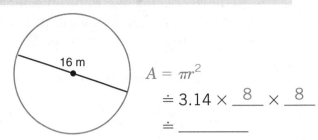

$A = \pi r^2$

$\doteq 3.14 \times \underline{\quad 8 \quad} \times \underline{\quad 8 \quad}$

$\doteq \underline{\qquad}$

The area is about _____ square units.

Find the approximate area of each circle below. Use 3.14 for π.

| a | b | c |

1.

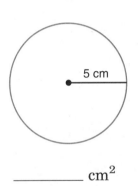

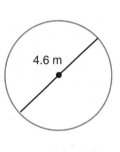

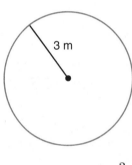

_____ cm^2 _____ m^2 _____ m^2

Find the approximate area of each circle described below. Use 3.14 for π.

| a | b |

	radius	approximate area		diameter	approximate area
2.	9 cm	_____ cm^2		28 mm	_____ mm^2
3.	14 mm	_____ mm^2		42 cm	_____ cm^2
4.	$3\frac{1}{2}$ m	_____ m^2		72 m	_____ m^2
5.	56 cm	_____ cm^2		126 mm	_____ mm^2
6.	5.3 mm	_____ mm^2		84 cm	_____ cm^2
7.	45 km	_____ km^2		1.8 km	_____ km^2

Lesson 5 Problem Solving   PRE-ALGEBRA

Solve each problem. Use 3.14 for π.

1. The Redfords would like to build a fence around a rectangular lot. The lot is 140 m long and 50 m wide. How much fencing is needed?

   _____ m of fencing are needed.

2. What is the area of the lot in problem **1**?

   The area is _____ m^2.

3. Mr. McDaniel wants to put carpeting in a room that is 4 m long and 3 m wide. How many square metres of carpeting does he need?

   He needs _____ m^2 of carpeting.

4. The lengths of the sides of a triangular-shaped garden are 17 m, 26 m, and 35 m. What is the perimeter of the garden?

   The perimeter is _____ m.

5. The diameter of a circular pond is 28 m. What is the circumference of the pond?

   The circumference is about _____ m.

6. What is the area of the pond in problem **5**?

   The area is about _____ m^2.

7. Mrs. Witt is refinishing a circular table with a radius of 60 cm. Find the area of the tabletop.

   The area is about _____ cm^2.

8. Find the circumference of the tabletop in problem **7**.

   The circumference is about _____ cm.

1.	2.
3.	4.
5.	6.
7.	8.

Lesson 6   Area of a Parallelogram   PRE-ALGEBRA

The area measure (A) of a parallelogram is equal to the product of the measure of its base (b) and the measure of its height (h). $A = bh$

Find A if $b = 14$ and $h = 9$.

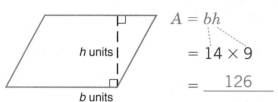

$A = bh$

$= 14 \times 9$

$= \underline{\quad 126 \quad}$

The area is _____ square units.

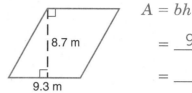

$A = bh$

$= \underline{\quad 9.3 \quad} \times \underline{\quad 8.7 \quad}$

$= \underline{\qquad}$

The area is _____ m^2.

Find the area of each parallelogram below.

a	b	c

1.

4.5 cm

5 cm

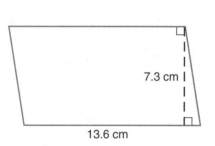

7.3 cm

13.6 cm

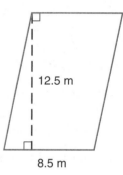

12.5 m

8.5 m

_____ cm^2 _____ cm^2 _____ m^2

Find the area of each parallelogram described below.

	base	height	area
2.	72 mm	24 mm	_____ mm^2
3.	7.5 cm	5 cm	_____ cm^2
4.	4.8 km	3.8 km	_____ km^2
5.	7.2 m	6 m	_____ m^2
6.	9.4 cm	6.7 cm	_____ cm^2
7.	9 m	7.3 m	_____ m^2
8.	16 km	12.4 km	_____ km^2

CHAPTER 11

Lesson 7 Surface Area of a Rectangular Prism

> The surface area (SA) of a rectangular prism is the sum of the areas of all its faces.

Find the surface area
of the figure shown.

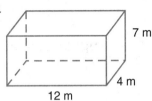

Imagine the rectangular prism as a flat surface.

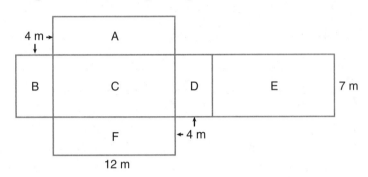

area A = 12 × 4 = 48

area B = 4 × 7 = 28

area C = 12 × 7 = 84

area D = 4 × 7 = 28

area E = 12 × 7 = 84

area F = 12 × 4 = 48

$SA = A + B + C + D + E + F$

SA = 48 + 28 + 84 + 28 + 84 + 48 = 320

The surface area is ____320____ m².

Find the surface area of each rectangular prism below.

a

1.

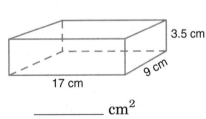

_____ cm²

b

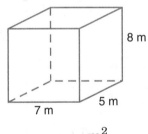

_____ m²

c

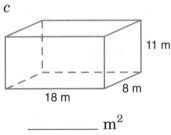

_____ m²

Find the surface area of each rectangular prism described below.

	length	width	height	surface area
2.	8 mm	11 mm	13 mm	_____ mm²
3.	24 cm	20 cm	37 cm	_____ cm²
4.	6.5 m	14.2 m	9.7 m	_____ m²
5.	4.5 cm	7.8 cm	12.3 cm	_____ cm²

Lesson 8 Surface Area of a Triangular Prism

The surface area (SA) of a triangular prism is the sum of the areas of all its faces.

Find the surface area of the figure shown.

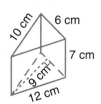

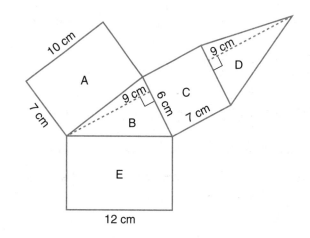

Imagine the triangular prism as a flat surface.

area $A = 7 \times 10 = 70$

area $B = \frac{1}{2} \times 6 \times 9 = 27$

area $C = 6 \times 7 = 42$

area $D = \frac{1}{2} \times 6 \times 9 = 27$

area $E = 12 \times 7 = 84$

$SA = A + B + C + D + E$

$SA = 70 + 27 + 42 + 27 + 84 = 250$

The surface area is ___250___ cm².

Find the surface area of each triangular prism below.

a	b	c

1.

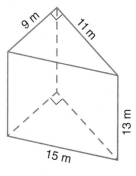

_____ m²

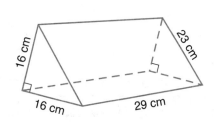

_____ cm²

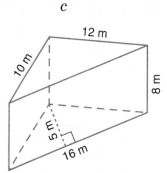

_____ m²

2.

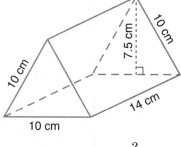

_____ cm²

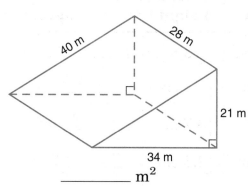

_____ m²

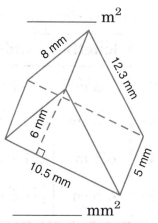

_____ mm²

CHAPTER 11

NAME _____

Lesson 9 Surface Area of a Cylinder

The surface area (SA) of a cylinder is the sum of the lateral area and twice the area of the circular base. $SA = 2\pi rh + 2\pi r^2$

Find the surface area of the figure shown. Use 3.14 for π.

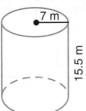

$$SA = 2\pi rh + 2\pi r^2$$
$$\doteq (2 \times 3.14 \times 7 \times 15.5) + (2 \times 3.14 \times 7^2)$$
$$\doteq 681.38 + 307.72$$
$$\doteq 989.1$$

The surface area is about ___989.1___ m².

Find the approximate surface area of each cylinder below. Use 3.14 for π.

a   b   c

1.

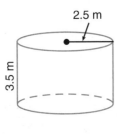
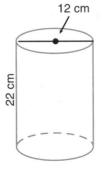
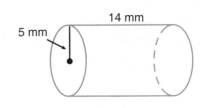

_____ m²   _____ cm²   _____ mm²

Find the approximate surface area of each cylinder described below. Use 3.14 for π.

	radius	height	approximate surface area
2.	5 cm	12 cm	_____ cm²
3.	18 m	12.5 m	_____ m²
4.	13.5 cm	5 cm	_____ cm²
5.	0.75 m	1.25 m	_____ m²
6.	53 cm	71 cm	_____ cm²
7.	8.15 mm	16.75 mm	_____ mm²

Lesson 10 Volume of a Rectangular Prism PRE-ALGEBRA

The volume measure (V) of a rectangular prism is equal to the product of the area measure of its base (B) and the measure of its height (h). $V = Bh$

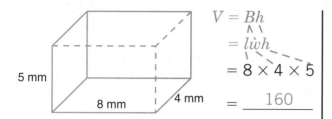

$V = Bh$
$= lwh$
$= 8 \times 4 \times 5$
$= \underline{\quad 160 \quad}$

The volume is _____ mm^3.

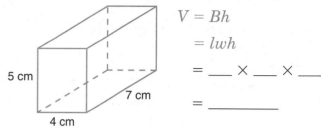

$V = Bh$
$= lwh$
$= \underline{\quad} \times \underline{\quad} \times \underline{\quad}$
$= \underline{\qquad}$

The volume is _____ cm^3.

Find the volume of each rectangular prism below.

a	b	c

1.

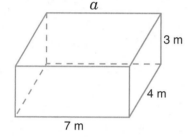

_____ m^3

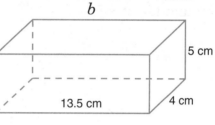

_____ cm^3

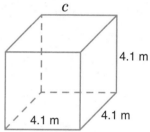

_____ m^3

2.

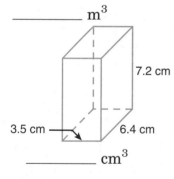

_____ cm^3

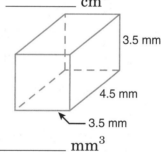

_____ mm^3

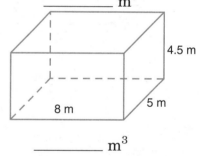

_____ m^3

Find the volume of each rectangular prism described below.

	length	width	height	volume
3.	6 cm	7 cm	8 cm	_____ cm^3
4.	4.1 m	3.7 m	2.6 m	_____ m^3
5.	3.5 cm	3.5 cm	3.5 cm	_____ cm^3
6.	28 mm	36 mm	14 mm	_____ mm^3
7.	7.3 m	2.5 m	5.7 m	_____ m^3

CHAPTER 11

Lesson 11   Volume of a Triangular Prism   PRE-ALGEBRA

The volume (V) of a triangular prism is equal to the product of the area measure of its base (B) and the measure of its height. $V = Bh$

Find the volume of the figure shown.

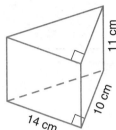

$V = Bh$
$V = (\frac{1}{2} \times 14 \times 10) \times 11$
$V = 70 \times 11$
$V = 770$

The formula for the area of the base (B) is $A = \frac{1}{2}bh$.

The volume is ____770____ cm^3.

Find the volume of each triangular prism below.

| a | b | c |

1.

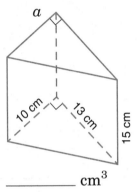
_____ cm^3

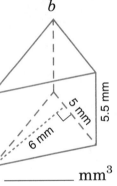
_____ mm^3

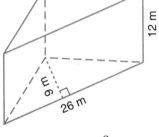
_____ m^3

2.

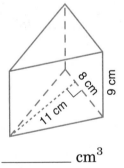
_____ cm^3

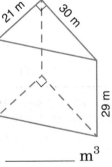
_____ m^3

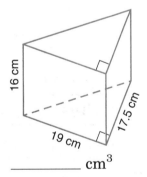
_____ cm^3

3.

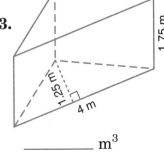
_____ m^3

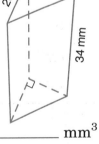
_____ mm^3

_____ m^3

Lesson 12 Volume of a Cylinder

NAME _____

PRE-ALGEBRA

The volume measure (V) of a cylinder is equal to the product of the area measure of its base (B) and the measure of its height (h). $V = Bh$

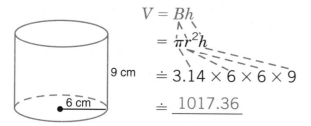

$V = Bh$

$= \pi r^2 h$

$\doteq 3.14 \times 6 \times 6 \times 9$

$\doteq \underline{1017.36}$

The volume is about _____ cm³.

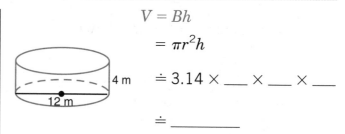

$V = Bh$

$= \pi r^2 h$

$\doteq 3.14 \times \underline{} \times \underline{} \times \underline{}$

$\doteq$ _____

The volume is about _____ m³.

Find the approximate volume of each cylinder. Use 3.14 for π.

           a   *b*   *c*

1.

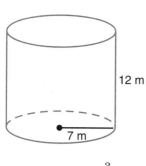

_____ m³

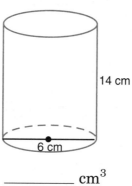

_____ cm³

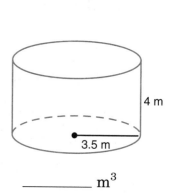

_____ m³

Find the approximate volume of each cylinder described below. Use 3.14 for π.

	radius	height	approximate volume
2.	8 cm	6 cm	_____ cm³
3.	18 mm	9 mm	_____ mm³
4.	1.7 m	3.4 m	_____ m³
5.	14 mm	6.5 mm	_____ mm³
6.	9 cm	14 cm	_____ cm³
7.	7 m	3.8 m	_____ m³

Lesson 12 Problem Solving   PRE-ALGEBRA

Solve each problem. Use 3.14 for π.

1. A box is 6 cm long, 4 cm wide, and 3 cm high. What is the volume of the box?

   The volume is _____ cm^3.

2. A cylindrical storage tank has a diameter of 7 m and a height of 5 m. What is the volume of the storage tank?

   The volume is about _____ m^3.

3. Cereal A comes in a rectangular box 20 cm wide, 6 cm deep, and 25 cm high. Find the volume of that box.

   The volume is about _____ cm^3.

4. Cereal B comes in a cylindrical box that has a diameter of 13 cm and a height of 25 cm. What is the volume of that box?

   The volume is about _____ cm^3.

5. Which cereal comes in the box with the larger volume? How much larger?

   Cereal _____ comes in a box that has a

   volume about _____ cm^3 larger.

6. A classroom is 11 m long, 8 m wide, and 3 m high. What is the volume of the classroom?

   The volume is _____ m^3.

7. Courtney has a cylindrical juice container with a diameter of 10 cm. Its height is 20 cm. How many cubic centimetres of juice will the container hold?

   The container will hold about _____ cm^3.

1.	2.
3.	4.
5.	6.
7.	

Lesson 13 Volume of a Cone

PRE-ALGEBRA

The volume (V) of a cone is equal to $\frac{1}{3}$ the volume of a cylinder with the same base. $V = \frac{1}{3}Bh$

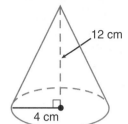

$$V = \frac{1}{3}Bh$$
$$= \frac{1}{3}\pi r^2 h$$
$$\doteq \frac{1}{3} \times 3.14 \times 4^2 \times 12$$
$$\doteq 200.96$$

The volume is about __200.96__ cm³.

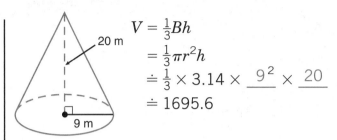

$$V = \frac{1}{3}Bh$$
$$= \frac{1}{3}\pi r^2 h$$
$$\doteq \frac{1}{3} \times 3.14 \times \underline{9}^2 \times \underline{20}$$
$$\doteq 1695.6$$

The volume is about __1695.6__ m³.

Find the approximate volume of each cone. Use 3.14 for π.

| a | b | c |

1.

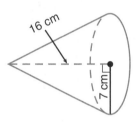

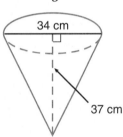

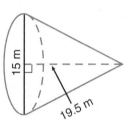

about _____ cm³

about _____ cm³

about _____ m³

Find the approximate volume of each cone described below. Use 3.14 for π.

	radius	height	approximate volume
2.	10 cm	15 cm	_____ cm³
3.	4 m	5.25 m	_____ m³
4.	34 mm	57 mm	_____ mm³
5.	11 m	1.5 m	_____ m³
6.	19 cm	24.75 cm	_____ cm³
7.	0.58 m	1.35 m	_____ m³

Lesson 14 Volume of a Pyramid   PRE-ALGEBRA

The volume (V) of a pyramid is equal to $\frac{1}{3}$ the volume of a rectangular prism with the same base. $V = \frac{1}{3}Bh$

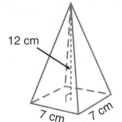

$V = \frac{1}{3}Bh$
$= \frac{1}{3} \times 7 \times 7 \times 12$
$= 196$

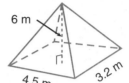

$V = \frac{1}{3}Bh$
$= \frac{1}{3} \times 3.2 \times \underline{4.5} \times \underline{6}$
$= 28.8$

The volume is ___196___ cm³.

The volume is ___28.8___ m³.

Find the volume of each pyramid.

| a | b | c |

1.

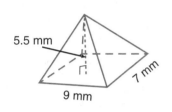

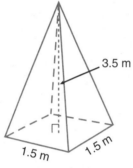

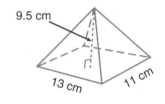

_____ mm³

_____ m³

_____ cm³

Find the volume of each pyramid described below.

	length of base	width of base	height	volume
2.	9 cm	9 cm	15 cm	_____ cm³
3.	12 mm	8 mm	10 mm	_____ mm³
4.	9 cm	15 cm	9.9 cm	_____ cm³
5.	0.6 m	0.4 m	0.8 m	_____ m³
6.	8.25 cm	10.5 cm	6 cm	_____ cm³
7.	12.75 mm	12.75 mm	5 mm	_____ mm³

Lesson 15 Perimeter, Area, and Volume   PRE-ALGEBRA

Find the perimeter or circumference of each figure below. Use 3.14 for π.

a

1. 8 m   16.5 m

22.3 m

_____ m

b

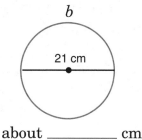
21 cm

about _____ cm

Find the area of each figure below. Use 3.14 for π.

a   b   c

2.

8 km

_____ km^2

7 m

13 m

_____ m^2

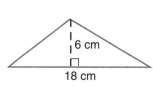
6 cm

18 cm

_____ cm^2

3.

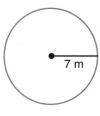
7 m

about _____ m^2

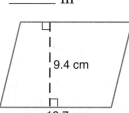
9.4 cm

12.7 cm

_____ cm^2

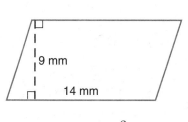
9 mm

14 mm

_____ mm^2

Find the volume of each figure below. Use 3.14 for π.

a   b

4.

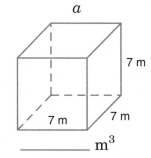
7 m

7 m   7 m

_____ m^3

3 cm

7 cm

5 cm

_____ cm^3

5.

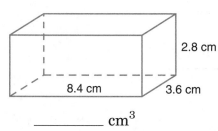 
2.8 cm

8.4 cm   3.6 cm

_____ cm^3

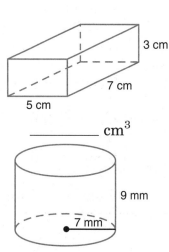
9 mm

7 mm

about _____ mm^3

CHAPTER 11

Lesson 15 Problem Solving   PRE-ALGEBRA

Solve each problem. Use 3.14 for π.

1. A carpenter cut a circular shelf from a square piece of wood as shown at the right. Find the area of the square piece of wood. Find the area of the circular piece of wood.

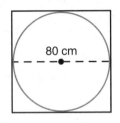
80 cm

   The area of the square piece is _____ cm^2.

   The area of the circular piece is about _____ cm^2.

2. The carpenter threw away the wood left over after cutting out the circular piece. How much wood was thrown away?

   _____ cm^2 were thrown away.

3. Find the circumference of the circular piece of wood in problem **1**.

   The circumference is about _____ cm.

4. A farmer has a field shaped like a parallelogram. The base is 1500 m. The height is 1200 m. Find the area of the field.

   The area is _____ m^2.

5. If the farmer puts a fence around the field in problem **4**, how much fencing will be needed?

   _____ m of fencing will be needed.

6. How many cubic metres of earth will be removed to dig a well 2 m in diameter and 28 m deep?

   About _____ m^3 of earth will be removed.

7. A tank is 150 cm long, 120 cm wide, and 185 cm deep. Find its volume.

   The volume is _____ cm^3.

1.

2.

3.

4.

5.

6.

7.

NAME _____

CHAPTER 11   PRACTICE TEST
Perimeter, Area, and Volume

Find the perimeter and area of each figure.

| | a | b | c |

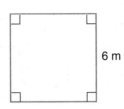 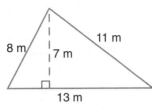 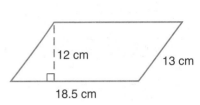

1.

perimeter: _____ m   _____ m   _____ cm

area: _____ m²   _____ m²   _____ cm²

Complete the table below. Use 3.14 for π. Find the approximate circumference and area.

	diameter	radius	approximate circumference	approximate area
2.	8 cm	_____ cm	about _____ cm	about _____ cm²
3.	_____ m	5 m	about _____ m	about _____ m²

Find the surface area of each figure. Use 3.14 for π.

a   b   c

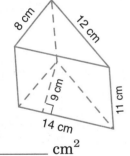 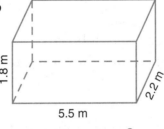 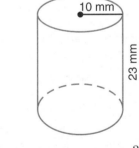

4.

_____ cm²   _____ m²   about _____ mm²

Find the volume of each figure. Use 3.14 for π.

5.

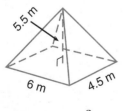  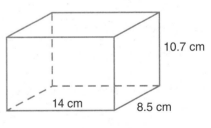

_____ m³   about _____ mm³   _____ cm³

CHAPTER 12 PRETEST
Graphs

Use the bar graph to answer each question.

Books Read Over Summer

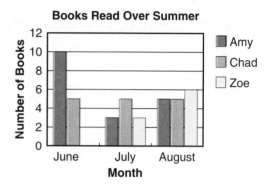

1. Who read the most books over the summer?

    _____

2. How many books did Zoe read in June? _____

3. Who read twice as many books in August as
    in July? _____

Use the line graph to answer each question.

Temperature Changes

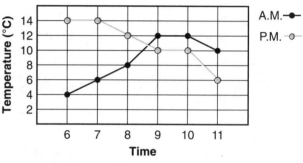

4. What was the general trend of
    temperature in the P.M. hours?

    _____

5. What was the temperature difference

    from 7 A.M. to 7 P.M.? _____

6. In a scatter plot, if the one set of data
    increases as the other set increases, the scatter plot has what type of correlation?

    _____

7. In a scatter plot, if the one set of data decreases as the other set increases, the
    scatter plot has what type of correlation? _____

8. The stronger the correlation, the more the points on the scatter plot resemble a

    _____.

9. A plot with a positive correlation slants _____ to the _____.

10. A plot with a negative correlation slants _____ to the _____.

11. Describe the type of correlation that the graph at the
     right shows.

     The graph shows a _____ correlation.

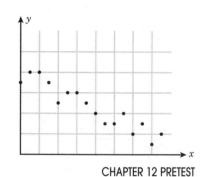

Lesson 1 Multiple Bar Graphs

Multiple bar graphs are used to compare data from more than one set of data. The graph provides a way to make visual comparisons among the data sets.

A different colour or pattern is used to identify each set of data in the bar graph.

3 children ages 9–12 chose BBQ sauce.

1 child age 9–12 chose honey sauce.

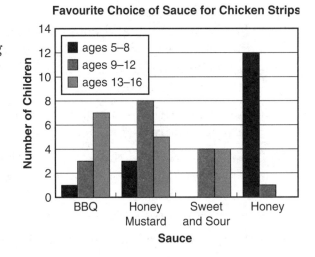
Favourite Choice of Sauce for Chicken Strips

Use the bar graph above to answer each question.

1. Which sauce did children ages 5–8 not choose? _____

2. How many children ages 9–12 chose honey mustard sauce? _____ children

3. Which sauce was the overwhelming favourite of children ages 5–8? _____

4. How many children ages 13–16 chose BBQ sauce? _____ children

5. Which age groups chose sweet and sour sauce equally? _____

6. How many more children ages 5–8 than children ages 13–16 chose honey sauce? _____ children

Use the information in the chart below to complete a multiple bar graph.

7. A hotel that provides breakfast kept track of the preferred breakfast juice for one Saturday morning.

	men	women	children
orange	30	16	28
apple	12	11	18
pineapple	5	12	4
grapefruit	3	10	0

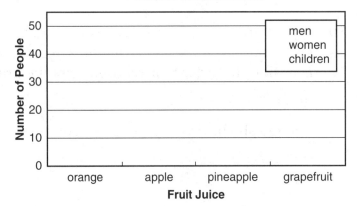
Preferred Breakfast Juice

CHAPTER 12

Lesson 2   Misleading Bar Graphs

Graphs that are presented as an orderly complete visual of data are usually easy to read. However, this does not always mean that the correct message is shown. Graphs can be manipulated to lead viewers to incorrect conclusions.

Look for use of titles, consistent treatment of data, and standardized scales.

Notice in the graph to the right that the scale along the horizontal axis is not standardized.

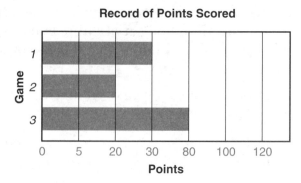

Record of Points Scored

Use the graph above to answer each question.

1. At first glance, what may you see as the points scored for game 1? Why?

   _____

2. Is the difference in points scored from game 1 to game 2 the same as the difference in points scored from game 1 to game 3? Explain. _____

   _____

   _____

3. If the games were shown as game 2, then game 1 and game 3, what conclusion might you draw? _____

   _____

Use the graph of Adam and Jamal's scores to answer each question.

4. How many increases of scores did Adam have? _____

5. Is this graph constructed correctly? Explain. _____

   _____

6. Does this presentation of the data make it easier or harder to compare one boy's progress? Why? _____

   _____

   _____

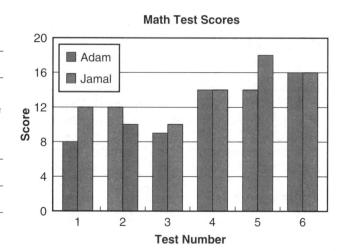

Math Test Scores

Lesson 3 Multiple Line Graphs

Multiple line graphs are used to compare numbers from more than one set of data. The graph provides a way to make visual comparisons among the numbers.

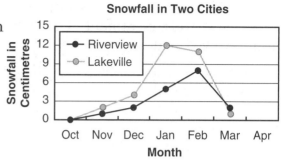

A different style of line is used for each city's snowfall. The key shows what each line represents.

Complete the multiple line graph for the month of April showing that Riverview had no snow and Lakeville had 1 cm of snow.

Use the line graph above to answer each question.

1. How many months did Riverview have more than 6 cm of snow? _____ month(s)

2. How many months did Riverview have more snow than Lakeville? _____ month(s)

3. In which two months did Lakeville have just 1 cm more of snow than Riverview?

    _____

4. Which city had the highest snowfall and in what month? _____

5. In which month did both cities have the same amount of snow? _____

6. In Lakeville, what month had twice as much snow as the previous month? _____

7. Did Riverview have its highest snowfall in the same month as Lakeville? _____

Use the information in the chart below to complete a double line graph.

8. Mrs. Smith charted the growth of her daughters' mass for two years.

	Jamie	Davida
birth	3.3	3.9
3 mo	3.9	4.8
6 mo	4.5	5.2
9 mo	6.4	7.3
1 year	8.0	8.5
15 mo	8.9	10
18 mo	10	11
21 mo	12	12
2 years	13	13

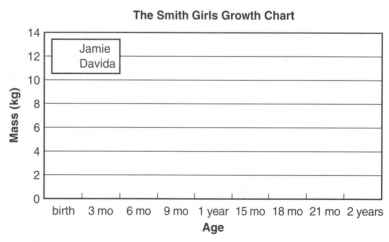

Lesson 4   Misleading Line Graphs

Line graphs can also be misleading. Look for use of titles, consistent treatment of data, and standardized scales.

Notice in the graph to the right that the months along the horizontal axis are out of sequence.

Furniture Sales

Use the graph above to answer each question.

1. If the months were listed in order, what trend would show?

_____

2. Name a reason why April may have been shown first. _____

_____

_____

Use the graph of rainfall in British Columbia to answer each question below.

3. It appears that Kelowna gets a lot more rain than Vancouver. Is that a fair statement to make based on reading this graph?

_____

_____

_____

4. Name one way to revise this graph to show a fair comparison of the rainfall in Kelowna

and Vancouver. _____

_____

_____

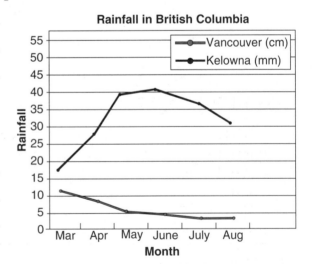

Rainfall in British Columbia

Lesson 5   Scatter Plots

Scatter plots are graphs that show the relationship of two variables in a set of data. Points are plotted on a coordinate grid to show how closely the variables are related.

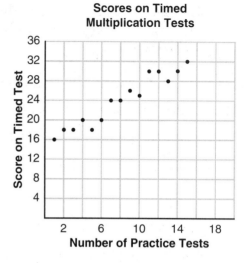

Scores on Timed
Multiplication Tests

Test Score	16	18	18	20	18	20	24	24	26	25	30	30	28	30	32	31	33	34	34	34
Number of Tests	1	2	3	4	5	6	7	8	9	10	11	12	13	14	15	16	17	18	19	20

To plot a pair of data, use the horizontal axis for one variable (in this case the number of practice tests) and the vertical axis for the other variable (score on timed test).

Complete the scatter plot for practice rounds greater than 14.

Use the scatter plot above to answer each question.

1. What score can a person who practised 18 or more rounds expect to get on the timed test? _____

2. What test score did the person who practised 10 rounds get? _____

3. Write a statement that explains the relationship between the practice rounds and the timed test score. _____

_____

4. If the most points possible for the timed test is 34, what advice would you give to someone who wants a perfect score? _____

_____

Use the data in the chart below to make a scatter plot.

5. Ben, Dr. Jackson's secretary, keeps track of visits to the dentist for cleanings and the number of cavities each patient has.

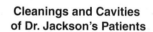

Cleanings and Cavities
of Dr. Jackson's Patients

Cleanings	2	3	6	7	8	9	10	2	3	1	9	5	4	5
Cavities	7	6	4	3	3	1	0	9	5	8	0	4	5	5

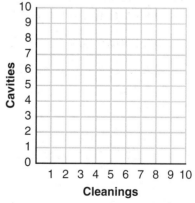

Lesson 6 Scatter Plots

If a straight line can be drawn following a pattern on a scatter plot, the data have a relationship, or **correlation.** This line is called a **line of best fit.**

If the line of best fit slants upward, the data have a **positive correlation.**

If the line of best fit slants downward, the data have a **negative correlation.**

When the data points are scattered throughout the graph, there is **no correlation.**

The closer the points on the scatter plot are to the line of best fit, the stronger the correlation.

Name the type of correlation that each graph shows.

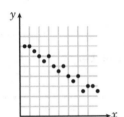   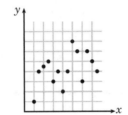   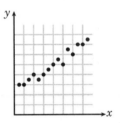

_____   _____   _____

Name the type of correlation that each graph shows.

a	*b*

1.
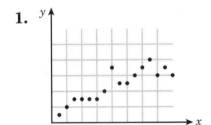
_____

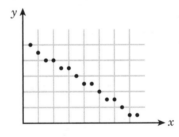
_____

2.
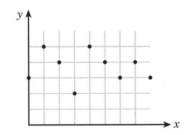

_____   _____

Lesson 7 Circles

A circle and its interior are called a **circular region.**

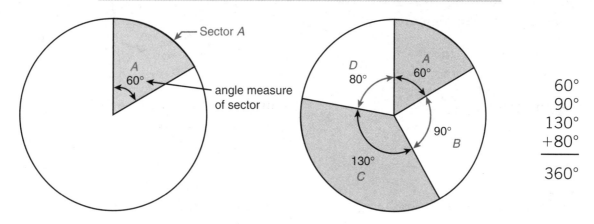

What is the angle measure of sector *B?* _____ Sector *C?* _____ Sector *D?* _____

The sum of the angle measures of all the sectors in a circular region is _____.

Use a protractor to help you separate each circular region as directed. Label each sector with the proper letter and angle measurement.

1. 4 sectors with angle measures as follows:

Sector *A*	30°
Sector *B*	60°
Sector *C*	120°
Sector *D*	150°

2. 5 sectors with angle measures as follows:

Sector *A*	20°
Sector *B*	25°
Sector *C*	45°
Sector *D*	90°
Sector *E*	180°

CHAPTER 12

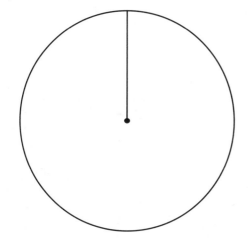

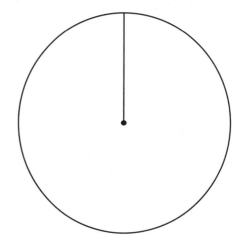

Lesson 8 Circles

Study how the circular region is separated into
four sectors representing 10%, 20%, 25%,
and 45% of the circular region.

$$10\% \text{ of } 360° = 36°$$
$$20\% \text{ of } 360° = 72°$$
$$25\% \text{ of } 360° = 90°$$
$$45\% \text{ of } 360° = 162°$$

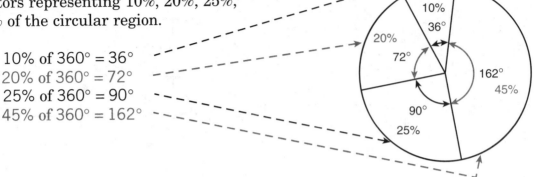

$$10\% + 20\% + 25\% + 45\% = \underline{\hspace{2cm}}\%$$ $$36° + 72° + 90° + 162° = \underline{\hspace{2cm}}°$$

Complete each sentence. Then write the correct angle measurement in the appropriate
sectors.

1. 10% of $360° = \underline{\hspace{2cm}}$

20% of $360° = \underline{\hspace{2cm}}$

30% of $360° = \underline{\hspace{2cm}}$

40% of $360° = \underline{\hspace{2cm}}$

$10\% + 20\% + 30\% + 40\% = \underline{\hspace{2cm}}$

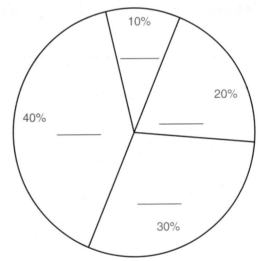

2. 5% of $360° = \underline{\hspace{2cm}}$

15% of $360° = \underline{\hspace{2cm}}$

35% of $360° = \underline{\hspace{2cm}}$

45% of $360° = \underline{\hspace{2cm}}$

$5\% + 15\% + 35\% + 45\% = \underline{\hspace{2cm}}$

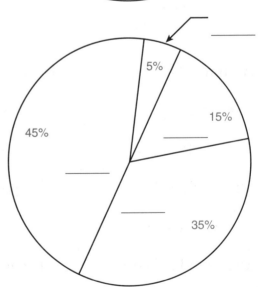

Lesson 9 Circle Graphs

Study how a **circle graph** is used to present the following information in a clear and interesting way.

Ashlee spends her allowance as follows: 25% for food, 50% for clothing, 15% for entertainment, and 10% for miscellaneous expenses.

Assume Ashlee's allowance is $20.

On clothing she would spend 50% of $20 or $_____.

On food she would spend 25% of $20 or $_____.

On entertainment she would spend 15% of $20 or $_____.

On miscellaneous expenses she would spend 10% of $20 or $_____.

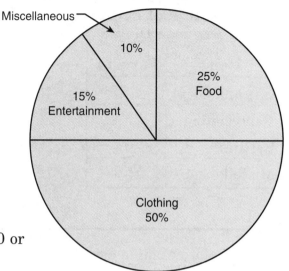

How Ashlee Spends Her Allowance

Complete each sentence.

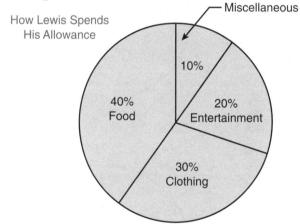

How Lewis Spends His Allowance

1. Assume Lewis' allowance is $25.

   He would spend $_____ for clothing.

   He would spend $_____ for food.

   He would spend $_____ for entertainment.

   He would spend $_____ for miscellaneous expenses.

2. Assume Ms. Adams' monthly income is $9000.

   She would spend $_____ for rent.

   She would spend $_____ for household expenses.

   She would spend $_____ for personal expenses.

   She would save $_____.

   She would spend $_____ for miscellaneous expenses.

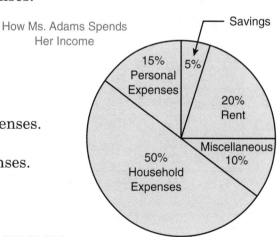

How Ms. Adams Spends Her Income

Lesson 10 Circle Graphs

Study how the information in the table can be presented on a circle graph.

Distribution of Each Auto Expense Dollar	
Item	**Percent**
Gas and Oil	40%
Depreciation	25%
Repairs	20%
Miscellaneous	15%

40% of 360° = $\underline{144°}$

25% of 360° = $\underline{90°}$

20% of 360° = _____

15% of 360° = _____

Miscellaneous

15%

40% Gas and Oil

20% Repairs

25% Depreciation

Use the information in each table to help you complete each circle graph.

1.

Distribution of Each Income Dollar	
Expense	**Percent**
Rent	30%
Personal	20%
Household	35%
Miscellaneous	15%

30% of 360° = _____

20% of 360° = _____

35% of 360° = _____

15% of 360° = _____

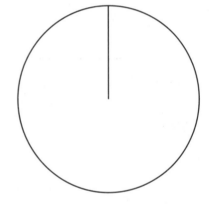

2.

Distribution of Activities on an Average School Day	
Activity	**Percent**
Sleeping	30%
School	25%
Eating	10%
Recreation	20%
Miscellaneous	15%

30% of 360° = _____

25% of 360° = _____

10% of 360° = _____

20% of 360° = _____

15% of 360° = _____

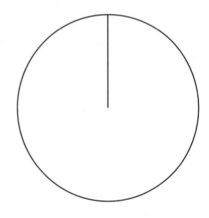

CHAPTER 12 PRACTICE TEST
Graphs

Use the bar graph to answer each question.

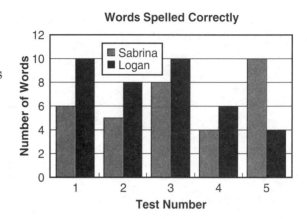

Words Spelled Correctly

1. On how many tests did Logan spell more words correctly than Sabrina? _____ tests

2. How many words did Sabrina spell correctly on the second test? _____ words

3. On which tests did Logan have the same score? _____

Use the line graph to determine how this graph is misleading.

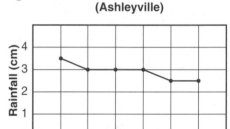

Average Monthly Rainfall (Ashleyville)

4. By looking at the points and line graphed, what conclusion would you draw about the rainfall in Ashleyville? _____

5. What is incorrect that causes you to reach the conclusion from question **4?**

_____

6. Use the chart to determine the number of degrees for each activity.

work = _____

travel = _____

eating = _____

recreation = _____

miscellaneous = _____

Average Work Day	
Activity	**Percent**
Work	40%
Travel	5%
Eating	10%
Recreation	15%
Miscellaneous	30%

7. Create a circle graph using the information from question **6.**

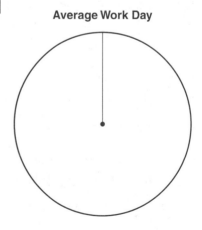

Average Work Day

CHAPTER 12

CHAPTER 13 PRETEST
Probability

You draw one of the cards without looking. Write the probability as a fraction in simplest form that you will draw

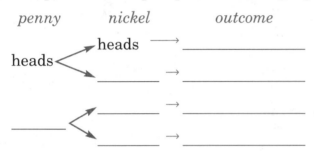

1. Janet _____

2. Jared _____

3. Juan _____

| Jared | Janet | Janet |
| Juan | Juan | Juan |

4. a card with a name that starts with *J* _____

5. a card with a name that does not start with *J* _____

6. Complete the sample space for tossing a penny and a nickel.

penny　　　*nickel*　　　　　*outcome*

heads ⟨ heads ⟶ _____

_____ → _____

_____ ⟨ _____ → _____

_____ → _____

Solve each problem. Write each probability as a percent.

7. You draw one of the marbles without looking. What is the probability of drawing a blue marble?

The probability is _____.

8. A company knows that 1% of the bolts they make are defective. If they produce 250 000 bolts, how many will be defective?

_____ bolts will be defective.

9. You spin the spinner at the right. What is the probability that the spinner will stop on 6?

The probability is _____.

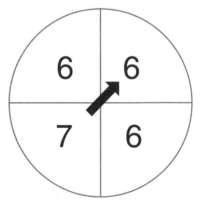

10. You spin the spinner at the right 20 times. Predict how many times the spinner will stop on 6.

The spinner will stop on 6 _____ times.

11. You spin the spinner at the right 200 times. Predict how many times the spinner will stop on 6.

The spinner will stop on 6 _____ times.

Lesson 1 Probability

You draw one of the cards shown at the right without looking. You would like to know your *chance* or **probability** of getting a card that shows an **A**.

Each card (possible result) is called an **outcome**. There are 6 cards. There are 6 possible outcomes. Since you have the same chance to draw any of the cards, the outcomes are **equally likely.**

number of outcomes that show **A**

number of possible outcomes

$\frac{2}{6}$ or $\frac{1}{3}$ Write the probability in simplest form.

The probability of drawing a card that shows an **A** is $\frac{1}{3}$.

You pick a marble without looking. In simplest form, write the probability of picking

1. white _____

2. black _____

3. blue _____

4. a marble that is **not** white _____

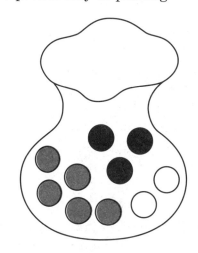

You spin the spinner shown at the right. Find the probability of the spinner stopping on

5. a blue section _____

6. a white section _____

7. a 1 _____

8. a 3 _____

9. a 2 _____

10. an odd number _____

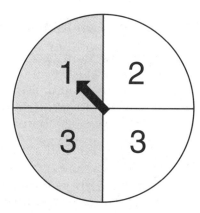

CHAPTER 13

Lesson 1   Problem Solving

Your company is having a box-lunch picnic. The company is furnishing free box lunches. The contents are on labels like those at the right. Solve each problem. Write each probability in simplest form.

Cheese Sandwich/ Apple	Roast Beef Sandwich/ Apple
Cheese Sandwich/ Pear	Roast Beef Sandwich/ Orange
Peanut Butter Sandwich/ Apple	Chicken Sandwich/ Pear
Taco/ Pear	Taco/ Apple

1. Suppose you do not care what kind of lunch you get, so you take one box without looking. What is the probability that you will get a cheese sandwich and an apple?

   The probability is _____.

2. You take one box without looking. What is the probability that you will get an apple?

   The probability is _____.

3. You take one box without looking. What is the probability that you will get a taco?

   The probability is _____.

4. You take one box without looking. What is the probability that you will get a pear?

   The probability is _____.

5. You take one box without looking. What is the probability that you will **not** get an orange?

   The probability is _____.

A game has a board like the one shown below. Use the board to answer each question. Write each probability in simplest form.

6. Are the outcomes equally likely? _____

Draw lines to make all of the rectangles the same size. Remember to label each section.

7. Now how many rectangles say *win?* _____

8. Now how many rectangles say *lose?* _____

9. You throw one dart. What is the probability of hitting a rectangle that says *win?*

   The probability is _____.

10. You throw one dart. What is the probability of **not** hitting a rectangle that says *win?*

    The probability is _____.

DART THROW		
win	lose	win
lose		lose
	win	
win	lose	win
lose		lose
	win	

Lesson 2   0 and 1 Probabilities

You spin the spinner at the right.

Probability of the spinner stopping on 2	Probability of the spinner stopping on a number less than 5	Probability of the spinner stopping on 6
$\frac{1}{4}$	$\frac{4}{4}$ or 1 A probability of 1 means the outcome is **certain** to happen.	$\frac{0}{4}$ or 0 A probability of 0 means the outcome will **never** happen.

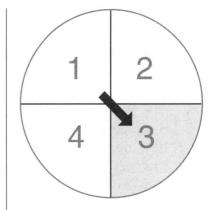

Solve each problem. Write each probability in simplest terms.

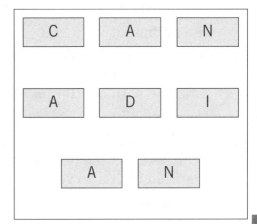

1. You pick one of the letter cards shown at the right without looking. What is the probability that you will pick a vowel (a, e, i, o, u)?

   The probability is _____.

2. You pick one of the letter cards without looking. What is the probability that you will pick an A?

   The probability is _____.

3. You pick one of the letter cards without looking. What is the probability that you will pick a B?

   The probability is _____.

4. You pick one of the letter cards without looking. What is the probability that the letter on the card is in the word *CANADIAN*?

   The probability is _____.

5. You pick one of the letter cards without looking. What is the probability that the letter on the card is **not** in the word *CANADIAN*?

   The probability is _____.

6. You pick one of the letter cards without looking. What is the probability that the letter on the card is in the word *AID*?

   The probability is _____.

Lesson 2 Problem Solving

Solve each problem. Write each probability in simplest form.

1. You are taking a multiple-choice test. Each item has six choices. You have no idea which is the correct answer. What is the probability that you will guess the correct answer?

   The probability is _____.

2. Suppose that each item on the test in problem **1** had four choices. You still have no idea which is the correct answer. What is the probability that you will guess the correct answer?

   The probability is _____.

3. You draw one marble from the bag shown at the right. What is the probability that you will draw a marble with a number on it?

   The probability is _____.

4. You draw one marble from the bag shown at the right. What is the probability that you will draw a marble with a letter on it?

   The probability is _____.

5. You draw one marble from the bag shown at the right. What is the probability that you will draw a marble with a vowel on it?

   The probability is _____.

6. You pick one of the number cards shown at the right without looking. What is the probability that you will pick a number greater than 30?

   The probability is _____.

7. You pick one of the number cards shown at the right without looking. What is the probability that you will pick a number less than 100?

   The probability is _____.

8. You pick one of the number cards shown without looking. What is the probability that you will pick a card with a 0 on it?

   The probability is _____.

9. You pick one of the number cards shown without looking. What is the probability that you will pick a card with a 7 on it?

   The probability is _____.

Test   Name _____

In the blank at the left, wri͟
that best completes the state͟

_____ 1. The busiest day at the͟
     a. Monday
     b. Tuesday
     c. Wednesday
     d. Thursday
     e. Friday
     f. Saturday

A   B   C

10	20	30
40	50	60

Lesson 3 Sample Spaces

Suppose you flip a penny and a dime. You can show all the possible outcomes in a table or in a tree diagram.

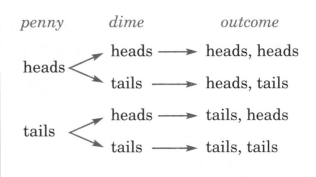

		dime	
		heads	tails
penny	heads	h, h	h, t
	tails	t, h	t, t

A list or a table of all the possible outcomes is called a **sample space.**

Use the sample spaces above to answer each question.

1. How many possible outcomes are there? _____

2. What is the probability that both coins will land with heads up? _____

3. What is the probability that one coin will land
   with heads up and the other will land with tails up? _____

Suppose you toss a penny, a nickel, and a dime. Complete the sample space below to show the possible outcomes.

4.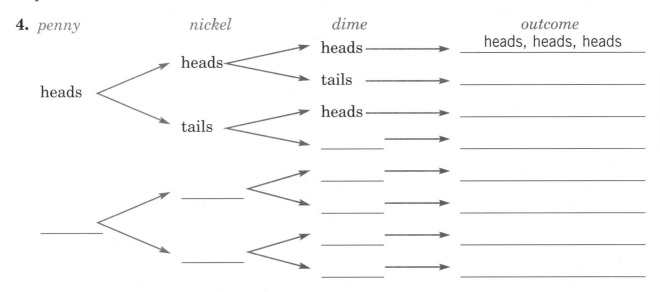

5. How many possible outcomes are there? _____

6. What is the probability of all heads? _____

7. What is the probability of two heads and one tail? _____

8. What is the probability of at least one tail? _____

Lesson 3   Problem Solving

Complete the sample space below to show all the possible outcomes of rolling a blue number cube and a black number cube. Then use the sample space to solve each problem. Write each probability in simplest form.

Blue Number Cube

	1	2	3	4	5	6
1	1,1	2,1	3,1	4,1		
2	1,2	2,2	3,2			
3	1,3					
4	1,4					
5						
6						

Black Number Cube

1. What is the probability of rolling two 5s?

    The probability is _____.

2. What is the probability of rolling the same number on both number cubes?

    The probability is _____.

3. What is the probability of rolling 4,5 or 5,4?

    The probability is _____.

4. What is the probability of rolling two number cubes that total 10?

    The probability is _____.

5. What is the probability of rolling two number cubes that total 20?

    The probability is _____.

6. What is the probability of rolling two number cubes that total less than 13?

    The probability is _____.

7. What is the probability of rolling two number cubes that total 7?

    The probability is _____.

8. What is the probability of rolling two different numbers?

    The probability is _____.

Lesson 4 Probability Experiments

Try this experiment.

Flip a coin 10 times.
How many times did you get heads? _____

Flip a coin 10 more times.
Out of the 20 flips, did you
get heads exactly 10 times? _____

Use tally marks (/) to record the results.

heads	
tails	

Mathematical probability (what you have found in previous lessons) tells what is likely to happen. It does not tell what will actually happen. **Experimental probability** tells what happened during a particular experiment.

Try this experiment. Record your results. Use your results to answer each question.

1. Make paper cards like those shown at the right. Be sure the cards are all the same size. Draw one card without looking, record the result, and put the card back. Repeat the experiment 30 times.

Apple	Orange

Apple	Orange

Apple	Peach

Apple	
Orange	
Peach	

2. Based on your experiment, what is the probability of picking a card that says *Apple?*   _____

3. What is the mathematical probability of picking a card that says *Apple?*   _____

4. Based on your experiment, what is the probability of picking a card that says *Orange?*   _____

5. What is the mathematical probability of picking a card that says *Orange?*   _____

6. Based on your experiment, what is the probability of picking a card that says *Peach?*   _____

7. What is the mathematical probability of picking a card that says *Peach?*   _____

8. Repeat the experiment 30 more times. Did your experimental probability results come closer to the mathematical probability after more draws?   _____

9. Compare your results with other class members'. Did you all get exactly the same results?   _____

CHAPTER 13

Lesson 4 Problem Solving

Try each experiment. Record your results. Use your results to answer each question.

1. Make paper cards like those shown at the right. Be sure the cards are all the same size. Draw one card without looking, record the result, and put the card back. Repeat the experiment 100 times. (You could work with a friend and each person make 50 draws.)

Red	Blue
Red	Blue
Red	Blue
Red	Black
White	Black

Red	
Blue	
White	
Black	

2. Based on your experiment, what is the probability of picking a card that says *Red?* _____

3. What is the mathematical probability of picking a card that says *Red?* _____

4. Based on your experiment, what is the probability of picking a card that says *Blue?* _____

5. What is the mathematical probability of picking a card that says *Blue?* _____

6. Based on your experiment, what is the probability of picking a card that says *White?* _____

7. Based on your experiment, what is the probability of picking a card that says *Black?* _____

8. Flip a penny and a dime. Record the results with tally marks. Repeat the experiment 25 times.

Penny	Dime	
heads	heads	
heads	tails	
tails	heads	
tails	tails	

9. Based on your experiment, what is the probability of both coins landing heads up? _____

10. Based on your experiment, what is the probability of at least one coin landing tails up? _____

Lesson 5 Probability and Percent   PRE-ALGEBRA

You are to draw one marble without looking. The probability of drawing a blue marble is $\frac{5}{10}$ or $\frac{1}{2}$. You can write the probability as a percent in either of these two ways.

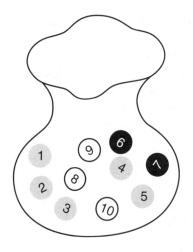

$$\frac{5}{10} = \frac{a}{100}$$

$$500 = 10a$$
$$50 = a$$

$$10\overline{)5.00} \quad \begin{array}{l} 0.50 = 50\% \\ \hline \end{array}$$
$$\underline{5\ 0}$$
$$00$$
$$\underline{00}$$
$$0$$

$$\frac{5}{10} = \frac{50}{100} = 50\%$$

The probability of drawing a blue marble is 50%.

Solve each problem. Write each probability as a percent.

1. Using the bag of marbles at the top of the page, what is the probability of drawing a black marble?

   The probability is _____.

2. Using the bag of marbles at the top of the page, what is the probability of drawing a marble with a number on it?

   The probability is _____.

You are to choose one of the cards at the right without looking. Write each probability as a percent.

3. What is the probability of choosing *win*?

   The probability is _____.

4. What is the probability of **not** choosing *win*?

   The probability is _____.

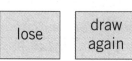

5. What is the probability of choosing *lose*?

   The probability is _____.

6. What is the probability of choosing *draw again*?

   The probability is _____.

7. What is the probability of choosing *go home*?

   The probability is _____.

Lesson 5 Problem Solving   PRE-ALGEBRA

Try each experiment. Record your results. Write each probability as a percent.

1. Make paper cards like those shown. Be sure the cards are all the same size. Draw one card without looking, record the result, and put the card back. Repeat the experiment 20 times.

Red	
Blue	
White	
Black	

Red	Blue
White	Blue
White	Blue
Black	Black
Black	Black

2. Based on your experiment, what is the probability of picking a card that says *Red?* _____

3. What is the mathematical probability of picking a card that says *Red?* _____

4. Based on your experiment, what is the probability of picking a card that says *Blue?* _____

5. What is the mathematical probability of picking a card that says *Blue?* _____

6. Based on your experiment, what is the probability of picking a card that says *White?* _____

7. What is the mathematical probability of picking a card that says *White?* _____

8. Based on your experiment, what is the probability of picking a card that says *Black?* _____

9. What is the mathematical probability of picking a card that says *Black?* _____

10. What is the experimental probability of picking a card that does **not** say *Black?* _____

11. What is the mathematical probability of picking a card that does **not** say *Black?* _____

12. What is the experimental probability of picking a card that says *Green?* _____

13. What is the mathematical probability of picking a card that says *Green?* _____

Lesson 6 Predicting with Probability

You roll a number cube once. What is the possibility of getting a 5?

Suppose you roll a number cube 60 times. You can predict how many times you would expect to get a 5 as follows:

probability of getting a 5 ⟶ number of rolls

$\frac{1}{6} \times 60 = 10$ ⟵ number of times you would expect to get a 5

A company finds that 2% of their calculators are defective. Predict how many calculators will be defective if they make 5000 calculators.

$$\begin{array}{r} 5\,0\,0\,0 \\ \times 0.0\,2 \\ \hline 1\,0\,0.0\,0 \end{array}$$

The company can expect 100 defective calculators.

Solve each problem. Write each probability as a fraction in simplest terms or as a percent.

1. You flip a coin once. What is the probability of getting heads?

   The probability is _____.

2. Suppose you flip a coin 200 times. Predict how many times you would expect to get tails.

   You should get tails about _____ times.

3. A company knows that $\frac{1}{2}$% of the batteries they make are defective. If they produce 100 000 batteries, how many will be defective?

   _____ batteries will be defective.

4. You spin the spinner at the right. What is the probability that the spinner will stop on *radio?*

   The probability is _____.

5. You spin the spinner at the right 20 times. Predict how many times the spinner will stop on *radio.*

   The spinner will stop on *radio* _____ times.

6. You spin the spinner at the right. What is the probability that the spinner will stop on *pencil?*

   The probability is _____.

7. You spin the spinner at the right 60 times. Predict how many times the spinner will stop on *pencil.*

   The spinner will stop on *pencil* _____ times.

1–2.

3.

4–7.

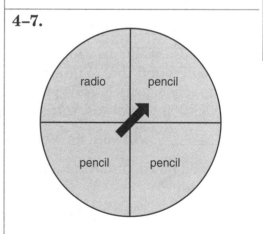

Lesson 6 Problem Solving

One hundred people were polled to see whom they preferred for union representative. The results are shown below. Use the results to solve each problem.

Candidate	Erickson	Nunez	Verdugo	Williams
Number of votes	34	27	25	14

1. What percent of those polled prefer Erickson?

   _____% prefer Erickson.

2. If 3000 people vote for union representative, predict how many will vote for Erickson.

   _____ will vote for Erickson.

3. What percent of those polled prefer Williams?

   _____% prefer Williams.

4. If 3000 people vote for union representative, predict how many will vote for Williams.

   _____ will vote for Williams.

5. If 3000 people vote for union representative, predict how many will vote for Nunez.

   _____ will vote for Nunez.

6. If 3000 people vote for union representative, predict how many will vote for Verdugo.

   _____ will vote for Verdugo.

7. Suppose Williams drops out of the election. A poll found that Williams's supporters now support Verdugo. Now predict how many of the 3000 voters will vote for Verdugo.

   _____ will vote for Verdugo.

8. Based on the information in problem **7**, who will win?

   _____ will win the election.

9. How many more votes will the winner get than Nunez will get?

   The winner will get _____ more votes than Nunez.

1–2.

3–4.

5.

6.

7.

8–9.

Lesson 7   More Probability Experiments

For some events it is hard to find a mathematical probability, so it is necessary to use experimental probability.

Make a cone from a piece of paper like this:

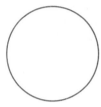

| Trace around a circular object with a diameter between 3 and 6 inches. | Cut out the circle. Fold it in half. Cut along the fold. | Tape the two edges of one semicircle together to make a cone. |

Now toss the cone in the air so it lands on a hard surface. Record the results in the table at the right. Repeat the experiment 50 times.

Landing	Tallies (50 times)
△ (on base)	
◁ (on side)	

Use the experiment above. Write each probability as a percent.

1. Based on 50 tries, what is the probability that the cone will land on its base?   _____

2. Based on 50 tries, what is the probability that the cone will land on its side?   _____

3. Either do the experiment 50 more times or combine your results with those of another student. Record the totals for the 100 tosses in the table at the right.

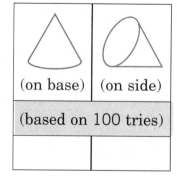

4. Based on 100 tries, what is the probability that the cone will land on its base?   _____

5. Based on 100 tries, what is the probability that the cone will land on its side?   _____

6. Are the results of **1** and **2** close to the results of **4** and **5**?   _____

Lesson 7 Problem Solving

Do this experiment. Use your results to solve each problem. Write each probability as a percent.

1. Use a sheet of typing paper and a hair pin
    or needle. On the paper, draw parallel
    lines so that they are just slightly farther
    apart than the length of the pin or needle.
    Hold the pin or needle about 15 cm
    above the paper and let it drop. Record
    the results. If the pin or needle does not
    land on the paper, that turn does not
    count. Repeat the experiment 50 times.

Touched a line	
Did not touch	

2. After 50 tries, what is the probability that the pin
    or needle landed so it touched a line?   _____

3. After 50 tries, what is the probability that the pin
    or needle landed so it did not touch a line?   _____

4. Repeat the experiment 50 more times, or combine
    your results with those of another student.

Touched a line	
Did not touch	

5. After 100 tries, what is the probability that the
    pin or needle landed so it touched a line?   _____

6. After 100 tries, what is the probability that the
    pin or needle landed so it did not touch a line?   _____

Try the experiment again. This time draw the lines so they are
only half as far apart. Record your results for 50 tries below.

Touched a line	
Did not touch	

7. After 50 tries, what is the probability that the pin
    or needle landed so it touched a line?   _____

8. After 50 tries, what is the probability that the pin
    or needle landed so it did not touch a line?   _____

Lesson 8 Problem Solving

NAME _____

Solve each problem. Write each probability as a fraction in simplest form.

1. You choose one of the cards at the right without looking. What is the probability that the card will say *go?*

   The probability is _____.

2. You choose one of the cards at the right without looking. What is the probability that the card will say *stop?*

   The probability is _____.

3. You choose one of the cards at the right without looking. What is the probability that the card will be *blue?*

   The probability is _____.

Solve each problem. Write each probability as a percent.

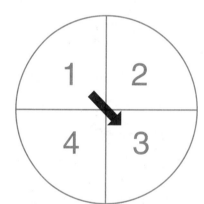

4. You spin the spinner at the right once. What is the probability that the spinner will stop on 4?

   The probability is _____.

5. You spin the spinner 80 times. Predict how many times the spinner will stop on 4.

   The spinner will stop on 4 _____ times.

6. A company knows that 2% of their computer disks are defective. The company produced 400 000 computer disks. How many of those disks will be defective?

   _____ computer disks will be defective.

Complete this experiment. Flip a coin. Record the results. Repeat the experiment 19 more times. Write each probability as a percent.

7. Based on 20 flips, what is the probability that the coin landed *heads up?*

   The probability is _____.

8. Based on 20 flips, what is the probability that the coin landed *tails up?*

   The probability is _____.

9. What is the mathematical probability that a coin will land *heads up?*

   The probability is _____.

PRISM MATHEMATICS
Purple Book

CHAPTER 13

CHAPTER 13   PRACTICE TEST
Probability

NAME _____

You roll a number cube with faces marked as shown at the right. Write the probability as a fraction in simplest form that you will roll

1. ahead 5 _____

2. back 3 _____

3. back any number _____

4. a face with an odd number _____

5. a face that does **not** say *back* _____

| ahead 5 | back 4 | ahead 3 |
| lose a turn | back 1 | ahead 2 |

Solve each problem. Write each probability as a percent.

6. Suppose you flip a coin 150 times. Predict how many times you would expect to get tails.

   You should get tails about _____ times.

7. A company knows that 3% of their doodads are defective. If they produce 300 000 doodads, how many will be defective?

   _____ doodads will be defective.

8. You spin the spinner at the right. What is the probability that the spinner will stop on *red?*

   The probability is _____.

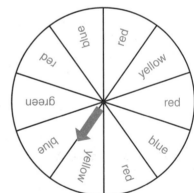

9. You spin the spinner at the right 20 times. Predict how many times the spinner will stop on *red.*

   The spinner will stop on *red* _____ times.

10. Complete the sample space for tossing a penny and a dime.

    penny   *dime*   *outcome*

    heads < heads ⟶ _____
              _____ ⟶ _____

    _____ < _____ ⟶ _____
                 _____ ⟶ _____

MID-TEST Chapters 1–6

Complete as indicated. Write each answer in simplest form.

	a	b	c	d	e
1.	83 920 +9 828	93 205 −28 591	4 9.235 +3 7.369	1.03 −0.9251	1 4 5.5 6 4 3.5 6 9.2 5 +3 2.3

| **2.** | 5 2 4 2
×9 3 | 6.2 6
×1 3 | $32\overline{)3360}$ | $0.04\overline{)50.3}$ | 1 2.5 9 3
×0.0 3 2 |

| **3.** | $\dfrac{5}{8}$
$\dfrac{7}{8}$
$+\dfrac{5}{8}$ | $\dfrac{3}{4}$
$-\dfrac{1}{3}$ | $5\dfrac{1}{6}$
$-2\dfrac{7}{8}$ | $5\dfrac{1}{4} \times 3\dfrac{1}{3}$ | $1\dfrac{3}{5} \div 2\dfrac{2}{15}$ |

Solve each equation.

a $\qquad\qquad\qquad$ b $\qquad\qquad\qquad$ c

4. $4b = 24$ $\qquad\qquad$ $\dfrac{a}{8} = 13$ $\qquad\qquad$ $d + 29 = 120$

5. $h - 5 = 3 \times 7$ $\qquad\quad$ $6j = 43 + 5$ $\qquad\qquad$ $\dfrac{s}{12} = 5 \times 6$

6. $7a + a = 80$ $\qquad\quad$ $n + n - 1 = 11$ $\qquad$ $r + 3r + 23 = 51$

MID-TEST CH. 1–6

Solve each of the following.

	a	*b*	*c*
7.	$\dfrac{2}{5} = \dfrac{n}{15}$	$\dfrac{9}{n} = \dfrac{1}{4}$	$\dfrac{12}{18} = \dfrac{6}{n}$

Complete each table. Write each fraction in simplest form.

8.

a

fraction	decimal	percent
$\dfrac{1}{4}$		

b

fraction	decimal	percent
		10%

Complete the following.

	a	*b*	*c*
9.	_____ is 15% of 40	36 is 75% of _____	43 is _____% of 86

Solve each problem.

10. A store sold 185 suits last month. Of those, 60% were women's suits. How many women's suits were sold?

_____ women's suits were sold.

10.

11. Naomi borrowed $2000 for one year at 12% annual interest. How much interest did she pay?

She paid $_____ interest.

11.

Write an equation for each problem. Solve each problem.

12. Anna made 12 more doodads than Aaron. Together they made 150 doodads. How many doodads did Anna make?

Equation: _____

Anna made _____ doodads.

12.

13. In the drawing at the right, how much mass would have to be applied at point A so the lever would be balanced?

Equation: _____

_____ kg would have to be applied at point A.

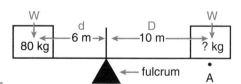

STOP

FINAL TEST Chapters 1-13

Complete as indicated. Write each answer in simplest form.

	a	b	c	d	e
1.	15 323 +5 628	8 685 −8 591	4 9.0 5 3 +5 8.3 6	5 1.5 −5.5 7	2.5 3 5 ×0.0 0 4

2.

496
×5 4

$62\overline{)12\ 834}$

$0.06\overline{)1.44}$

$1\frac{1}{2}$
$+3\frac{1}{2}$

$6\frac{1}{3}$
$-4\frac{1}{2}$

3.

$\frac{1}{5} \times 6\frac{2}{3}$

$1\frac{1}{2} \div 2\frac{1}{4}$

6 h 20 min
+2 h 2 min

3 h 10 min
×3

10 min 20 s
−7 min 35 s

Solve each of the following.

	a	b	c
4.	$6n = 24$	$\frac{a}{3} = 43$	$e + 9 = 12$
5.	$h - 9 = 2 \times 5$	$2j = 23 - 7$	$\frac{s}{8} = 4 \times 3$
6.	$2a + a = 30$	$n + n - 5 = 15$	$r + 7r + 14 = 30$
7.	$\frac{2}{7} = \frac{n}{14}$	$\frac{9}{n} = \frac{1}{7}$	$\frac{12}{30} = \frac{6}{n}$

FINAL TEST   Chapters 1-13 (continued)

Complete each table. Write each fraction in simplest form.

a

fraction	decimal	percent
$\frac{1}{2}$		

b

fraction	decimal	percent
		75%

8.

Complete the following.

	a	b	c
9.	_____ is 25% of 80	105 is 75% of _____	66 is _____% of 275
10.	6 m = _____ cm	8 km = _____ m	100 L = _____ kL
11.	100 mg = _____ g	2.3 kg = _____ g	5600 mL = _____ L
12.	60 cm = _____ m	3 L = _____ mL	4 h 15 min = _____ min
13.	2 t = _____ kg	2000 g = _____ kg	3 kL = _____ L

Round as indicated.

	nearest thousand	*nearest hundred*	*nearest ten*
14. 32 546	_____	_____	_____

Write an estimate for each exercise. Then find the answer.

15.
```
  2342
  +923
  _____
```
```
  40412
  -9342
  _____
```
```
  923
  ×31
  _____
```

16. Water freezes at _____ °C.

On the _____ before each name below, write the letter of the figure it describes.

17. _____ line segment

18. _____ circle

19. _____ acute angle

20. _____ right triangle

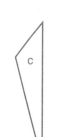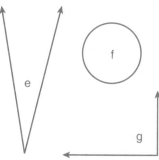

Use the similar triangles below to help you complete the following.

21. If $a = 16$, $b = 8$, and $d = 12$, then $e =$ _____.

22. If $b = 3$, $c = 5$, and $e = 9$, then $f =$ _____.

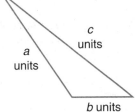

$$\frac{a}{d} = \frac{b}{e} = \frac{c}{f}$$

Find the area of each figure below. Use 3.14 for π.

a	b	c

23.

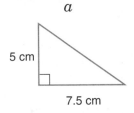 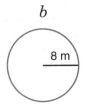 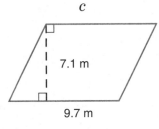

_____ cm^2 about _____ m^2 _____ m^2

Find the surface area of each figure below. Use 3.14 for π.

24.

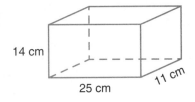 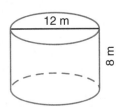 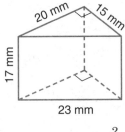

_____ cm^2 about _____ m^2 _____ mm^2

Find the volume of each figure below. Use 3.14 for π.

25.

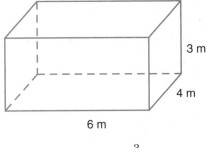 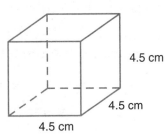 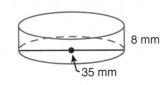

_____ m^3 _____ cm^3 about _____ mm^3

GO

Use the circle graph to complete each sentence.

The Bentons'
Vacation Expenses

26. The Bentons spent $2500 on vacation.

    The Bentons spent $_____ on food.

    The Bentons spent $_____ on a hotel.

    The Bentons spent $_____ on souvenirs.

    The Bentons spent $_____ on transportation.

    The Bentons spent $_____ on entertainment.

Hotel
36%

Souvenirs
7%

Transportation
16%

Entertainment
12%

Food
29%

Use the cards at the right to solve each problem.

27. You draw one of the cards without looking. What is the probability of drawing a card that

    has stripes? _____

    has dots? _____

    ```
    1   2   3
    4   5   6
    ```

28. You make 30 draws, replacing the card after each draw. Predict how many times you will draw each card that

    is a multiple of 3. _____

    has dots and an odd number. _____

Solve each problem.

29. A company made 40 000 batteries. It knows 2% are defective. How many defective batteries did the company make?

    The company made _____ defective batteries.

    29.

30. Jami borrowed $4000 for one year at 15% annual interest. How much interest did she pay?

    Jami paid $_____ in interest.

    30.

31. Aliya is 2 years older than D'Marco. If you add their ages together, the sum is 40. How old is Aliya?

    Equation: _____

    Aliya is _____ years old.

    31.

STOP

NAME _____

Do each problem.
Find the correct answer.
Mark the space for the answer.

Part 1 **Concepts**	Part 2 **Computation**

1. In which of these problems can the dividend be divided evenly by the divisor?

  A $134 \div 8$
  B $135 \div 9$
  C $127 \div 7$
  D $136 \div 6$

5.   30 426
          891
      +6 055

  A   37 372
  B   38 662
  C   38 364
  D   39 462

2. What number should replace the ☐ to make the following a true statement?

10 462 = ☐ + 3219 + 4763

  A   3490
  B   7982
  C   2472
  D   2480

6.   94 028
         −659

  A   94 368
  B   93 369
  C   94 479
  D   93 479

3. What difference is more than 4500 and less than 4700?

  A   41 366 − 37 086
  B   42 230 − 37 605
  C   69 638 − 64 859
  D   37 579 − 33 097

7.   7132
        ×101

  A   737 766
  B   720 433
  C   719 423
  D   720 332

4. What digit is in the ten thousands place in the product 4579×746?

  A   1
  B   9
  C   5
  D   4

8. 22)‾894‾

  A   40 r14
  B   41 r6
  C   40 r21
  D   39 r17

ANSWER ROW   **1** Ⓐ Ⓑ Ⓒ Ⓓ   **3** Ⓐ Ⓑ Ⓒ Ⓓ   **5** Ⓐ Ⓑ Ⓒ Ⓓ   **7** Ⓐ Ⓑ Ⓒ Ⓓ
                       2 Ⓐ Ⓑ Ⓒ Ⓓ   **4** Ⓐ Ⓑ Ⓒ Ⓓ   **6** Ⓐ Ⓑ Ⓒ Ⓓ   **8** Ⓐ Ⓑ Ⓒ Ⓓ

9. 16.937
+4.584

A 20.411
B 22.612
C 21.521
D 23.481

10. 4.9018
−2.9765

A 2.0353
B 1.9253
C 1.8342
D 2.1453

11. 52.62
×0.33

A 18.0556
B 17.4678
C 16.8396
D 17.3646

12. 2.4)8.832

A 3.24
B 3.68
C 3.96
D 4.12

Part 3 **Applications**

13. There are 56 943 people who live in the city where Candace works, and there are 39 017 people who live in the city where Candace was born. How many more people live in the city where Candace works than in the city where she was born?

A 16 336   C 17 926
B 16 535   D 18 016

14. If Daniel delivered 455 phone books each day for 4 days, how many phone books did he deliver altogether?

A 1820   C 1455
B 1660   D 1290

15. While testing tires at the R.J. Rubber Company, a new tire was rotated 1612 km for 26 hours. How fast was the tire rotating?

A 55 km/h   C 60 km/h
B 58 km/h   D 62 km/h

16. The thickness of Isaiah's piece of bread is 2.065 cm. The thickness of his stack of turkey is 1.158 cm. How thick will Isaiah's sandwich be when he combines the turkey with two pieces of bread?

A 4.963 cm   C 4.399 cm
B 5.288 cm   D 5.636 cm

17. Bianca and Lydia are counting the kilojoules (kJ) in what they eat. For dinner, they bought two roast beef subs with 2616 kJ each and two garden salads with 491 kJ each. How many calories were in the entire dinner?

A 6214   C 6652
B 7657   D 5439

18. Each jar of spaghetti sauce costs $2.55. How many jars can you buy with $20.40?

A 8   C 10
B 9   D 11

ANSWER ROW   **9** Ⓐ Ⓑ Ⓒ Ⓓ   **11** Ⓐ Ⓑ Ⓒ Ⓓ   **13** Ⓐ Ⓑ Ⓒ Ⓓ   **15** Ⓐ Ⓑ Ⓒ Ⓓ   **17** Ⓐ Ⓑ Ⓒ Ⓓ
10 Ⓐ Ⓑ Ⓒ Ⓓ   **12** Ⓐ Ⓑ Ⓒ Ⓓ   **14** Ⓐ Ⓑ Ⓒ Ⓓ   **16** Ⓐ Ⓑ Ⓒ Ⓓ   **18** Ⓐ Ⓑ Ⓒ Ⓓ

NAME _____

Do each problem.
Find the correct answer.
Mark the space for the answer.

| Part 1 **Concepts** | Part 2 **Computation** |

1. What is the least number that is evenly divisible by 16 and 24?

  A   384
  B   48
  C   64
  D   8

2. Which of these names the greatest number?

  A   two and four tenths
  B   nine tenths
  C   one and nine tenths
  D   two and nine hundredths

3. What number is in the numerator in the quotient $1\frac{6}{7} \div 2\frac{3}{8}$?

  A   19
  B   56
  C   104
  D   133

4. What is the reciprocal of $\frac{4}{9}$?

  A $\frac{1}{9}$

  B $\frac{9}{4}$

  C $\frac{5}{9}$

  D $\frac{1}{4}$

5.   89 621
     48 306
   +5 774

  A   142 810
  B   152 741
  C   140 355
  D   143 701

6.   342
        ×56

  A   18 810
  B   19 152
  C   19 096
  D   23 892

7.   28.651
      4.009
    +17.560

  A   50.220
  B   48.210
  C   51.020
  D   49.110

8.   62.381
      −7.947

  A   55.524
  B   54.434
  C   52.863
  D   55.444

ANSWER ROW   **1** Ⓐ Ⓑ Ⓒ Ⓓ   **3** Ⓐ Ⓑ Ⓒ Ⓓ   **5** Ⓐ Ⓑ Ⓒ Ⓓ   **7** Ⓐ Ⓑ Ⓒ Ⓓ
             2 Ⓐ Ⓑ Ⓒ Ⓓ   **4** Ⓐ Ⓑ Ⓒ Ⓓ   **6** Ⓐ Ⓑ Ⓒ Ⓓ   **8** Ⓐ Ⓑ Ⓒ Ⓓ

9. 19.061
   ×24

   A 428.354
   B 487.554
   C 457.464
   D 381.224

10. 1.6)‾39.536‾

    A 25.34
    B 21.62
    C 28.95
    D 24.71

11. $1\frac{4}{5}$
    $-\frac{2}{3}$

    A $1\frac{2}{15}$
    B $1\frac{4}{15}$
    C $1\frac{1}{5}$
    D $\frac{11}{15}$

12. $2\frac{1}{6} \times 3\frac{2}{5}$

    A $6\frac{1}{15}$
    B $6\frac{1}{10}$
    C $7\frac{11}{30}$
    D $7\frac{7}{30}$

Part 3 Applications

13. Desiree's car averages 6.9 km per litre of gasoline in the city. How many miles would she be able to travel on 33.1 L of gasoline?

    A 228.39   C 220.39
    B 228.28   D 220.29

14. At the stadium, there are 84 243 seats. At Tuesday night's game, 59 567 seats were filled. How many seats were empty?

    A 22 636   C 26 215
    B 24 676   D 27 897

15. If you were to travel from Ottawa, to Berlin, Germany, you would travel 7050 km. From Berlin to Hong Kong, it is 10 100 km. How many kilometres would you travel from Ottawa to Hong Kong, by way of Berlin?

    A 16 690   C 17 150
    B 16 080   D 14 650

16. On Saturday, Jasmine spent $1\frac{2}{3}$ h driving her son to and from a soccer game, $\frac{3}{5}$ h driving her dog to the veterinarian, and $1\frac{2}{15}$ h driving her daughter to and from a softball game. How long did Jasmine drive on Saturday?

    A 3 h   C $2\frac{11}{15}$ h
    B $4\frac{1}{5}$ h   D $3\frac{2}{5}$ h

17. The boys' record for the high jump at Piston High School is 1.95 m. The girls' record is 1.61 m. How much more distance do the girls need to tie the boys' record?

    A 0.26 m   C 0.53 m
    B 0.34 m   D 0.56 m

18. Hal's football practice runs $2\frac{1}{4}$ h for 4 days a week. How many hours does Hal practise each week?

    A $8\frac{1}{4}$ C 9
    B $8\frac{1}{2}$ D $9\frac{3}{4}$

ANSWER ROW   **9** Ⓐ Ⓑ Ⓒ Ⓓ   **11** Ⓐ Ⓑ Ⓒ Ⓓ   **13** Ⓐ Ⓑ Ⓒ Ⓓ   **15** Ⓐ Ⓑ Ⓒ Ⓓ   **17** Ⓐ Ⓑ Ⓒ Ⓓ
             10 Ⓐ Ⓑ Ⓒ Ⓓ   **12** Ⓐ Ⓑ Ⓒ Ⓓ   **14** Ⓐ Ⓑ Ⓒ Ⓓ   **16** Ⓐ Ⓑ Ⓒ Ⓓ   **18** Ⓐ Ⓑ Ⓒ Ⓓ

PRISM MATHEMATICS
Purple Book

216

CHAPTER 2
CUMULATIVE REVIEW

NAME _____

Do each problem.
Find the correct answer.
Mark the space for the answer.

| Part 1 **Concepts** | Part 2 **Computation** |

1. Which of the following products has a 7 in the thousands place?

 A 417×335
 B 908×47
 C 387×149
 D 216×816

2. Which of these is less than $\frac{4}{9}$?

 A $\frac{1}{3}$
 B $\frac{1}{2}$
 C $\frac{3}{4}$
 D $\frac{5}{8}$

3. Which of the following expressions represents the phrase "18 more than a number"?

 A $18 \times n$
 B $18 - n$
 C $n \div 18$
 D $n + 18$

4. Which equation has a solution of 23?

 A $40 = x + 17$
 B $154 = 7x$
 C $x - 9 = 16$
 D $x + 36 = 55$

5. 68 542
     $-59\ 763$

 A 8779
 B 19 889
 C 10 078
 D 9869

6. $314.98
     $+78.28$

 A $381.37
 B $376.86
 C $393.26
 D $382.16

7. 146.3
     $\times 17.8$

 A 2319.64
 B 2604.14
 C 2163.76
 D 2111.24

8. $4\frac{1}{6}$

     $3\frac{3}{8}$

     $+5\frac{1}{2}$

 A $13\frac{5}{6}$
 B $12\frac{1}{8}$
 C $14\frac{5}{24}$
 D $13\frac{1}{24}$

CUMULATIVE REVIEW

ANSWER ROW   **1** Ⓐ Ⓑ Ⓒ Ⓓ   **3** Ⓐ Ⓑ Ⓒ Ⓓ   **5** Ⓐ Ⓑ Ⓒ Ⓓ   **7** Ⓐ Ⓑ Ⓒ Ⓓ
            2 Ⓐ Ⓑ Ⓒ Ⓓ   **4** Ⓐ Ⓑ Ⓒ Ⓓ   **6** Ⓐ Ⓑ Ⓒ Ⓓ   **8** Ⓐ Ⓑ Ⓒ Ⓓ

9. $2\frac{3}{4} \times 4\frac{1}{4}$

A $8\frac{3}{16}$

B $11\frac{11}{16}$

C $9\frac{1}{2}$

D $10\frac{5}{16}$

10. $4\frac{1}{5} \div 3\frac{2}{3}$

A $1\frac{3}{10}$

B $2\frac{1}{15}$

C $1\frac{8}{55}$

D $1\frac{2}{15}$

11. $\frac{z}{6} = 7$

A $z = 42$

B $z = 49$

C $z = 54$

D $z = 48$

12. $250 - 70 = x + 100$

A $x = 70$

B $x = 80$

C $x = 180$

D $x = 95$

Part 3 Applications

13. When Lonnie won the lottery, he decided to divide his $50 000 evenly among eight charities. How much money will each charity receive?

A $8175   C $5950

B $7325   D $6250

14. In the previous problem, if Lonnie had decided to buy a new car for $27 487.95, how much money would he have left from his winnings?

A $33 623.15   C $26 534.05

B $22 512.05   D $20 423.05

15. The garden centre parking lot holds 325 cars. On Saturday evening, the lot was $\frac{3}{5}$ full. How many cars were in the parking lot?

A 195   C 225

B 210   D 240

16. Celeste lost 7 kg in $3\frac{1}{2}$ months. How many kilograms did she lose per month?

A 9 kg   C 10 kg

B 2 kg   D 5 kg

17. Josh and Logan are filling plastic eggs with candy pieces to give out at school. If Josh fills 110 of the 225 eggs, how many eggs will Logan need to fill?

A 95   C 105

B 100   D 115

18. Twelve rooms were reserved yesterday at the Townsend Hotel. If that is $\frac{1}{6}$ of all the rooms, how many rooms are there at the hotel?

A 65   C 72

B 68   D 76

STOP

ANSWER ROW 9 Ⓐ Ⓑ Ⓒ Ⓓ 11 Ⓐ Ⓑ Ⓒ Ⓓ 13 Ⓐ Ⓑ Ⓒ Ⓓ 15 Ⓐ Ⓑ Ⓒ Ⓓ 17 Ⓐ Ⓑ Ⓒ Ⓓ
10 Ⓐ Ⓑ Ⓒ Ⓓ 12 Ⓐ Ⓑ Ⓒ Ⓓ 14 Ⓐ Ⓑ Ⓒ Ⓓ 16 Ⓐ Ⓑ Ⓒ Ⓓ 18 Ⓐ Ⓑ Ⓒ Ⓓ

PRISM MATHEMATICS
Purple Book

218

CHAPTER 3
CUMULATIVE REVIEW

CHAPTER 4   CUMULATIVE REVIEW

NAME _____

Do each problem.
Find the correct answer.
Mark the space for the answer.

Part 1 **Concepts**

1. What number is 10 000 more than 23 971 056?

   A 23 961 056
   B 23 972 056
   C 23 981 056
   D 24 081 056

2. What digit is in the <u>hundredths</u> place in the quotient $0.034\overline{)0.21012}$?

   A 1
   B 6
   C 3
   D 8

3. What is the value of d in the following equation?

   $7d + 2d + 13 = 85$

   A 8
   B 9
   C 10.3
   D 72

4. If $a = 7$, then $3a - 6 = $ ____?

   A 4
   B 21
   C 15
   D 18

Part 2 **Computation**

5. $27\overline{)32\ 481}$

   A 1203
   B 1217 r18
   C 1226
   D 1196 r6

6. $\begin{array}{r} 10.748 \\ -0.967 \\ \hline \end{array}$

   A 10.881
   B 9.671
   C 9.781
   D 11.715

7. $8\frac{3}{10} - 6\frac{2}{5}$

   A $2\frac{1}{5}$
   B $2\frac{1}{10}$
   C $1\frac{9}{10}$
   D $1\frac{2}{5}$

8. $4\frac{1}{9} \times 2\frac{1}{2}$

   A $8\frac{1}{9}$
   B $10\frac{5}{18}$
   C $8\frac{1}{18}$
   D $9\frac{7}{18}$

CUMULATIVE REVIEW

ANSWER ROW   **1** Ⓐ Ⓑ Ⓒ Ⓓ   **3** Ⓐ Ⓑ Ⓒ Ⓓ   **5** Ⓐ Ⓑ Ⓒ Ⓓ   **7** Ⓐ Ⓑ Ⓒ Ⓓ
                          2 Ⓐ Ⓑ Ⓒ Ⓓ   **4** Ⓐ Ⓑ Ⓒ Ⓓ   **6** Ⓐ Ⓑ Ⓒ Ⓓ   **8** Ⓐ Ⓑ Ⓒ Ⓓ

PRISM MATHEMATICS
Purple Book

CHAPTER 4
CUMULATIVE REVIEW

219

9. $15m = 255$

A $m = 14$
B $m = 15$
C $m = 16$
D $m = 17$

10. $\dfrac{x}{3} = 65 + 25$

A $x = 90$
B $x = 270$
C $x = 30$
D $x = 180$

11. $9e - 3e =$

A $6e$
B $27e$
C 6
D $11e$

12. $2s + s + 16 = 49$

A $s = 6$
B $s = 9$
C $s = 11$
D $s = 14$

Part 3 **Applications**

13. If each ticket in a bundle of 1800 tickets costs 65¢, what is the cost of the bundle?

A $1075
B $1250
C $1170
D $1105

14. Ricky spent $2\frac{1}{3}$ h doing homework on Monday, $1\frac{3}{4}$ h on Tuesday, and $2\frac{1}{6}$ h on Wednesday. How long did he spend doing homework in those three days?

A $6\frac{1}{4}$ h
B $5\frac{5}{12}$ h
C $5\frac{1}{2}$ h
D $6\frac{2}{3}$ h

15. An electrician has just finished $\frac{6}{7}$ of a 77-h job. How many hours has he finished?

A   55
B   62
C   59
D   66

16. Katrina has earned 52 stars in school this year for good behaviour. She has earned four times as many as Brooklyn. How many stars has Brooklyn earned?

A   11
B   13
C   208
D   18

17. William is twice as old as his son, Elijah. Their combined age is 78. How old is Elijah?

A   20
B   23
C   26
D   30

18. In the previous problem, how old is William?

A   60
B   52
C   46
D   40

ANSWER ROW **9** Ⓐ Ⓑ Ⓒ Ⓓ   **11** Ⓐ Ⓑ Ⓒ Ⓓ   **13** Ⓐ Ⓑ Ⓒ Ⓓ   **15** Ⓐ Ⓑ Ⓒ Ⓓ   **17** Ⓐ Ⓑ Ⓒ Ⓓ
10 Ⓐ Ⓑ Ⓒ Ⓓ   **12** Ⓐ Ⓑ Ⓒ Ⓓ   **14** Ⓐ Ⓑ Ⓒ Ⓓ   **16** Ⓐ Ⓑ Ⓒ Ⓓ   **18** Ⓐ Ⓑ Ⓒ Ⓓ

NAME _____

Do each problem.
Find the correct answer.
Mark the space for the answer.

Part 1 **Concepts**	Part 2 **Computation**

1. Which of the following fractions is not equivalent to $\frac{3}{7}$?

A $\frac{9}{21}$

B $\frac{12}{27}$

C $\frac{6}{14}$

D $\frac{15}{35}$

5.
$$\begin{array}{r} 29\ 601 \\ 357 \\ +8\ 273 \\ \hline \end{array}$$

A 39 241
B 41 321
C 36 142
D 38 231

2. $1.05 =$

A $\frac{10}{15}$

B $\frac{15}{10}$

C $\frac{100}{105}$

D $\frac{105}{100}$

6.
$$\begin{array}{r} 1342.05 \\ \times 34.6 \\ \hline \end{array}$$

A 47 851.341
B 49 342.821
C 46 434.930
D 44 562.620

3. Which of the following phrases represents the expression $n \div 3$?

A three divided by a number
B three less than a number
C a number divided by three
D a number increased by three

7. $5\frac{1}{3} \div 2\frac{1}{6}$

A $2\frac{1}{6}$

B $2\frac{6}{13}$

C $2\frac{5}{6}$

D $3\frac{1}{11}$

4. Which of the following decimals is greater than $3\frac{2}{7}$?

A 3.35
B 3.25
C 2.7
D 3.099

8. $8 \times 5 = \frac{r}{4}$

A $r = 160$
B $r = 175$
C $r = 40$
D $r = 205$

CUMULATIVE REVIEW

ANSWER ROW **1** Ⓐ Ⓑ Ⓒ Ⓓ   **3** Ⓐ Ⓑ Ⓒ Ⓓ   **5** Ⓐ Ⓑ Ⓒ Ⓓ   **7** Ⓐ Ⓑ Ⓒ Ⓓ
            2 Ⓐ Ⓑ Ⓒ Ⓓ   **4** Ⓐ Ⓑ Ⓒ Ⓓ   **6** Ⓐ Ⓑ Ⓒ Ⓓ   **8** Ⓐ Ⓑ Ⓒ Ⓓ

PRISM MATHEMATICS
Purple Book

CHAPTER 5
CUMULATIVE REVIEW

221

9. $4x + x + 22 = 62$

A $x = 20$
B $x = 5$
C $x = 200$
D $x = 8$

10. $t + (2t + 7) = 16$

A $t = 4$
B $t = 6$
C $t = 3$
D $t = 5$

11. $\frac{2}{5} = \frac{v}{125}$

A $v = 50$
B $v = 75$
C $v = 25$
D $v = 100$

12. 35 is 20% of ___.

A 190
B 175
C 168
D 160

Part 3 Applications

13. Joaquin needed four new tires for his car. The tires cost $86.97 each. How much did Joaquin pay for his tires?

A $347.88
B $386.75
C $456.98
D $412.08

14. Angela's trip was 605 km and took 11 h. She drove the same distance each hour. What was her average travelling speed?

A 55 km/h
B 50 km/h
C 61 km/h
D 64 km/h

15. Last Year, Renee could run $3\frac{2}{3}$ laps around the track in 10 min. This year she can run $4\frac{7}{9}$ laps. How many more laps can she run this year than last year?

A $1\frac{1}{3}$
B $1\frac{1}{9}$
C $1\frac{1}{2}$
D $1\frac{8}{9}$

16. Derek has noticed that the temperature has risen 6 degrees since he woke up this morning. The thermometer now reads 27°C. What was the temperature when Derek woke up?

A 33°C
B 29°C
C 24°C
D 21°C

17. The goalie for the red hockey team had 12 saves out of 15 shots last week. At that rate, how many saves will she have if there are 25 shots?

A 18
B 19
C 20
D 21

18. The grade 4s at Current Elementary School raised $3250 for new playground equipment. They needed $195 of that total to pay for expenses. What percent of the total was used for expenses?

A 4%
B 6%
C 7%
D 9%

ANSWER ROW **9** Ⓐ Ⓑ Ⓒ Ⓓ **11** Ⓐ Ⓑ Ⓒ Ⓓ **13** Ⓐ Ⓑ Ⓒ Ⓓ **15** Ⓐ Ⓑ Ⓒ Ⓓ **17** Ⓐ Ⓑ Ⓒ Ⓓ
10 Ⓐ Ⓑ Ⓒ Ⓓ **12** Ⓐ Ⓑ Ⓒ Ⓓ **14** Ⓐ Ⓑ Ⓒ Ⓓ **16** Ⓐ Ⓑ Ⓒ Ⓓ **18** Ⓐ Ⓑ Ⓒ Ⓓ

PRISM MATHEMATICS
Purple Book

222

CHAPTER 5
CUMULATIVE REVIEW

NAME _____

Do each problem.
Find the correct answer.
Mark the space for the answer.

Part 1 **Concepts**

1. What number should replace the ☐ to make the following a true statement?

$54\ 709 = ☐ + 34\ 855 + 1648$

  A 18 200

  B 36 503

  C 33 207

  D 18 206

2. What number is 500 000 less than 362 745 309?

  A 362 245 309

  B 362 695 309

  C 357 745 309

  D 362 145 309

3. How would you write 37% as a fraction?

  A $\frac{3}{7}$

  B $\frac{37}{100}$

  C $\frac{.37}{100}$

  D $\frac{37}{100}$

4. Which formula can you use to find the interest on a loan?

  A $i = \dfrac{p \times r}{t}$

  B $i = p + r + t$

  C $i = p \times r \times t$

  D $i = \dfrac{r \times t}{p}$

Part 2 **Computation**

5. 52 013
      $-9\ 874$

  A 61 887

  B 53 249

  C 42 139

  D 47 658

6. $3\frac{1}{9}$

    $4\frac{2}{3}$

    $+5\frac{7}{18}$

  A $13\frac{5}{6}$

  B $13\frac{1}{6}$

  C $12\frac{11}{18}$

  D $14\frac{2}{9}$

7. $33 = \frac{f}{9}$

  A $f = 297$

  B $f = 3.667$

  C $f = 231$

  D $f = 363$

8. $2x + 4x + 6 = 42$

  A $x = 4$

  B $x = 6$

  C $x = 8$

  D $x = 10$

ANSWER ROW   **1** Ⓐ Ⓑ Ⓒ Ⓓ   **3** Ⓐ Ⓑ Ⓒ Ⓓ   **5** Ⓐ Ⓑ Ⓒ Ⓓ   **7** Ⓐ Ⓑ Ⓒ Ⓓ
             2 Ⓐ Ⓑ Ⓒ Ⓓ   **4** Ⓐ Ⓑ Ⓒ Ⓓ   **6** Ⓐ Ⓑ Ⓒ Ⓓ   **8** Ⓐ Ⓑ Ⓒ Ⓓ

9. ___ is 41% of 600.

A 258

B 14.63

C 683

D 246

10. $\frac{1}{8}$ is ___% of $1\frac{1}{4}$.

A 5

B 20

C 10

D 18

11. What is the rate on a loan if interest = $72, principal = $200, and time = 2 years?

A 26%

B 31%

C 22%

D 18%

12. What is the time on a loan if interest = $3780, principal = $21 000, and rate = 9%?

A 1 year

B 2 years

C $1\frac{1}{2}$ years

D 3 years

Part 3 Applications

13. Aliana found a wall oven she would like to buy for $365.95. The clerk told her it had a small dent in the back of it, so they would take $18.30 off of the price. How much did Aliana pay for the oven?

A $347.65   C $321.75

B $317.55   D $357.65

14. A recipe to make bread requires $1\frac{1}{4}$ packets of yeast. Sandra is making $2\frac{1}{2}$ times the amount of bread that the recipe calls for. How much yeast will she need?

A $2\frac{3}{4}$ packets   C $2\frac{7}{8}$ packets

B $3\frac{1}{2}$ packets   D $3\frac{1}{8}$ packets

15. Last month, Geraldine delivered three times as many newspapers as Ralph. They delivered a total of 2088 newspapers. How many newspapers did Ralph deliver?

A 436   C 522

B 481   D 579

16. When Elsie and Trish were 5 years old, Elsie's mass was 5 kg more than Trish. Their combined mass was 49 kg. What was Elsie's mass?

A 21 kg   C 24 kg

B 22 kg   D 27 kg

17. Keenan saved and deposited $10\frac{1}{2}$% of $1200 he earned mowing lawns. How much did he deposit?

A $126   C $198

B $160   D $210

18. At an annual interest rate of $6\frac{1}{4}$%, Luigi earned $56 in 2 years. How much did he deposit to do this?

A $422   C $506

B $448   D $524

STOP

ANSWER ROW **9** Ⓐ Ⓑ Ⓒ Ⓓ **11** Ⓐ Ⓑ Ⓒ Ⓓ **13** Ⓐ Ⓑ Ⓒ Ⓓ **15** Ⓐ Ⓑ Ⓒ Ⓓ **17** Ⓐ Ⓑ Ⓒ Ⓓ
10 Ⓐ Ⓑ Ⓒ Ⓓ **12** Ⓐ Ⓑ Ⓒ Ⓓ **14** Ⓐ Ⓑ Ⓒ Ⓓ **16** Ⓐ Ⓑ Ⓒ Ⓓ **18** Ⓐ Ⓑ Ⓒ Ⓓ

PRISM MATHEMATICS
Purple Book

CHAPTER 6
CUMULATIVE REVIEW

224

NAME _____

Do each problem.
Find the correct answer.
Mark the space for the answer.

Part 1 **Concepts**	Part 2 **Computation**

1. Which of these is another name for six and fifteen thousandths?

   A 6.15

   B 6.000 15

   C 6015

   D 6.015

2. What is the value of n in the following proportion?

$$\frac{27}{n} = \frac{108}{136}$$

   A 34

   B 21

   C 31

   D 544

3. $17b + 5b - 9b =$

   A $22b$

   B $8b$

   C $13b$

   D $31b$

4. What operation do you perform to convert grams to milligrams?

   A multiply by 100

   B divide by 100

   C multiply by 1000

   D divide by 1000

5. $3.6\overline{)432.036}$

   A 104.31

   B 152.10

   C 120.01

   D 134.11

6. $2\frac{1}{5} \times 3\frac{1}{3}$

   A $6\frac{1}{15}$

   B $7\frac{1}{3}$

   C $6\frac{1}{5}$

   D $7\frac{2}{15}$

7. $82 - 16 = 11c$

   A $c = 10$

   B $c = 8$

   C $c = 5$

   D $c = 6$

8. $x + 3x + 7 = 79$

   A $x = 18$

   B $x = 21$

   C $x = 19$

   D $x = 15$

CUMULATIVE REVIEW

ANSWER ROW   **1** Ⓐ Ⓑ Ⓒ Ⓓ   **3** Ⓐ Ⓑ Ⓒ Ⓓ   **5** Ⓐ Ⓑ Ⓒ Ⓓ   **7** Ⓐ Ⓑ Ⓒ Ⓓ

                2 Ⓐ Ⓑ Ⓒ Ⓓ   **4** Ⓐ Ⓑ Ⓒ Ⓓ   **6** Ⓐ Ⓑ Ⓒ Ⓓ   **8** Ⓐ Ⓑ Ⓒ Ⓓ

9. $5\frac{3}{4}\% =$

A 5.75
B 0.575
C 0.0575
D 0.00575

10. What is the interest on a loan if principal = $700, rate = 6%, and time = 2 years?

A $42
B $79
C $82
D $84

11. In problem **10,** if interest was compounded annually, what is the total amount at the end of two years?

A $784.00
B $786.52
C $742.00
D $744.52

12. 0.639 kL =

A 639 L
B 6.39 L
C 63.9 L
D 0.0639 L

Part 3 Applications

13. Keesha borrowed $1200 for one year. Interest on the first $500 of the loan was 12%. It was 9% interest on the rest. How much interest did she pay?

A $188
B $154
C $123
D $96

14. In a certain village, $\frac{3}{5}$ of the men are married. If 85 men live in the village, how many are married?

A 39
B 46
C 51
D 60

15. The Davidson triplets and the Johnson twins were absent on Thursday. They make up $\frac{1}{5}$ of the entire class. How many students are in the class?

A 20
B 25
C 30
D 35

16. At Rosemont Junior High School, 1 out of every 6 children rides their bikes to and from school. There are 438 children who attend Rosemont. How many ride their bikes?

A 73
B 58
C 102
D 82

17. The president of a large corporation spent $1071.00 on baseball tickets for his employees. If each ticket costs $12.75, how many employees does he have?

A 75
B 84
C 91
D 106

18. Yasmine's father said she could not go swimming until the temperature reached 25°C. Yasmine read the thermometer and it said 23°C. How many degrees does the temperature have to rise for her to be allowed to go swimming?

A 5°C
B 4°C
C 3°C
D 2°C

ANSWER ROW   **9** Ⓐ Ⓑ Ⓒ Ⓓ   **11** Ⓐ Ⓑ Ⓒ Ⓓ   **13** Ⓐ Ⓑ Ⓒ Ⓓ   **15** Ⓐ Ⓑ Ⓒ Ⓓ   **17** Ⓐ Ⓑ Ⓒ Ⓓ

10 Ⓐ Ⓑ Ⓒ Ⓓ   **12** Ⓐ Ⓑ Ⓒ Ⓓ   **14** Ⓐ Ⓑ Ⓒ Ⓓ   **16** Ⓐ Ⓑ Ⓒ Ⓓ   **18** Ⓐ Ⓑ Ⓒ Ⓓ

NAME _____

Do each problem.
Find the correct answer.
Mark the space for the answer.

Part 1 **Concepts**	Part 2 **Computation**

1. What difference is more than 11 000 and less than 11 500?

   A   47 541 − 35 891

   B   33 564 − 22 619

   C   75 930 − 64 580

   D   59 797 − 48 267

5. 3650.2
   ×16

   A   54 753.2

   B   58 403.2

   C   58 563.2

   D   58 404.8

2. If $y = 11$, then $4y - 22 =$ _____?

   A   44

   B   22

   C   20

   D   37

6. $3\frac{5}{6} - 2\frac{1}{3}$

   A $\frac{5}{6}$

   B $1\frac{2}{3}$

   C $1\frac{1}{6}$

   D $1\frac{1}{2}$

3. How many complete minutes are in 675 s?

   A   13

   B   12

   C   11

   D   22

7. $\dfrac{x}{110} = 18 - 13$

   A $x = 440$

   B $x = 330$

   C $x = 550$

   D $x = 660$

4. Which of the following is a measurement of mass?

   A   grams

   B   kilolitres

   C   Celsius

   D   decimetres

8. $f + 5f = 126$

   A $f = 18$

   B $f = 21$

   C $f = 23$

   D $f = 27$

CUMULATIVE REVIEW

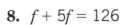

ANSWER ROW   **1** Ⓐ Ⓑ Ⓒ Ⓓ   **3** Ⓐ Ⓑ Ⓒ Ⓓ   **5** Ⓐ Ⓑ Ⓒ Ⓓ   **7** Ⓐ Ⓑ Ⓒ Ⓓ

                 2 Ⓐ Ⓑ Ⓒ Ⓓ   **4** Ⓐ Ⓑ Ⓒ Ⓓ   **6** Ⓐ Ⓑ Ⓒ Ⓓ   **8** Ⓐ Ⓑ Ⓒ Ⓓ

9. 124 is 25% of ____.

   A 496
   B 330
   C 422
   D 478

10. What is the principal on a loan if interest = \$312, rate = 13%, and time = 3 years?

   A \$1200
   B \$1400
   C \$600
   D \$800

11. 14.5 g =

   A 14 500 mg
   B 1450 mg
   C 145 mg
   D 1.45 mg

12. 2 h 20 min
     ×4

   A 8 h 40 min
   B 8 h 20 min
   C 9 h 20 min
   D 9 h 40 min

Part 3 **Applications**

13. Keith ran $16\frac{3}{4}$ laps around the track. Harold ran $14\frac{5}{6}$ laps. How many more laps did Keith run than Harold?

   A $1\frac{1}{6}$
   C $2\frac{1}{4}$
   B $1\frac{7}{12}$
   D $1\frac{11}{12}$

14. After their dart game, Jason had 48 points which was $\frac{1}{4}$ the number of points that Derek had. How many points did Derek have?

   A 164
   C 12
   B 192
   D 238

15. Marie and her friends are watching the city pool being filled. The pool holds 162 000 L. If the pool is 75% full, how many gallons are in it?

   A 113 400 L
   C 121 500 L
   B 129 600 L
   D 137 700 L

16. Ricardo deposited \$400 in a two-year account at 8%. If this account were compounded annually, how much interest would be in the account after two years?

   A \$66.56
   C \$32.00
   B \$64.00
   D \$34.56

17. A recipe for chocolate fudge calls for 60 g of cocoa powder. How many milligrams would that be?

   A 20 000 mg
   C 40 000 mg
   B 60 000 mg
   D 30 000 mg

18. It takes 20 h 30 min to drive from Halifax to Toronto. It takes 10 h 45 min to drive from Halifax to Quebec City. How long does it take to drive from Quebec City to Toronto?

   A 10 h 45 min
   C 30 h 15 min
   B 31 h 15 min
   D 9 h 45 min

STOP

ANSWER ROW   9 Ⓐ Ⓑ Ⓒ Ⓓ   11 Ⓐ Ⓑ Ⓒ Ⓓ   13 Ⓐ Ⓑ Ⓒ Ⓓ   15 Ⓐ Ⓑ Ⓒ Ⓓ   17 Ⓐ Ⓑ Ⓒ Ⓓ
           10 Ⓐ Ⓑ Ⓒ Ⓓ   12 Ⓐ Ⓑ Ⓒ Ⓓ   14 Ⓐ Ⓑ Ⓒ Ⓓ   16 Ⓐ Ⓑ Ⓒ Ⓓ   18 Ⓐ Ⓑ Ⓒ Ⓓ

PRISM MATHEMATICS
Purple Book

CHAPTER 8
CUMULATIVE REVIEW

228

NAME _____

Do each problem.
Find the correct answer.
Mark the space for the answer.

Part 1 **Concepts**

1. What is the least number that is evenly divisible by 12 and 32?

   A 64

   B 96

   C 128

   D 192

2. What digit is in the thousandths place in the product 1.0678×3.14?

   A 2

   B 7

   C 5

   D 8

3. What operation do you perform to convert litres to kilolitres?

   A multiply by 1000

   B divide by 1000

   C multiply by 100

   D divide by 10

4. What type of triangle has angle measures 98°, 46°, and 36°?

   A acute

   B right

   C isosceles

   D obtuse

Part 2 **Computation**

5.
$$\begin{array}{r} 740.12 \\ 3.48 \\ +96.75 \\ \hline \end{array}$$

   A 728.35

   B 739.25

   C 839.45

   D 840.35

6. $8\frac{1}{3} \div 2\frac{1}{4}$

   A $4\frac{1}{3}$

   B $3\frac{19}{27}$

   C $4\frac{3}{4}$

   D $3\frac{1}{12}$

7. $a + a + 17 = 55$

   A $a = 19$

   B $a = 22$

   C $a = 18$

   D $a = 16$

8. $\dfrac{m}{7} = \dfrac{72}{84}$

   A $m = 8.16$

   B $m = 4$

   C $m = 864$

   D $m = 6$

ANSWER ROW **1** Ⓐ Ⓑ Ⓒ Ⓓ **3** Ⓐ Ⓑ Ⓒ Ⓓ **5** Ⓐ Ⓑ Ⓒ Ⓓ **7** Ⓐ Ⓑ Ⓒ Ⓓ

            2 Ⓐ Ⓑ Ⓒ Ⓓ **4** Ⓐ Ⓑ Ⓒ Ⓓ **6** Ⓐ Ⓑ Ⓒ Ⓓ **8** Ⓐ Ⓑ Ⓒ Ⓓ

9. What is the time of a loan if interest = $162, principal = $900, and rate = 8%?

A 3 years

B $2\frac{3}{4}$ years

C $2\frac{1}{4}$ years

D $1\frac{3}{4}$ years

10. 13 dm =

A 0.13 m

B 1.3 m

C 130 m

D 0.013 m

11. 18 kg =

A 10 800 g

B 1800 g

C 18 000 g

D 1.8 g

12. A(n) _____ triangle never has sides the same length.

A isosceles

B equilateral

C scalene

D straight

Part 3 Applications

13. Mrs. Sarma made three deposits for the home and school association last month. The first deposit was $325.65, next was $519.43, and the last deposit was $272.18. How much money did Mrs. Sarma deposit all together?

A $1003.36

B $1096.14

C $1117.26

D $1204.15

14. During the $3\frac{1}{4}$ h soccer camp, the players worked on dribbling, passing, and shooting activities. How much time was spent on each activity, if the time was divided evenly?

A $1\frac{1}{12}$ h

B $\frac{11}{12}$ h

C $1\frac{1}{2}$ h

D $1\frac{1}{4}$ h

15. The 14th hole at the Winterwax Golf Course is 190 m long. How long would it be on a model with a scale of 2 cm to 76 m?

A 4 cm

B 5 cm

C 6 cm

D 7 cm

16. Mr. Newman has $1300 in a savings account that pays 6% interest compounded annually. How much will Mr. Newman have in his account after two years?

A $1378.00

B $1498.09

C $1535.21

D $1460.68

17. In Warehouse #5, Chandler counted 52 boxes with a mass of 113 kg each. If his boss needs an estimate of the mass for all the boxes, what would Chandler tell him?

A 5500 kg

B 5650 kg

C 550 kg

D 5720 kg

18. If you put a right angle and an angle that measures 36° together with one common ray, what would be the angle measure they form?

A 81°

B 156°

C 126°

D 111°

ANSWER ROW   **9** Ⓐ Ⓑ Ⓒ Ⓓ   **11** Ⓐ Ⓑ Ⓒ Ⓓ   **13** Ⓐ Ⓑ Ⓒ Ⓓ   **15** Ⓐ Ⓑ Ⓒ Ⓓ   **17** Ⓐ Ⓑ Ⓒ Ⓓ

10 Ⓐ Ⓑ Ⓒ Ⓓ   **12** Ⓐ Ⓑ Ⓒ Ⓓ   **14** Ⓐ Ⓑ Ⓒ Ⓓ   **16** Ⓐ Ⓑ Ⓒ Ⓓ   **18** Ⓐ Ⓑ Ⓒ Ⓓ

Do each problem.
Find the correct answer.
Mark the space for the answer.

Part 1 **Concepts**

1. In which of these problems can the dividend be evenly divided by the divisor?

A $3481 \div 19$
B $2149 \div 23$
C $3318 \div 32$
D $2523 \div 29$

2. What number does x represent to make the equation true?

$\frac{7}{9} - \frac{x}{9} = \frac{2}{9}$

A 5
B 1
C 8
D 9

3. The prefix 'hecto' means

A 0.1
B 10
C 100
D 1000

4. The value of $\sqrt{27}$ is between _____.

A 6 and 7
B 20 and 30
C 2 and 14
D 5 and 6

Part 2 **Computation**

5. $\begin{array}{r} \$2978.10 \\ -\ 1989.63 \\ \hline \end{array}$

A $1099.57
B $1989.66
C $988.47
D $899.47

6. $9\frac{4}{5} + 8\frac{5}{6}$

A $18\frac{19}{30}$
B $17\frac{2}{15}$
C $17\frac{3}{10}$
D $18\frac{1}{6}$

7. $d = 310.5 \times 8$

A $d = 2412$
B $d = 2484$
C $d = 2564$
D $d = 2173.5$

8. ____ is 145% of 120.

A 177
B 170
C 168
D 174

GO

ANSWER ROW   **1** Ⓐ Ⓑ Ⓒ Ⓓ   **3** Ⓐ Ⓑ Ⓒ Ⓓ   **5** Ⓐ Ⓑ Ⓒ Ⓓ   **7** Ⓐ Ⓑ Ⓒ Ⓓ
                        2 Ⓐ Ⓑ Ⓒ Ⓓ   **4** Ⓐ Ⓑ Ⓒ Ⓓ   **6** Ⓐ Ⓑ Ⓒ Ⓓ   **8** Ⓐ Ⓑ Ⓒ Ⓓ

9. $112 - 17 = r + 45$

    A $r = 38$
    B $r = 42$
    C $r = 47$
    D $r = 50$

10. What is the interest on a loan if principal = $400, rate = $9\frac{1}{2}\%$, and time = $3\frac{1}{2}$ years?

    A $133
    B $126
    C $114
    D $119

11.
    3 h 45 min
    +4 h 45 min

    A 7 h 45 min
    B 8 h 30 min
    C 8 h 15 min
    D 8 h 45 min

12. $21^2 =$

    A 529
    B 42
    C 484
    D 441

Part 3 Applications

13. Last week, Branham ran $42\frac{1}{2}$ times around the block. The block is 2 km around. How many kilometres did Branham run?

    A 40 km
    C 21 km
    B 85 km
    D 2 km

14. Leah answered 34 out of 40 questions correct on her driver's test. What percent of the test did she get right?

    A 81%
    C 92%
    B 88%
    D 85%

15. What kind of rate will Mr. Nardiello receive if he'll pay $714 in interest after $3\frac{1}{2}$ years if he borrows $3400?

    A 4%
    C 6%
    B 5%
    D 7%

16. For the carnival, eight tables were placed end to end. Each table is 2 m long. What is the total length of the tables?

    A 4 m
    C 10 m
    B 16 m
    D 6 m

17. What is the square root of 9?

    A 3
    C 87
    B 6
    D 12

18. The fire department ladder leans against a building. The bottom of the ladder rests 5 m from the building, and the top of his ladder rests 12 m up on the building wall. How long is the ladder?

    A 14 m
    C 16 m
    B 15 m
    D 13 m

ANSWER ROW   **9** Ⓐ Ⓑ Ⓒ Ⓓ   **11** Ⓐ Ⓑ Ⓒ Ⓓ   **13** Ⓐ Ⓑ Ⓒ Ⓓ   **15** Ⓐ Ⓑ Ⓒ Ⓓ   **17** Ⓐ Ⓑ Ⓒ Ⓓ

            10 Ⓐ Ⓑ Ⓒ Ⓓ   **12** Ⓐ Ⓑ Ⓒ Ⓓ   **14** Ⓐ Ⓑ Ⓒ Ⓓ   **16** Ⓐ Ⓑ Ⓒ Ⓓ   **18** Ⓐ Ⓑ Ⓒ Ⓓ

NAME _____

Do each problem.
Find the correct answer.
Mark the space for the answer.

Part 1 **Concepts**

1. Which of the following expressions represents the phrase "34 decreased by twice a number"?

   A $34 + 2 + n$

   B $34 - 2n$

   C $2n - 34$

   D $34 \div 2n$

2. Which of these is greater than $5\frac{3}{8}$?

   A $5\frac{6}{11}$

   B $5\frac{1}{4}$

   C $5\frac{2}{7}$

   D $5\frac{7}{20}$

3. Two angles that have the same size are called _____ angles.

   A isosceles

   B acute

   C congruent

   D equilateral

4. What is the formula for the area of a triangle?

   A $A = bh$

   B $A = \frac{1}{2}bh$

   C $A = \frac{1}{2} + b + h$

   D $A = \pi r^2$

Part 2 **Computation**

5. $47\overline{)11\,938}$

   A 254

   B 303 r18

   C 286

   D 269 r39

6. $\frac{15}{16} - \frac{3}{4}$

   A $\frac{1}{4}$

   B $\frac{7}{16}$

   C $\frac{3}{16}$

   D $\frac{1}{2}$

7. $9 \times 6 = 18p$

   A $p = 5$

   B $p = 2$

   C $p = 4$

   D $p = 3$

8. $18\frac{1}{4}\% =$

   A 0.018 25

   B 1.825

   C 18.25

   D 0.1825

ANSWER ROW   **1** Ⓐ Ⓑ Ⓒ Ⓓ   **3** Ⓐ Ⓑ Ⓒ Ⓓ   **5** Ⓐ Ⓑ Ⓒ Ⓓ   **7** Ⓐ Ⓑ Ⓒ Ⓓ

  2 Ⓐ Ⓑ Ⓒ Ⓓ   **4** Ⓐ Ⓑ Ⓒ Ⓓ   **6** Ⓐ Ⓑ Ⓒ Ⓓ   **8** Ⓐ Ⓑ Ⓒ Ⓓ

9.   7 min 40 s
              ×3

A 22 min 20 s
B 23 min
C 22 min
D 21 min 40 s

10. $\sqrt{4356} =$

A 66
B 62
C 55
D 68

11. What is the perimeter of a square if s = 11 cm?

A 22 cm
B 60.5 cm
C 44 cm
D 33 cm

12. What is the approximate surface area of a cylinder if height = 3 cm and radius = 2 cm? Use 3.14 for π.

A 12.56 cm^2
B 62.80 cm^2
C 51.40 cm^2
D 31.40 cm^2

Part 3 Applications

13. When Mrs. Jackson was sick, her daughter, Laura, drove back and forth to see her five times in one month. If the distance was 116 km from Laura's house to her mother's, how many kilometres did Laura drive to see her mother in that one month?

A 955 km
B 580 km
C 1160 km
D 660 km

14. Diedri bought 4.5 kg of mixed nuts. The store clerk said she was guaranteed to find 25% of that mixture to be cashews. At least how many kilogram of cashews did Diedri get?

A 1.125 kg
B 1.25 kg
C 2.125 kg
D 0.9 kg

15. For how many years did Alfonzo have a loan of $900 at 5% interest if the interest is $45?

A 4
B 3
C 2
D 1

16. Mr. Omar showed a movie on physics to his science students. The first day, they watched 47 min. The second day, they watched the remaining 73 min. If Mr. Omar showed the movie to four classes, how many total hours did the movie play?

A 6
B 8
C 4
D 10

17. Myra and her friends left the dock in their sailboat and sailed 4 km west and then 3 km south. How far was the sailboat from the dock then?

A 5 km
B 6 km
C 7 km
D 8 km

18. Tony is responsible for mowing the vacant lot across the street. The lot is rectangular and measures 155 m by 36 m. How many square metre does Tony mow?

A 382 m^2
B 2451 m^2
C 5580 m^2
D 7320 m^2

ANSWER ROW   **9** Ⓐ Ⓑ Ⓒ Ⓓ   **11** Ⓐ Ⓑ Ⓒ Ⓓ   **13** Ⓐ Ⓑ Ⓒ Ⓓ   **15** Ⓐ Ⓑ Ⓒ Ⓓ   **17** Ⓐ Ⓑ Ⓒ Ⓓ
                          10 Ⓐ Ⓑ Ⓒ Ⓓ   **12** Ⓐ Ⓑ Ⓒ Ⓓ   **14** Ⓐ Ⓑ Ⓒ Ⓓ   **16** Ⓐ Ⓑ Ⓒ Ⓓ   **18** Ⓐ Ⓑ Ⓒ Ⓓ

CHAPTER 12 CUMULATIVE REVIEW

NAME _____

Do each problem.
Find the correct answer.
Mark the space for the answer.

Part 1 Concepts

1. What number is in the numerator when you write the product of $8\frac{3}{11} \times 6\frac{1}{5}$ as a mixed numeral?

   A 55
   B 2821
   C 51
   D 16

2. What type of triangle has angle measures 67°, 58°, and 55°?

   A acute
   B right
   C isosceles
   D obtuse

3. Perpendicular lines form _____ angles.

   A 120°
   B 90°
   C 45°
   D 60°

4. Which of the following sector measurements represent a whole circle?

   A 170°, 120°, 60°, 30°
   B 150°, 90°, 45°, 25°, 20°
   C 168°, 90°, 72°, 36°
   D 130°, 90°, 80°, 60°

Part 2 Computation

5. $3251.06
    −973.48
    ‾‾‾‾‾‾‾

    A $2387.58
    B $3388.68
    C $2267.77
    D $2277.58

6. $8\frac{9}{11} =$

   A $\frac{97}{11}$
   B $\frac{109}{11}$
   C $\frac{95}{11}$
   D $\frac{171}{11}$

7. $\frac{2}{x} = \frac{170}{425}$

   A $x = 7$
   B $x = 0.8$
   C $x = 5$
   D $x = 2.5$

8. 146.8 m =

   A 14 680 cm
   B 1468 cm
   C 14.68 cm
   D 1.468 cm

ANSWER ROW   1 ⒶⒷⒸⒹ   3 ⒶⒷⒸⒹ   5 ⒶⒷⒸⒹ   7 ⒶⒷⒸⒹ
             2 ⒶⒷⒸⒹ   4 ⒶⒷⒸⒹ   6 ⒶⒷⒸⒹ   8 ⒶⒷⒸⒹ

PRISM MATHEMATICS
Purple Book

CHAPTER 12
CUMULATIVE REVIEW

235

CUMULATIVE REVIEW

9. $4\frac{3}{4} \div 2\frac{1}{2}$

A $2\frac{1}{4}$

B $1\frac{9}{10}$

C $2\frac{3}{8}$

D $1\frac{3}{16}$

10. $29^2 =$

A 729

B 58

C 116

D 841

11. What is the approximate area of a circle if the radius = 30 cm? Use 3.14 for π.

A 188.4 cm^2

B 706.5 cm^2

C 2826 cm^2

D 3017.5 cm^2

12. 55% of a circular region =

A 162°

B 198°

C 216°

D 234°

Part 3 **Applications**

13. In three days, Georgina got 18 h of sleep. At this rate, how many h of sleep would she get in 7 days?

A 31 h   C 39 h

B 36 h   D 42 h

14. Mrs. Fay has 22 more papers to mark than Mr. Spencer. Together, they have 216 papers to mark. How many papers does Mrs. Fay have to mark?

A 101   C 127

B 119   D 97

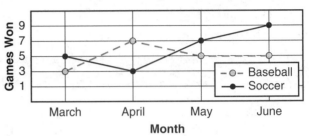

Games Won by the Two Teams

15. In which month did the soccer team win seven games?

A May   C March

B June   D April

16. There are 24 pain reliever tablets in a bottle. Each tablet contains 200 mg of an active ingredient called ibuprofen. How many grams of ibuprofen are there in the bottle?

A 320 g   C 4.8 g

B 4800 g   D 48 g

17. The Nicholsons have an above-ground circular swimming pool in their backyard. The diameter of the pool is 7 m. What is the approximate circumference of the pool? Use 3.14 for π.

A about 10.99 m   C about 14 m

B about 21.98 m   D about 43.96 m

18. Monique is making a circle graph to represent how she spends her day. She spends 35% of a day sleeping. What should be the measure of the sector that represents the sleep?

A 126°   C 97.2°

B 103°   D 75°

ANSWER ROW   **9** Ⓐ Ⓑ Ⓒ Ⓓ   **11** Ⓐ Ⓑ Ⓒ Ⓓ   **13** Ⓐ Ⓑ Ⓒ Ⓓ   **15** Ⓐ Ⓑ Ⓒ Ⓓ   **17** Ⓐ Ⓑ Ⓒ Ⓓ

              10 Ⓐ Ⓑ Ⓒ Ⓓ   **12** Ⓐ Ⓑ Ⓒ Ⓓ   **14** Ⓐ Ⓑ Ⓒ Ⓓ   **16** Ⓐ Ⓑ Ⓒ Ⓓ   **18** Ⓐ Ⓑ Ⓒ Ⓓ

Do each problem.
Find the correct answer.
Mark the space for the answer.

| Part 1 **Concepts** | Part 2 **Computation** |

1. How much would the value of 825 910 be decreased by if you replaced the 8 with a 7?

A   10 000

B   100 000

C   1000

D   1

2. Which of these is not equal to the others?

A   65%

B $\frac{65}{100}$

C   0.065

D   65 ÷ 100

3. What is the formula for the volume of a cylinder?

A $V = Bh$

B $V = 2\pi rh + 2\pi r^2$

C $V = \frac{1}{3} Bh$

D $V = 2\pi r^2 h$

4. How many possible outcomes are there if you flip a coin and roll a number cube?

A   6

B   8

C   12

D   24

5. $\frac{5}{6} \div 1\frac{2}{3}$

A $\frac{1}{3}$

B $\frac{1}{6}$

C $\frac{2}{9}$

D $\frac{1}{2}$

6. $81 + 19 = \dfrac{300}{x}$

A $x = 2$

B $x = 10$

C $x = 3$

D $x = 30$

7. $3\frac{3}{4}$ is ___% of 5.

A   50

B   62

C   71

D   75

8. 1.650 km =

A   1650 m

B   165 m

C   16.5 m

D   0.165 m

CUMULATIVE REVIEW

ANSWER ROW   **1** Ⓐ Ⓑ Ⓒ Ⓓ   **3** Ⓐ Ⓑ Ⓒ Ⓓ   **5** Ⓐ Ⓑ Ⓒ Ⓓ   **7** Ⓐ Ⓑ Ⓒ Ⓓ

2 Ⓐ Ⓑ Ⓒ Ⓓ   **4** Ⓐ Ⓑ Ⓒ Ⓓ   **6** Ⓐ Ⓑ Ⓒ Ⓓ   **8** Ⓐ Ⓑ Ⓒ Ⓓ

PRISM MATHEMATICS
Purple Book

CHAPTER 13
CUMULATIVE REVIEW

237

9.
6 h 2 min
+4 h 2 min

A 10 h 2 min
B 11 h 1 min
C 11 h
D 10 h 1 min

10. $11^2 =$

A 22
B 110
C 121
D 132

11. What is the approximate area of a circle if the radius = 10 cm? Use 3.14 for π.

A 31.4 cm^2
B 314 cm^2
C 78.5 cm^2
D 62.8 cm^2

12. If you roll a number cube 30 times, how many times would you expect to roll a 3?

A 10
B 6
C 4
D 5

Part 3 Applications

13. Food prices are expected to rise 4% in the next year. If this happens, how much will a cart of groceries that cost $175 today cost in one year?

A $198
B $189
C $182
D $180

14. Samantha drew a triangle with different length measurements on all three sides. What type of triangle did Samantha draw?

A isosceles
B equilateral
C scalene
D pyramid

15. When the Rodriquez family flew to Aruba, the flight there took 3 h 48 min and the flight home took 3 hours 55 min. How long did the Rodriquez family spend flying on their vacation?

A 7 h 43 min
C 6 h 33 min
B 7 h 15 min
D 6 h 58 min

16. Marcus spent $1\frac{1}{2}$ h on his math homework, $1\frac{3}{4}$ h on his science project, and $1\frac{2}{3}$ h on his essay. How did Marcus spend on schoolwork in all?

A $3\frac{3}{4}$ h
C $4\frac{1}{4}$ h
B $4\frac{11}{12}$ h
D $4\frac{1}{2}$ h

17. In a circle graph, Roger's farm is divided into percentages of different farm animals. Roger has 15% cows, 25% chickens, 35% horses, 15% pigs, and 10% goats. If Roger has 160 farm animals in all, how many chickens does he have?

A 24
C 56
B 40
D 16

18. At Carmen's Ice Cream Shoppe, the owner said that 12% of the total dips of ice cream sold are rocky road. If 225 dips were sold tomorrow, how many would you predict to be rocky road?

A 17
C 23
B 20
D 27

STOP

ANSWER ROW **9** Ⓐ Ⓑ Ⓒ Ⓓ **11** Ⓐ Ⓑ Ⓒ Ⓓ **13** Ⓐ Ⓑ Ⓒ Ⓓ **15** Ⓐ Ⓑ Ⓒ Ⓓ **17** Ⓐ Ⓑ Ⓒ Ⓓ
10 Ⓐ Ⓑ Ⓒ Ⓓ **12** Ⓐ Ⓑ Ⓒ Ⓓ **14** Ⓐ Ⓑ Ⓒ Ⓓ **16** Ⓐ Ⓑ Ⓒ Ⓓ **18** Ⓐ Ⓑ Ⓒ Ⓓ

ALGEBRA READINESS
Variables, Expressions, Equations

In algebra,

- a **variable** is a symbol, usually a letter of the alphabet, that stands for an unknown number. x
- an **algebraic expression** is a combination of variables, numbers, and at least one operation. $x + 6$
- an **equation** is a sentence that contains an equal sign. $x + 6 = 13$

Write *expression* or *equation* for each of the following.

	a	b	c
1.	$n + 13 = 20$ _equation_	$6ab$ _____	$25 + x$ _____
2.	$9 \times n = 63$ _____	$8 + x - y$ _____	$34 + 79 = 113$ _____

Translate each phrase into an algebraic expression.

a

3. ten more than x _$x + 10$_   7 decreased by n _____

4. twelve less than a _____   the product of 15 and 34 _____

5. the sum of five and six _____   a number divided by 13 _____

b

Translate each sentence into an equation.

6. Eleven times a number is 132. _$11 \times n = 132$_

7. Twenty minus fourteen equals six. _____

8. Ten less than a number equals forty. _____

Write the following in words.

9. $n + 5$ _____

10. $6 - a$ _____

11. $35 \times 25 = 875$ _____

ALGEBRA READINESS
Properties of Numbers

Commutative Properties of Addition and Multiplication
The order in which numbers are added does not change the sum. $a + b = b + a$
The order in which numbers are multiplied does not change the product. $x \times y = y \times x$

Associative Properties of Addition and Multiplication
The grouping of addends does not change the sum. $(a + b) + c = a + (b + c)$
The grouping of factors does not change the product. $(x \times y) \times z = x \times (y \times z)$

Identity Properties of Addition and Multiplication
The sum of an addend and zero is that addend. $a + 0 = a$
The product of a factor and one is that factor. $a \times 1 = a$

Properties of Zero
The product of a factor and zero is zero. $a \times 0 = 0$
The quotient of zero and any non-zero number is zero. $0 \div a = 0$

Name the property shown by each statement.

                        a b

1. $x \times 1 = x$ _____ $(12 \times a) \times b = 12 \times (a \times b)$ _____

2. $54m + n = n + 54m$ _____ $0 \div 3xy = 0$ _____

3. $(7a + b) + 5 = (b + 7a) + 5$ _____ $\dfrac{15x}{y} \times 0 = 0$ _____

4. $(w + x) + 0 = (w + x)$ _____ $\frac{1}{3}c + \frac{2}{5}d = \frac{2}{5}d + \frac{1}{3}c$ _____

Rewrite each expression using the property indicated.

                        a b

5. property of zero: $8a \times 0 =$ _____   commutative: $7d + 13e =$ _____

6. identity: $1 \times (3x + 11) =$ _____   associative: $(x \times 2y) \times z =$ _____

7. identity: $\frac{3}{5}w + 0 =$ _____   commutative: $m \times 2n =$ _____

8. associative: $a + (4b + c) =$ _____   property of zero: $0 \div (8xy) =$ _____

ALGEBRA READINESS
The Distributive Property

Distributive Property
If one factor in a product is a sum, multiplying each addend by the other factor before adding does not change the product.

$$a \times (b + c) = (a \times b) + (a \times c)$$

For example, $4 \times (15 + 9) = (4 \times 15) + (4 \times 9)$
$$4 \times \quad 24 \quad = \quad 60 \quad + \quad 36$$
$$96 = 96$$

Rewrite each expression using the distributive property.

	a	b
1.	$x \times (y + 15) =$ _____	$(35 \times 4x) + (35 \times 6y) =$ _____
2.	$(d \times 7) + (d \times 2e) =$ _____	$z \times (23 + 5y) =$ _____
3.	$j \times (3k + m) =$ _____	$(46 \times b) + (46 \times c) =$ _____
4.	$(17 \times s) + (17 \times t) =$ _____	$(42 \times x) + (42 \times y) =$ _____
5.	$132 \times (a + d) =$ _____	$(x + y) \times z =$ _____

Replace each w with 11, x with 0, y with 7, and z with 20.
Then evaluate each expression.

	a	b
6.	$z \times (w + x) =$ _____	$(x \times w) + (x \times z) =$ _____
7.	$y \times (w + x) =$ _____	$(y \times w) + (y \times z) =$ _____
8.	$w \times (x + y) =$ _____	$(w \times z) + (w \times y) =$ _____
9.	$(w \times z) + (w \times x) =$ _____	$x \times (z + y) =$ _____
10.	$(z \times y) + (z \times z) =$ _____	$(z \times x) + (z \times w) =$ _____
11.	$w \times (z + x + y) =$ _____	$(z \times w) + (z \times x) + (z \times y) =$ _____

ALGEBRA READINESS
Evaluating Expressions

Algebraic expressions can be evaluated using the rules called **Order of Operations.**

    1. Do all operations within parentheses. $(3 + 6) \times 3 = 27$
    2. Do all multiplications and divisions from left to right. $5 \times 4 + 2 = 22$
    3. Do all additions and subtractions from left to right. $12 - 3 + 5 = 14$

Name the operation that should be done first. Then find the value.

	a		*b*
1. $16 - (4 \times 2)$	multiply ; 8	$8 + 6 \div 3$	_____ ; _____
2. $9 \times 6 - 3$	_____ ; _____	$4 + 6 \times 7 - 1$	_____ ; _____
3. $(3 + 4) \times (6 - 3)$	_____ ; _____	$8 \div 2 + (3 - 1)$	_____ ; _____

Evaluate each expression if $a = 8$, $b = 4$, and $c = 2$.

	a		*b*
4. $b \times c - a$	0	$a \div b + c$	_____
5. $4 + b - c$	_____	$3 \times a \div 4$	_____
6. $8 \times (b + c)$	_____	$a + a \div c$	_____
7. $(a + a) \div c$	_____	$(a + b) \div c$	_____
8. $9 - (a \div b)$	_____	$(b + c) \times a$	_____
9. $b \div c + a - b$	_____	$(b + c) \times (a + b)$	_____
10. $c \times (a + b)$	_____	$(c \times a) + (c \times b)$	_____

Write true or false.

	a		*b*
11. $8 + 24 \div 4 - 2 = 12$	_____	$18 \div 3 + (5 - 2) = 3$	_____
12. $24 - 10 - 3 \times 4 = 2$	_____	$42 \div 7 \times 6 = 1$	_____

ALGEBRA READINESS
Solving Equations Using Addition and Subtraction

Subtraction Property of Equality
If you subtract the same number from each side of an equation, the two sides remain equal.

$$x + 8 = 14$$

To undo the addition of 8, subtract 8.

$$x + 8 - 8 = 14 - 8$$
$$x + 0 = 6$$
$$x = 6$$

Addition Property of Equality
If you add the same number to each side of an equation, the two sides remain equal.

$$n - 6 = 7$$

To undo the subtraction of 6, add 6.

$$n - 6 + 6 = 7 + 6$$
$$n - 0 = 13$$
$$n = 13$$

Write the operation that would undo the operation in the equation.

a	*b*

1. $x - 16 = 20$ ___addition___ $24 + n = 38$ _____

2. $14 = n - 32$ _____ $a + 50 = 84$ _____

Solve each equation.

a	*b*

3. $n - 7 = 12$ ___19___ $x + 17 = 25$ _____

4. $a - 11 = 6$ _____ $32 + b = 40$ _____

5. $x + 9 = 18$ _____ $n - 45 = 90$ _____

6. $16 + a = 54$ _____ $12 + x = 24$ _____

7. $b - 15 = 0$ _____ $83 + n = 83$ _____

8. $16 + b = 32$ _____ $52 = a - 5$ _____

9. $35 = n + 15$ _____ $x + 18 = 19$ _____

Write and solve an equation for each situation.

10. A total of 97 students tried out for the debate team. If 45 of the students were girls, how many were boys? _____

11. Three members left the debate team during the year. If 12 members remained, how many were on the team originally? _____

ALGEBRA READINESS
Solving Equations Using Multiplication and Division

Division Property of Equality
If you divide each side of an equation by the same nonzero number, the two sides remain equal.

$$3 \times n = 15$$

To undo multiplication by 3, divide by 3.

$$\frac{3 \times n}{3} = \frac{15}{3}$$

$$n = 5$$

Multiplication Property of Equality
If you multiply each side of an equation by the same number, the two sides remain equal.

$$\frac{a}{3} = 9$$

To undo division by 3, multiply by 3.

$$\frac{a}{3} \times 3 = 9 \times 3$$

$$a = 27$$

Write the operation that would undo the operation in the equation.

	a			*b*	

1. $6 \times a = 24$ ___division___ $\dfrac{x}{4} = 16$ _____

2. $4 = \dfrac{n}{3}$ _____ $42 = 7 \times a$ _____

3. $x \times 8 = 56$ _____ $\dfrac{a}{8} = 16$ _____

Solve each equation.

        a   *b*

4. $\dfrac{x}{3} = 4$ ___12___ $6 \times a = 54$ _____

5. $x \times 12 = 144$ _____ $\dfrac{n}{6} = 16$ _____

6. $\dfrac{x}{8} = 24$ _____ $9 \times n = 81$ _____

7. $54 = x \times 6$ _____ $8 = \dfrac{n}{7}$ _____

8. $72 = 9 \times a$ _____ $n \times 16 = 160$ _____

9. $356 \times n = 356$ _____ $34 \times a = 544$ _____

10. $\dfrac{n}{15} = 38$ _____ $x \times 53 = 3445$ _____

ALGEBRA READINESS
Solving Two-Step Equations

A **two-step equation** is solved by undoing each operation in the equation.

$$4n + 5 = 17$$

To undo the addition of 5, subtract 5.

$$4n + 5 - 5 = 17 - 5$$

$$4n = 12$$

To undo the multiplication of 4, divide by 4.

$$\frac{4n}{4} = \frac{12}{4}$$

$$n = 3$$

$$\frac{n}{4} - 1 = 2$$

To undo the subtraction of 1, add 1.

$$\frac{n}{4} - 1 + 1 = 2 + 1$$

$$\frac{n}{4} = 3$$

To undo the division by 4, multiply by 4.

$$\frac{n}{4} \times 4 = 3 \times 4$$

$$n = 12$$

Solve each equation.

	a	b	c
1.	$2x + 5 = 11$ ___3___	$3a - 5 = 7$ _____	$6n + 8 = 50$ _____
2.	$2b - 9 = 7$ _____	$5x + 15 = 35$ _____	$\frac{a}{5} - 3 = 0$ _____
3.	$\frac{n}{6} + 12 = 15$ _____	$7 + 3x = 28$ _____	$2n - 4 = 6$ _____
4.	$\frac{a}{12} - 10 = 2$ _____	$\frac{n}{10} - 9 = 1$ _____	$6n - 12 = 18$ _____
5.	$\frac{n}{6} - 12 = 0$ _____	$\frac{a}{7} - 3 = 1$ _____	$4 + 10x = 74$ _____
6.	$8a - 50 = 6$ _____	$\frac{a}{3} - 6 = 6$ _____	$12 = 9x - 15$ _____
7.	$\frac{n}{9} - 9 = 0$ _____	$\frac{a}{12} - 15 = 3$ _____	$18a - 6 = 30$ _____

Write the equation. Then solve.

8. Seven more than two times a number is 23. _____

9. Three times a number, increased by 4, equals 31. _____

10. Eight less than five times a number is 27. _____

11. Twice a number, decreased by 16, is 54. _____

ALGEBRA READINESS
Solving Equations

Some equations contain multiple steps.

$2 + 6 + 4x = 80$

Combine $2 + 6 = 8$.

$$8 + 4x = 80$$
$$8 - 8 + 4x = 80 - 8$$
$$4x = 72$$
$$\frac{4x}{4} = \frac{72}{4}$$
$$x = 18$$

$$\frac{a}{4 + 6} - 3 = 11$$

Simplify the denominator.

$$\frac{a}{10} - 3 = 11$$
$$\frac{a}{10} - 3 + 3 = 11 + 3$$
$$\frac{a}{10} = 14$$
$$10 \times \frac{a}{10} = 14 \times 10$$
$$a = 140$$

Solve each equation.

	a		b	
1. $\dfrac{n}{15 - 8} + 31 = 45$	$n =$ _____	$7 + 18 + 3x = 34$	$x =$ _____
2. $\dfrac{x}{11 - 3} + 7 = 16$	$x =$ _____	$5d + 15 + 5 = 45$	$d =$ _____
3. $6a - 37 = 3 + 2$	$a =$ _____	$8 + 4b + 21 = 33$	$b =$ _____
4. $7 + \dfrac{u}{24 - 18} = 12$	$u =$ _____	$33 - 15 + 3z = 57$	$z =$ _____
5. $8c + 108 - 95 = 45$	$c =$ _____	$\dfrac{h}{34 - 17} - 27 = 3$	$h =$ _____
6. $\dfrac{w}{8 - 5} - 21 = 14$	$w =$ _____	$11y + 53 - 30 = 78$	$y =$ _____
7. $27 + 23 + 10d = 60$	$d =$ _____	$49 - 44 + 13x = 96$	$x =$ _____
8. $123 + \dfrac{r}{7 + 9} = 131$	$r =$ _____	$85 - 67 = 9 + \dfrac{w}{14}$	$w =$ _____
9. $\dfrac{m}{36 - 19} - 11 = 6$	$m =$ _____	$24 - 11 = \dfrac{n}{3} + 6$	$n =$ _____
10. $15 + 37 - 8 + 9b = 98$	$b =$ _____	$39 + \dfrac{z}{26 + 8 - 11} = 58$	$z =$ _____

ALGEBRA READINESS
Solving Inequalities

An **inequality** is a mathematical sentence that contains an inequality symbol ($>$, $<$, $\geq$, $\leq$).
$>$ means *is greater than*. $<$ means *is less than*.
$\geq$ means *is greater than or equal to*. $\leq$ means *is less than or equal to*.
An inequality is solved the same way an equation is solved.

$x - 3 > 10$ $a + 5 \leq 8$
Add 3 to both sides of the inequality.   *Subtract 5 from both sides of the inequality.*
$x - 3 + 3 > 10 + 3$ $a + 5 - 5 \leq 8 - 5$
$x > 13$ $a \leq 3$

An inequality can have more than one solution.

x is any number greater than 13. a is any number less than or equal to 3.

Write *true* or *false*.

	a	*b*	*c*
1.	$7 > 2$ _____	$5 < 3$ _____	$4 \geq 2$ _____
2.	$6 \leq 5$ _____	$0 > 2$ _____	$9 \leq 9$ _____

Use the given value to tell if each inequality is *true* or *false*.

	a	*b*
3.	$n + 2 \geq 7$ if $n = 6$ _____	$14 \geq x + 6$ if $x = 4$ _____
4.	$3a \geq 7$ if $a = 0$ _____	$2 < 2x - 5$ if $x = 3$ _____

Give a value for the variable in each inequality.

	a	*b*
5.	$n + 4 > 5$ a number greater than 1	$x - 3 < 7$ _____
6.	$a + 8 < 11$ _____	$n - 5 > 3$ _____
7.	$x + 6 > 8$ _____	$a - 6 < 9$ _____
8.	$n \leq 5$ _____	$x \geq 12$ _____
9.	$a \geq 3$ _____	$n \leq 10$ _____
10.	$a + 1 > 9$ _____	$n - 1 \leq 7$ _____

ALGEBRA
READINESS

ALGEBRA READINESS
Inequalities on a Number Line

You can graph the solution of an inequality on a number line.

The following graphs compare x and 5.

An open dot means that 5 is not a solution.

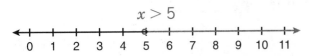

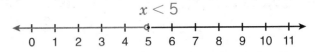

A closed dot means that 5 is a solution.

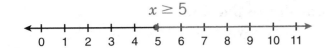

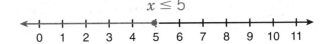

Graph each inequality on a number line.

a b

1. $d > 3$

$y \leq 8$

2. $x > 11$

$n < 4$

3. $h \geq 0$

$p > 15$

Solve each inequality. Graph the solution on a number line.

a b

4. $a - 3 \geq 5$ _____

$g + 11 < 20$ _____

5. $3 + u \leq 6$ _____

$7 + x < 15$ _____

6. $j + 7 > 7$ _____

$p + 18 - 9 \geq 20$ _____

ALGEBRA READINESS
Integers

Negative and positive whole numbers are called **integers.**

Integers are often shown on a number line with zero as a starting point.

The greater of two integers is always the one farther to the right on a number line.

Say: −2 is less than 5.
Write: −2 < 5

Say: 5 is greater than −2.
Write: 5 > −2

Use integers to name each point on a number line.

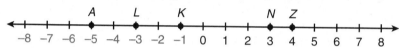

1. N _____ L _____ Z _____ K _____ A _____

Graph each point on the number line below.

2. $B, -7$ $F, 1$ $M, 4$ $P, -4$ $S, 5$

<---+--->
  −10 −9 −8 −7 −6 −5 −4 −3 −2 −1 0 1 2 3 4 5 6 7 8 9 10

Write < or > in each ☐.

	a	b	c	d
3.	-1 ☐ -3	4 ☐ 2	0 ☐ 5	0 ☐ -1
4.	-4 ☐ -2	-8 ☐ 0	4 ☐ -4	-1 ☐ -7
5.	-6 ☐ 1	2 ☐ -6	-5 ☐ 0	-7 ☐ -8

List each set of integers in order from least to greatest.

        a b

6. $4, 0, -2, -1$ _____ $-6, -1, 1, -5$ _____

7. $1, 0, -1, -7, -3$ _____ $-2, 2, 0, -3, 3$ _____

ALGEBRA READINESS

ALGEBRA READINESS
Absolute Value

The **absolute value** of a number is the distance that number is from zero on the number line. The absolute value of a number is always positive.

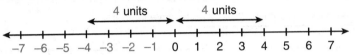

Say: The absolute value of −4 is 4.
Write: $|-4| = 4$

Say: The absolute value of 4 is 4.
Write: $|4| = 4$

Write the absolute value of each number.

	a	b	c
1.	$\lvert -7 \rvert =$ _____	$\lvert 14 \rvert =$ _____	$\lvert 0 \rvert =$ _____
2.	$\lvert 25 \rvert =$ _____	$\lvert -16 \rvert =$ _____	$\lvert -33 \rvert =$ _____
3.	$\lvert -78 \rvert =$ _____	$\lvert 118 \rvert =$ _____	$\lvert -250 \rvert =$ _____

Write < or > in each ☐.

	a	b	c
4.	$\lvert -6 \rvert$ ☐ $\lvert 4 \rvert$	$\lvert 5 \rvert$ ☐ $\lvert -4 \rvert$	$\lvert 9 \rvert$ ☐ $\lvert -13 \rvert$
5.	$\lvert 0 \rvert$ ☐ $\lvert -5 \rvert$	$\lvert -6 \rvert$ ☐ $\lvert -3 \rvert$	$\lvert 11 \rvert$ ☐ $\lvert 15 \rvert$
6.	$\lvert -25 \rvert$ ☐ $\lvert -23 \rvert$	$\lvert -10 \rvert$ ☐ $\lvert 0 \rvert$	$\lvert -7 \rvert$ ☐ $\lvert -9 \rvert$
7.	$\lvert 35 \rvert$ ☐ $\lvert 47 \rvert$	$\lvert 55 \rvert$ ☐ $\lvert -45 \rvert$	$\lvert -34 \rvert$ ☐ $\lvert 37 \rvert$
8.	$\lvert -84 \rvert$ ☐ $\lvert -81 \rvert$	$\lvert 103 \rvert$ ☐ $\lvert -98 \rvert$	$\lvert -138 \rvert$ ☐ $\lvert -157 \rvert$

List in order from least to greatest.

	a		b
9.	$-5, 7, \lvert -9 \rvert, 0$ _____		$\lvert -3 \rvert, -8, 5, \lvert -7 \rvert$ _____
10.	$0, \lvert 5 \rvert, -7, \lvert -6 \rvert$ _____		$-11, 10, \lvert -9 \rvert, 11$ _____

ALGEBRA READINESS
Adding and Subtracting Integers

The sum of two positive integers is a **positive** integer.

$3 + 2 = 5$

The sum of two negative integers is a **negative** integer.

$-4 + (-2) = -6$

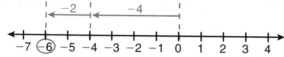

To add integers with different signs, **subtract** their absolute values. Give
the result the same sign as the integer with the greatest absolute value.

$6 + (-2) = 4$

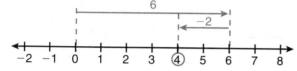

To subtract an integer, **add** its opposite.
The subtraction problem $-8 - 3 = -11$ can be rewritten as the addition problem
$-8 + (-3) = -11$. -3 is the opposite of 3.

Add.

	a	*b*	*c*	*d*
1.	$7 + (-3) = \underline{4}$	$5 + 3 = \underline{}$	$-9 + 4 = \underline{}$	$-6 + (-2) = \underline{}$
2.	$-12 + 9 = \underline{}$	$-4 + (-6) = \underline{}$	$3 + 18 = \underline{}$	$3 + (-9) = \underline{}$
3.	$-1 + (-6) = \underline{}$	$12 + 14 = \underline{}$	$8 + (-6) = \underline{}$	$-4 + 8 = \underline{}$
4.	$-12 + 0 = \underline{}$	$-14 + (-2) = \underline{}$	$0 + (-1) = \underline{}$	$14 + (-14) = \underline{}$
5.	$68 + (-42) = \underline{}$	$-97 + 38 = \underline{}$	$-16 + (-16) = \underline{}$	$48 + 52 = \underline{}$

Subtract.

	a	*b*	*c*	*d*
6.	$8 - (-4) = \underline{12}$	$10 - 6 = \underline{}$	$-8 - 5 = \underline{}$	$9 - (-6) = \underline{}$
7.	$21 - 15 = \underline{}$	$18 - (-9) = \underline{}$	$10 - (-5) = \underline{}$	$-6 - (-5) = \underline{}$
8.	$-4 - 9 = \underline{}$	$-8 - 6 = \underline{}$	$-12 - (-7) = \underline{}$	$5 - 11 = \underline{}$
9.	$16 - 31 = \underline{}$	$-8 - 12 = \underline{}$	$-4 - 0 = \underline{}$	$-5 - 2 = \underline{}$
10.	$2 - (-15) = \underline{}$	$-8 - (-18) = \underline{}$	$9 - (-17) = \underline{}$	$0 - 8 = \underline{}$

ALGEBRA READINESS
Multiplying and Dividing Integers

The product of two integers with **like** signs
is **positive**.

The product of two integers with **unlike** signs
is **negative**.

$3 \times 5 = 15$ $-3 \times (-5) = 15$

$-6 \times 3 = -18$ $6 \times (-3) = -18$

The quotient of two integers with **like** signs
is **positive**.

The quotient of two integers with **unlike** signs
is **negative**.

$8 \div 4 = 2$ $-8 \div (-4) = 2$

$6 \div (-3) = -2$ $-6 \div 3 = -2$

State whether each answer is positive or negative.

	a	b	c
1.	$18 \times (-7) =$ ___negative___	$6 \times (-48) =$ _____	$-12 \times (-15) =$ _____
2.	$-18 \div (-9) =$ _____	$54 \div (-6) =$ _____	$-56 \div 7 =$ _____

Multiply or divide.

	a	b	c
3.	$8 \times (-9) =$ ___-72___	$-9 \times (-6) =$ _____	$-12 \times 8 =$ _____
4.	$-56 \div (-7) =$ _____	$-54 \div 9 =$ _____	$96 \div (-8) =$ _____
5.	$11 \times (-8) =$ _____	$72 \div 9 =$ _____	$10 \times (-10) =$ _____
6.	$63 \div (-9) =$ _____	$-35 \div 5 =$ _____	$126 \times (-1) =$ _____
7.	$7 \times (-7) =$ _____	$235 \div (-1) =$ _____	$-634 \times 0 =$ _____
8.	$-64 \div (-8) =$ _____	$0 \div (-147) =$ _____	$-12 \times (-12) =$ _____

Write *true* or *false*. If false, state the reason.

9. The product of two positive integers is never negative. _____

10. The product of two negative integers is always negative. _____

11. The quotient of two negative integers is always positive. _____

ALGEBRA READINESS
Powers and Exponents

NAME _____

Numbers can be expressed in different ways. $10\,000 = 10 \times 10 \times 10 \times 10$
A shorter way to express $10\,000$ is by using **exponents.** $10\,000 = 10^4$
An exponent tells how many times a number, called the **base,** is used as a factor.

$$\text{base} \longrightarrow 10^6 = 10 \times 10 \times 10 \times 10 \times 10 \times 10 = 1\,000\,000$$
$$2^4 = \qquad 2 \times 2 \times 2 \times 2 \qquad = 16$$

Numbers that are expressed using exponents are called **powers.**

Write each power as the product of the same factor.

	a		b
1. 8^4	$8 \times 8 \times 8 \times 8$	9^3	_____
2. 23^2	_____	1^6	_____
3. 10^5	_____	2^7	_____
4. 6^3	_____	49^4	_____

Use exponents to express the following.

	a		b
5. $3 \times 3 \times 3 \times 3$	3^4	$9 \times 9 \times 9$	_____
6. 15×15	_____	$2 \times 2 \times 2 \times 2 \times 2 \times 2$	_____
7. $1 \times 1 \times 1 \times 1$	_____	$4 \times 4 \times 4 \times 4 \times 4$	_____
8. $12 \times 12 \times 12$	_____	$10 \times 10 \times 10$	_____

Evaluate each expression.

	a		b
9. x^3 if $x = 5$	125	n^2 if $n = 9$	_____
10. a^5 if $a = 2$	_____	b^7 if $b = 10$	_____
11. x^2 if $x = 15$	_____	n^4 if $n = 3$	_____

ALGEBRA READINESS

PRISM MATHEMATICS
Purple Book

ALGEBRA READINESS
Powers and Exponents

253

ALGEBRA READINESS
Negative Exponents

NAME _____

Numbers between 0 and 1 can be expressed using **negative exponents.**

Any nonzero number raised to a negative power is the same as 1 divided by that number raised to the absolute value of the power.

$$x^{-a} = \frac{1}{x^a}$$

$$10^{-3} = \frac{1}{10^3} = \frac{1}{10 \times 10 \times 10} = \frac{1}{1000}$$

$$3^{-5} = \frac{1}{3^5} = \frac{1}{3 \times 3 \times 3 \times 3 \times 3} = \frac{1}{243}$$

Rewrite each expression using a positive exponent. Then write it in expanded form.

a $\hspace{10cm}$ b

1. $10^{-2} = $ ___ $\dfrac{1}{10^2} = \dfrac{1}{10 \times 10}$ ___ $8^{-4} = $ _____

2. $6^{-3} = $ _____ $11^{-4} = $ _____

3. $5^{-5} = $ _____ $18^{-3} = $ _____

4. $2^{-7} = $ _____ $12^{-5} = $ _____

Use negative exponents to rewrite the following.

a $\hspace{10cm}$ b

5. $\dfrac{1}{5 \times 5 \times 5}$ _5^{-3}_ $\dfrac{1}{3 \times 3 \times 3 \times 3}$ _____

6. $\dfrac{1}{14 \times 14 \times 14 \times 14}$ _____ $\dfrac{1}{8 \times 8 \times 8}$ _____

7. $\dfrac{1}{10 \times 10 \times 10 \times 10 \times 10}$ _____ $\dfrac{1}{2 \times 2 \times 2 \times 2 \times 2 \times 2 \times 2 \times 2}$ _____

8. $\dfrac{1}{24 \times 24 \times 24 \times 24}$ _____ $\dfrac{1}{15 \times 15 \times 15 \times 15 \times 15 \times 15}$ _____

Evaluate each expression.

a $\hspace{10cm}$ b

9. a^{-2} if $a = 3$ _$\frac{1}{9}$_ x^{-4} if $x = 2$ _____

10. b^{-3} if $b = 5$ _____ m^{-4} if $m = 4$ _____

ALGEBRA READINESS
Multiplying and Dividing Powers

To **multiply** powers *that have the same base,* **add** the exponents.

$$a^m \times a^n = a^{m+n}$$
$$10^3 \times 10^2 = 10^{3+2} = 10^5$$

To **divide** powers *that have the same base,* **subtract** the exponents.

$$a^m \div a^n = a^{m-n}$$
$$10^3 \div 10^2 = 10^{3-2} = 10^1$$

Find each product.

	a		*b*		*c*	
1.	$5^3 \times 5^6$	5^9	$3^2 \times 3^4$	_____	$n^6 \times n^2$	_____
2.	$9^3 \times 9^1$	_____	$x \times x$	_____	$10^4 \times 10^4$	_____
3.	$12^3 \times 12^4$	_____	$a \times a^5$	_____	$15^5 \times 15^3$	_____

Verify each product by replacing the powers with their values.

	a		*b*	
4.	$3^3 \times 3^2 = 3^5$	$27 \times 9 = 243$	$2^2 \times 2^3 = 2^5$	_____
5.	$3 \times 3^4 = 3^5$	_____	$5 \times 5 = 5^2$	_____
6.	$2^4 \times 2^2 = 2^6$	_____	$3^2 \times 3^2 = 3^4$	_____

Find each quotient.

	a		*b*		*c*	
7.	$7^7 \div 7^2$	7^5	$a^4 \div a^2$	_____	$8^3 \div 8^1$	_____
8.	$9^5 \div 9^2$	_____	$6^{12} \div 6^6$	_____	$5^8 \div 5^3$	_____
9.	$4^4 \div 4$	_____	$7^6 \div 7^5$	_____	$15^4 \div 15^3$	_____

Verify each quotient by replacing the powers with their values.

	a		*b*	
10.	$3^4 \div 3^2 = 3^2$	$81 \div 9 = 9$	$2^5 \div 2^3 = 2^2$	_____
11.	$4^3 \div 4 = 4^2$	_____	$5^2 \div 5 = 5$	_____
12.	$3^3 \div 3 = 3^2$	_____	$10^5 \div 10^2 = 10^3$	_____

ALGEBRA READINESS

ALGEBRA READINESS
Scientific Notation

NAME _____

A number written in **scientific notation** is shown as the product of a factor between 1 and 10 and a power of 10.

30 000   Move the decimal point 4 places to the left. Multiply by 10^4.

3×10^4

$5\,780\,000 = 5.78 \times 10^6$

0.0003   Move the decimal point 4 places to the right. Multiply by 10^{-4}.

3×10^{-4}

$0.006\,23 = 6.23 \times 10^{-3}$

Express each of the following in scientific notation.

	a		b		c	
1. 6300	6.3×10^3	7000	_____	540	_____
2. 0.5	_____	0.006	_____	0.0007	_____
3. 690	_____	0.20	_____	50 000	_____
4. 0.0017	_____	0.064	_____	8 000 000	_____
5. 0.609	_____	0.003	_____	0.0852	_____

Express each scientific notation as indicated.

	a		b		c	
6. 7.5×10^2	750	3×10^3	_____	9×10^4	_____
7. 5×10^{-3}	_____	8×10^{-1}	_____	4×10^{-2}	_____
8. 6.5×10^2	_____	9.04×10^3	_____	7×10^{-1}	_____
9. 6.47×10^2	_____	1.2×10^3	_____	5.8×10^{-2}	_____
10. 2×10^{-2}	_____	0.2×10^3	_____	8.1×10^3	_____

ALGEBRA READINESS
Ordered Pairs

The location of any point on a grid can be indicated by an **ordered pair** of numbers. Point A on the grid at the right is indicated by the ordered pair (2, 4) because it is located at 2 on the horizontal scale x, and at 4 on the vertical scale y. The number on the horizontal scale x is always named first in an ordered pair. (0, 0) is called the **origin.**

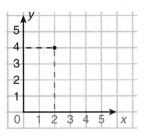

Use Grid 1 to name the point for each ordered pair.

Grid 1

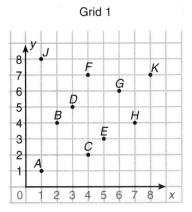

	a		b
1.	(4, 2) ____C____	(7, 4) _____
2.	(8, 7) _____	(2, 4) _____
3.	(6, 6) _____	(3, 5) _____
4.	(5, 3) _____	(1, 1) _____
5.	(4, 7) _____	(1, 8) _____

Use Grid 2 to find the ordered pair for each labelled point.

Grid 2

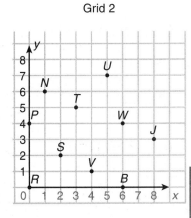

	a		b
6.	J __(8, 3)__	N _____
7.	S _____	W _____
8.	R _____	B _____
9.	T _____	V _____
10.	U _____	P _____

Locate four points on the grid and name each ordered pair.

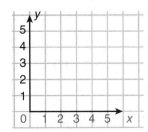

	a		b
11.	A _____	C _____
12.	Z _____	R _____

ALGEBRA READINESS

ALGEBRA READINESS
Graphing in Four Quadrants

NAME _____

A **coordinate plane** is formed by two number lines that are perpendicular. The horizontal line is the **x-axis.** The vertical line is the **y-axis.** The axes intersect at the **origin.** The axes divide the coordinate plane into four **quadrants.** The first number in an ordered pair is the **x-coordinate.** The second number is the **y-coordinate.**

To plot the point $(6, -3)$ on a coordinate plane, start at 0 and move 6 units right then 3 units down.

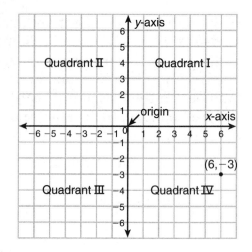

Use Grid 1 to name the point for each ordered pair.

	a	b	**Grid 1**

1. $(1, -6)$ _____ $(-3, -7)$ _____

2. $(-5, 0)$ _____ $(4, 2)$ _____

3. $(-7, -3)$ _____ $(5, 0)$ _____

4. $(-6, 1)$ _____ $(-4, 3)$ _____

Plot each ordered pair on Grid 2.

a	b	**Grid 2**

5. $T(6, -5)$ $R(-4, 0)$

6. $U(-3, 1)$ $P(-7, 2)$

7. $S(0, -7)$ $W(1, -2)$

8. $Q(0, 0)$ $V(2, 7)$

State the quadrant in which each ordered pair would be located.

	a	b	c

9. $(-9, 4)$ _____ $(5, -1)$ _____ $(-3, -3)$ _____

10. $(18, -33)$ _____ $(12, 20)$ _____ $(-34, 42)$ _____

ALGEBRA READINESS
Making Function Tables

A **function** is a rule that states for each value of one variable that there is exactly one related value for the other variable.

For example, $y = 3x - 6$ is a function.

A **function table** organizes values of a function.

Each x-value and its corresponding y-value can be thought of as ordered pairs.

x	y
1	−3
2	0
3	3
4	6

$y = 3x - 6$
let x = 1, 2, 3, 4
$y = 3(1) - 6$
$y = -3$

Make a function table for each function and the given values of x.

	a	b	c

1. $y = 8 + 2x$ $\qquad\qquad$ $y = \dfrac{3x}{2}$ $\qquad\qquad$ $y = 12 - 8x$

let $x = -4, -2, 0, 2, 4$ $\qquad$ let $x = -2, -1, 0, 1, 2$ $\qquad$ let $x = 0, 1, 2, 3, 4$

2. $y = 5x - 15$ $\qquad\qquad$ $y = \dfrac{x}{4} - 5$ $\qquad\qquad$ $y = \dfrac{x}{3} + 4$

let $x = -5, 0, 1, 3, 8$ $\qquad$ let $x = -8, -4, 0, 4, 8$ $\qquad$ let $x = -9, -3, 0, 6, 12$

Write the function that is represented by each function table.

3.

x	y
−2	−9
−1	−8
0	−7
1	−6
2	−5

_____

x	y
0	0
2	−6
4	−12
6	−18
8	−24

_____

x	y
−1	−1
0	1
1	3
2	5
3	7

_____

ALGEBRA READINESS

ALGEBRA READINESS
Graphing Linear Functions

A **linear function** is one that can be represented on a coordinate plane as a straight line.

To graph a linear function, create a function table with at least two ordered pairs. Then plot these ordered pairs on a coordinate plane and draw a line through the points.

Graph the linear function $y = 6 - 2x$.

x	y
-1	8
0	6
1	4

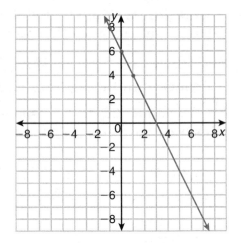

Graph each linear function.

        a   *b*

1. $y = -2x$ $y = 7 - \dfrac{x}{2}$

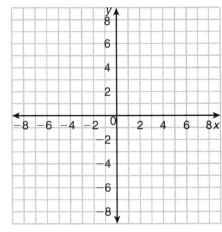   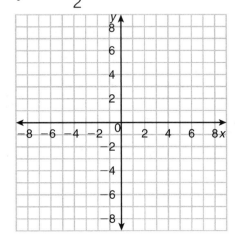

2. $y = 5x - 4$ $y = \dfrac{3}{4}x + 5$

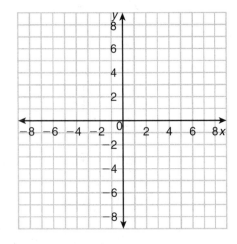   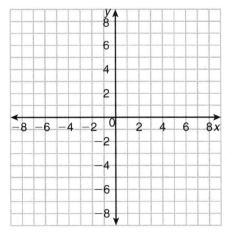

ALGEBRA READINESS
Slope

The slope of a line is the ratio of the change in y to the corresponding change in x.

$$\text{slope} = \frac{\text{change in } y}{\text{change in } x}$$

In Quadrant I, the change in y is 2 and the corresponding change in x is 3. Therefore, the slope of the line is $\frac{2}{3}$.

The slope of the line is the same in Quadrant III.

$$\frac{\text{change in } y}{\text{change in } x} = \frac{-2}{-3} \text{ or } \frac{2}{3}$$

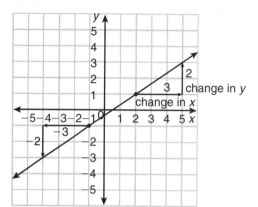

To find the slope of a line when given two ordered pairs on that line: find the ratio of the difference in the y-coordinates and the difference in the x-coordinates.

Find the slope of the line passing through $(6, -4)$ and $(3, 2)$.

$$\text{Slope} = \frac{-4 - 2}{6 - 3} = \frac{-6}{3} = \frac{-2}{1}$$

Find the slope of each graphed line.

1.

a	b	c
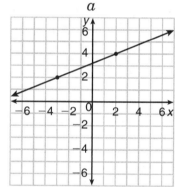	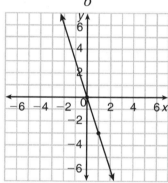	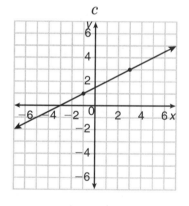

slope = _____   slope = _____   slope = _____

Find the slope of the line passing through each pair of points.

         a b c

2. $(5, -7), (3, 2)$ $(3, -1), (-3, -4)$ $(-4, -2), (8, -6)$

     slope = _____   slope = _____   slope = _____

3. $(6, -5), (7, -3)$ $(-4, 1), (0, 0)$ $(1, -3), (4, -1)$

     slope = _____   slope = _____   slope = _____

ALGEBRA READINESS
Slope-Intercept Form

The **slope-intercept form** of a linear equation is $y = mx + b$, where m is the slope and b is the y-intercept. The **y-intercept** of a line is the point where the line crosses the y-axis.

You can use the slope and y-intercept to graph a line.

Graph the line $y = \frac{2}{3}x + 2$.

The slope is $\frac{2}{3}$. The y-intercept is 2.

Step 1: Place a point at the y-intercept, 2.
Step 2: Use the slope to plot another point.
    The slope is $\frac{2}{3}$.
Step 3: Draw a line through the two points.

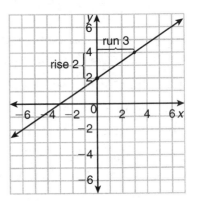

Name the slope and y-intercept of each line. Then graph the line.

| a | b |

1. $y = -\frac{1}{2}x + 3$ $y = 3x - 2$

slope = _____ y-intercept = _____   slope = _____ y-intercept = _____

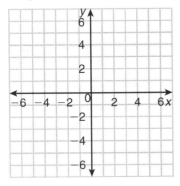
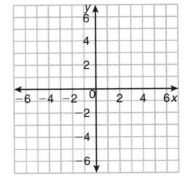

2. $y = \frac{3}{4}x - 5$ $y = -4x + 1$

slope = _____ y-intercept = _____   slope = _____ y-intercept = _____

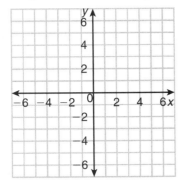
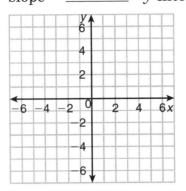

PRISM MATHEMATICS
Purple Book

262

ALGEBRA READINESS
Slope-Intercept Form